Reporting Islam

Gender and Islam

Series Editors
Professor Nadia Al-Bagdadi, Central European University, Hungary
Professor Randi Deguilhem, National Institute of Scientific Research (CNRS), France
Professor Bettina Dennerlein, University of Zurich, Switzerland

Advisory Board
Madawi Al-Rasheed, Middle East Centre, London School of Economics, UK
Kathryn Babayan, University of Michigan, USA
Jocelyne Cesari, Berkley Center, Georgetown University, USA, and University of Birmingham, UK
Dawn Chatty, University of Oxford, UK
Nadia El Cheikh, American University of Beirut, Lebanon
Hoda Elsadda, Cairo University, Egypt
Ratna Ghosh, McGill University, Canada
Suad Joseph, UC Davis, USA

Published and Forthcoming Titles
Queer Muslims in Europe: Sexuality, Religion and Migration in Belgium, Wim Peumans
Mainstreaming the Headscarf: Islamist Politics and Women in the Turkish Media, Ezra Ozcan
Masculinities and Displacement in the Middle East: Syrian Refugees in Egypt, Magdalena Suerbaum
Sex and Desire in Muslim Cultures: Beyond Norms and Transgression from the Abbasids to the Present Day, Aymon Kreil, Lucia Sorbera, and Serena Tolino (Eds)
The Politics of the Female Body in Contemporary Turkey: Reproduction, Maternity, Sexuality, Hilal Alkan, Ayşe Dayı, Sezin Topcu, and Betül Yarar (Eds)
Muslim Masculinities in Literature and Film: Transcultural Identity and Migration in Britain, Peter Cherry
Reporting Islam: Muslim Women in the New York Times, *1979–2011*, Suad Joseph (Ed.)

Reporting Islam

Muslim Women in the New York Times,
1979–2011

Edited by

Suad Joseph

BLOOMSBURY ACADEMIC
LONDON · NEW YORK · OXFORD · NEW DELHI · SYDNEY

BLOOMSBURY ACADEMIC
Bloomsbury Publishing Plc
50 Bedford Square, London, WC1B 3DP, UK
1385 Broadway, New York, NY 10018, USA
29 Earlsfort Terrace, Dublin 2, Ireland

BLOOMSBURY, BLOOMSBURY ACADEMIC and the Diana logo are trademarks of
Bloomsbury Publishing Plc

First published in Great Britain 2023
Paperback edition first published 2024

Copyright © Suad Joseph, 2023

Suad Joseph and contributors have asserted their right under the Copyright, Designs and Patents Act, 1988, to be identified as Editor of this work.

For legal purposes the Acknowledgments on pp. vii–ix constitute an extension of this copyright page.

Series design by Adriana Brioso
Cover image © Dipak Pankhania / Alamy Stock Photo

All rights reserved. No part of this publication may be reproduced or transmitted in any form or by any means, electronic or mechanical, including photocopying, recording, or any information storage or retrieval system, without prior permission in writing from the publishers.

Bloomsbury Publishing Plc does not have any control over, or responsibility for, any third-party websites referred to or in this book. All internet addresses given in this book were correct at the time of going to press. The author and publisher regret any inconvenience caused if addresses have changed or sites have ceased to exist, but can accept no responsibility for any such changes.

A catalogue record for this book is available from the British Library.

A catalog record for this book is available from the Library of Congress.

ISBN: HB: 978-0-7556-4783-5
PB: 978-0-7556-4787-3
ePDF: 978-0-7556-4784-2
eBook: 978-0-7556-4785-9

Series: Gender and Islam

Typeset by Newgen KnowledgeWorks Pvt. Ltd., Chennai, India

To find out more about our authors and books visit www.bloomsbury.com and sign up for our newsletters.

Contents

Acknowledgments   vii

1. Reporting Islam: Decolonizing the Representation of Muslim Women in News Media   1
   Suad Joseph
2. Maturing Islam: Turkey as the Site of Islamic Liberalization in the *New York Times*, 1980–2011   37
   Caroline McKusick
3. The Material Life of Representation: "Veiled Muslim Women" in the *New York Times*, 1980–2011   67
   Lena Meari
4. Anti-Islamist (Re)Presentations in the *New York Times* and Academic Feminism, 1979–2011   105
   Tanzeen Rashed Doha
5. Friends and Foes: The Pragmatic Liberal Biases in Representation of Saudi Women vs. Iranian Women in the *New York Times*, 1980–2011   141
   Hakeem Naim
6. The Islamic World Is Flat(tened): Contesting Islam in South Asia in the *New York Times*, 1980–2011   165
   Rajbir Singh Judge

List of Contributors   201
Index   205

Acknowledgments

I would like to acknowledge the work of the following University of California, Davis interns in the Joseph Lab for the *New York Times* Media project from 2001 to 2022: Abdul Majid Aziz, Abigail Turner, Abir Sabbagh, Alex Chavez, Ambika Kandasamy, Amira Elmallah, Anna Hamilton, Azka Fayyaz, Azza Malik, Brandon Rapoza, Brittany Kingman, Brittney Tapia-Nunez, Carina Alexandra Mkrtchiyan, Chelsea Snow, Christopher Alam, Nour Taha, Dalal Audesh-Scarbrough, Elise Boyle, Elham Bakhtary, Eman Ateyeh, Emily Abraham, Erik Kennedy, Faisal Alghassab, Gheed Saeed, Gizem Basar, Hanna Khalil, Hannah Phillips, Imran Ahmad, Jazzmin Fragiacomo, Jessica Babaknia, Jessica Bray, Jonathan Pan, Josh Wizman, Julia Bagget, Juliet Bost, Ka Hin Wong, Karla Marquez, Karina Piser, Kavika Kapoor, Karissa Oliver, Kevin Woldhagen, Kimia Akhbari, Krystina Baudrey, Kymberley Chu, Lara Kiswani, Layla Mustafa, Luana Coberg, Layla Mustafa, Madina Stanackzai, Majid Aziz, Manpreet Singh, Marion Everidge, Marjan Ansari, Nancy Juarez, Natalie Hovsepian, Nia Robertson, Noor Halabi, Noor Adilla Jamaludin, Nour Taha, Othman Elgarguri, Puja Prathi, Rachel Diamond, Rima Akras, Maahum Shahab, Raheel Hayat, Reem Suleiman, Rita Maalouf, Sabrina Shupp, Saliem Shehadeh, Samir Halteh, Sandy Hage, Sara AlJassar, Sarah Couvalt, Sarah Sharif, Saranjit Uppal, Serena Stashak, Shana Khan, Sheeba Desai, Sohail Morar, Sophia Luskin, Soulaima Dennawi, Tara Saghir, Taylor Ward, William Northrup, Yara Kaadan, Yasaman Nourkhalaj, and Yasmine Orangi. For those interns whose names may have been unintentionally missed, I apologize.

The interns in the Joseph Lab typically worked six to eight hours a week, using ProQuest, to search for *New York Times* articles based on key terms and key decades that they were assigned. They met weekly and typically worked for a minimum of one academic year. A number of interns worked for two to three years on the project. They were required to write their own papers and present those papers in the University of California Davis Undergraduate Research Conference as well as in the Middle East/South Asia Studies Student

Research Symposium annually held in spring, until the pandemic of 2020. Some of those papers or abstracts are posted on https://sjoseph.ucdavis.edu/new-york-times-media-project.

Several early articles from the media project were coauthored with Benjamin D'Harlingue, a UCD graduate student in Cultural Studies at the time. In addition, graduate students who helped with formatting, editing, and background work include: Aleksandra Taranov, Justin Malachowski, Karin Root, Meghan Klasic, Rachel Feldman, Kevin Smith, Suzanne Guiod, Tarecq Amer, Tory Brykalski, and Zuzanna Turowska. I most especially thank Joseph Lab UCD undergraduate intern Elise Boyle and UCD graduate student Meghan Klasic for their discipline and commitment to all my book projects over several years, and specifically to the formatting and editing of this book. They were a dream team without whom multiple book projects would have languished even more than they already had. Meghan Klasic carried out the final formatting, while working full time at her postdoctoral position, and working as the graduate student researchers team lead on my Mapping the Production of Knowledge on Women and Gender in the Arab Region project. Amazing multitasker!

UCD librarian Adam Siegel helped train students and guide our use of ProQuest. He met with the team in the Joseph Lab a number of times and helped us puzzle out the limits and constraints of ProQuest and the NYT archive. His help was invaluable. The project collaborated with Profs. Laurent El Ghaoui and Babak Ayazifar's engineering Lab at the University of California, Berkeley for several years developing tools to quantify key word searches, funded by a UC Berkeley CITRIS grant. The conversations with El Ghaoui and Ayazifar were immensely productive, even though, ultimately, the Media Analysis project team elected to focus on qualitative analysis.

Many deans of the UCD College of Letters and Sciences and the many chairs of the Department of Anthropology supported the Joseph Lab with space and other resources over the 20 years of the Media Analysis project. I am most grateful for their support and the support of their staff. I wish to thank also the College of Letters and Sciences IT staff for their unstinting decades-long support of the Joseph Lab. Without their patience and persistence, this, and many other Lab projects, would have come to a technical halt.

There were many others involved in the Media Analysis project over the 20 years of this project. For names missed, I offer apologies.

Lastly, I would like specially to thank our I.B. Tauris editor Sophie Rudland. Sophie consistently reached out to me, patiently, for several years as the book was being finalized, keeping tabs on the progress, and repeatedly expressing her faith and interest in the project. That motivation is in no small measure responsible for the completion of this book. She was at every point encouraging and supportive. I.B. Tauris staff Yasmin Garcha guided us through production with gentle hands and spirit, along with Faye Robinson. I am most grateful to them all.

Davis, California
May 2022

1

Reporting Islam: Decolonizing the Representation of Muslim Women in News Media

Suad Joseph

Historic Escalated Islamophobia

The past two decades have witnessed a massive escalation of Islamophobia in the United States and Europe (Jamal and Naber 2008; Kumar 2021; Ramadan 2021; Shyrock 2010). Islamophobia is a form of racism that discriminates against Muslim persons (Kumar 2021, 7). Nadine Naber adds that Islamophobia is a manifestation of cultural racism—it racializes culture, religion, and national origin (2008). Islamophobic discourses and representations—and Islamophobic hate crimes—have disproportionally targeted Muslim women (Hamze 2016). Religion has become racialized (Bayoumi 2006); Muslims are racialized as people of color (Jamal and Naber 2008); and Muslim women are their iconic representatives (Joseph and D'Harlingue 2007; Soltani 2016). News media have contributed significantly to the racialization of Islam (Poole and Richardson 2006; Said 1997) and the targeting of Muslim women as representatives of that religion. This book is concerned with two critical developments. First are the linkages between the escalation in Islamophobia and the racialization of religion. Second is the representation of Islam, Muslims, and Muslim women in US print news media—specifically representation of Muslim women in the *New York Times* (NYT). Both developments are analyzed by the authors of this book in terms of colonialism, neocolonialism, global and regional geopolitics, capitalism, security investments, the rise of the populism and the far right in the United States and Europe, and race/gender/class politics and discourses.

No small measure of this escalated Islamophobia can be attributed to the heightened hate speech directed toward Muslims in the United States in the lead up to the 2016 presidential elections, widely reported and often enhanced in the news media. Race-baiting and anti-Muslim hate had been merged and mobilized eight years earlier against the Barack Obama presidency, the first Black American president, with the false claims that he was a closet Muslim (Moody and Holmes 2015). The aftermath of the Obama presidency saw then President Donald Trump's "Muslim Ban," a ban that the US Supreme Court upheld in 2018. The Muslim Ban restricted travel from several Muslim majority countries—Iran, Libya, Somalia, Syria, and Yemen. The US State Department reported that 40,000 people were denied entry to the United States from 2017 to 2021 as a result of the Muslim Ban (rescinded by President Joe Biden in 2021) (Alfonseca 2021).

The electoral politics of Islamophobia rhetoric is evident in the treatment of Rep. Ilhan Omar, Democratic representative from Minnesota, and Rep. Rashida Tlaib, Democratic representative from Michigan, both elected to Congress in 2018—the first Muslim women elected to Congress. Two Muslim men had been elected to Congress a decade earlier: Rep. Keith Ellison, Democrat from Minnesota in 2006, and Rep. Andre Carson, Democrat from Indiana in 2008. Both men faced Islamophobic attacks (Ellison 2016; National Press Club 2016); yet the level of hate directed at the two Muslim women representatives has seemed to be in a universe of its own (Omar 2021; Smith 2019). The conflation of Islamophobia, racism, and sexism in the attacks on Omar and Tlaib intensified each discriminatory form, amounting to intersectional discrimination (Aziz 2022).

The intensification of Islamophobia in the United States and Europe is evident in a number of opinion polls. Breitbart (2015) reported that 63 percent of the US population believe Muslim refugees should not be allowed to enter the United States. To whatever degree that their survey is accurate (given that Breitbart has fed the flames of Islamophobia), it reflects, to some degree, the impact of media misrepresentation. That large numbers of the sampling group (63 percent) were Hispanics, who themselves are often misrepresented in immigration discourses, is even more telling of the hysteria that the media rhetoric and the Muslim Ban incited toward Muslims in America (Lee 2015).

The escalation of Islamophobia in the United States and Europe comes at a time of increased Muslim populations in these regions, intensified populism, and increased anti-immigration rhetoric in national elections. The Pew Research Center estimated the Muslim population of the United States reached 3.85 million in 2020, or about 1.1 percent of the population (the third largest religion in the United States) and reported that the number of Islamic houses of worship increased from 1,209 in 2000 to 2,769 in 2020 (Mohamed 2021). The Pew Research Center projects that by 2040 Muslims will be America's second largest religious group, outnumbering Jews (Mohamed 2018). By 2050, they project that the Muslim population in the United States will be 8.1 million, equaling 2.1 percent of the population, doubling their current figures in 30 years. Despite the increased presence of Muslims in the United States, the majority (53 percent) of American say they do not personally know a Muslim (Mohamed 2021).

In Europe, a number of countries have significant Muslim populations—especially France, Germany, Italy, and England. Muslims accounted for 5 percent of the population of Europe in 2017 and are projected to grow to between 7.5 percent (with no further migration) and 14 percent (with migration) by 2050 (Pew Research Center 2017a). Globally, the Muslim population is over two billion. While Christians currently outnumber Muslims globally, many researchers project that Muslims will outnumber Christians by 2050 (World Population Review 2022). These figures alone draw attention to the importance of understanding Islamophobia and its increasing deployment in politics.

Playing to Islamophobia has become a political tactic among some American and European politicians. According to a report in the *Washington Post* (Leetaru 2015), Donald Trump's media coverage had plateaued for the six weeks prior to the San Bernardino killings in 2 December 2015. As soon as he launched his attack on Muslims, his ratings "reached a new record for the 2016 presidential race, accounting for 76 percent of all mentions of candidates of either party on national television networks and 82 percent of mentions of the GOP candidates" (Leetaru 2015). Leetaru argues that the surge in coverage for Mr. Trump came after he suggested the creation of a national database to track Muslims in America (before the San Bernardino attack). After he made this proposal, on 19 November 2015, "he went from 24 percent of all mentions of GOP candidates (which placed him under Jeb Bush) to 50 percent in just 48 hours. He then rocketed further—to 82 percent," after the San Bernardino attack (Leetaru 2015). Trump followed with a proposal to ban Muslims from entering the United States, until the "problem" was solved, a part of his general anti-immigrant rhetoric that included brutal disparagement of Mexicans and other South Americans. He even claimed he saw televised footage of Muslims in New Jersey cheering after the 9/11 attacks on New York—a claim that no television network validated (Bobic 2015). Donald Trump and Ted Cruz, both Republican presidential candidates in 2016, escalated their discriminatory remarks about Muslims in the wake of the 22 March 2016 Brussels bombing, with Ted Cruz calling for police to patrol and "secure" US Muslim neighborhoods. Both benefited from the increased news media coverage following their Islamophobic remarks and proposals. It appeared the more Islamophobic their campaigns, the more news media attention they received—further escalating and normalizing Islamophobia.

While much of Europe breathed a sigh of relief when Emmanuel Macron won a second term as president of France in 2022 (winning 58.5 percent of the vote), the stunning news was that far-right candidate Marine Le Pen garnered 41.5 percent on an anti-European Union and anti-immigrant platform. This was a significant improvement from her 33.9 percent in 2017. As the NYT reported, Le Pen's anti-immigrant platform was largely anti-Muslim and included proposals to disallow Muslim women students from wearing hijab (Cohen 2022).

Islamophobia Is Material

The impact of distorted discourses and representations, in electoral politics and especially in respected news media, is material and dangerous. According to the FBI, hate crimes perpetrated against Muslims in the United States rose by 1,617 percent from 2000 to 2001 (Alfonseca 2021). On 22 December 2015, the NYT reported that the rate of suspected hate crimes against Muslims had tripled, with 38 attacks on Muslims reported in a short period of time (Siemaszko 2015; Stack 2015). According to research referenced above, carried out by Brian Levin, a professor at California State University San Bernardino and former New York City police officer, between 11 September 2001 and 31 December 2001, there were 481 hate crimes against Muslims reported (40.1 per month). Between 2010 and 2014, there was a monthly average of 12.6 anti-Muslim hate crimes reported. The 38 hate crimes in December of 2015 represented a tripling of the average hate crimes against Muslims—based on FBI statistics that Levin compiled. The FBI reported a 67 percent increase of hate crimes against Muslims from 2014 to 2015—for a total of 5,850 incidents. Of these, the FBI indicated that 57 percent were trigged by race or ethnicity and 20 percent were motivated by religious bias (Lichtbau 2016). In 2016, 48 percent of Muslim American adults reported they had personally experienced Islamophobic discrimination in the first months of the Donald Trump administration. Most Americans acknowledge that Muslims face more discrimination than other religious groups. In 2016, the FBI reported a 67 percent increase of hate crimes against Muslims from 2014 to 2015—for a total of 5,850 incidents (Lichtbau 2016). In 2017 the Pew Research Center reported that assaults against Muslims in the United States between 2015 and 2016 surpassed the highest number of assaults following the 9/11 terrorist attacks in 2001 (Pew Research Center 2017b).

In 2017 three-fourths of Muslim adults in the United States asserted there is "a lot" of discrimination against Muslims. Seventy percent of US adults agreed with them (Pew Research Center 2017b). In 2017 hate crimes against Muslim Americans increased 17 percent from 2016. The 2019 FBI Hate Crimes Statistics Report again found an increase in hate crimes, with hate crimes against Muslim Americans second only to those against Jews (FBI 2020). In August 2021, the FBI reported a decline in hate crimes against Muslims and Arabs, but a 37 percent increase in hate crimes against Sikhs. Sikhs are often mistaken as Muslims (Hastings 2021). Race, ethnicity, and religion are often conflated in public perceptions—and often the conflation is written on the bodies of women.

The populist, conservative turn in Europe, with its anti-immigrant focal point, has produced similar material consequences. In the UK, Tell MAMA, a group that monitors anti-Muslim hate crimes, reported a 326 percent increase in hate crimes against Muslims in 2015, linked to the Brexit vote (Jeory 2016). In France there was a reported 223 percent increase in anti-Muslim threats and attacks in 2015 over 2014 (Glasser 2016). Reactions to Muslims are often trigged by nonlocal events. Oliver Wright (2015) found a spike of 300 percent of attacks on British Muslims in the week right after the November 2015 Paris attacks. The European Union Minorities and Discrimination Survey, conducted in 2017, reported that one in three European Muslims had experienced discrimination and that 27 percent had faced a racist crime (EU MDS 2017). Narzanin Massoumi, in a NYT Opinion piece, found that there was a 52 percent increase in Islamophobic events in France in 2018, a 74 percent increase in Austria, a 54 percent increase in Germany, and a 53 percent increase in Italy (Massoumi 2020). The 866-page European Islamophobia Report of 2020 found that Islamophobia in Europe has only worsened under the pandemic and is at a "tipping point" (Bayrakli and Hafez 2020). That report included the contributions of 37 experts on racism and gathered data on 31 countries.

Gendering Islamophobia

Muslim women have become a stand-in for Islam. They have become a highly magnetized target for Islamophobes. Anoosh Soltani points out that "veiled Muslim women become emblematic of Islam and are often the target of physical and verbal Islamophobic hate crimes" (2016). As Sahar Aziz observes, the media association of the "veil" with terrorism heightened the vulnerability of Muslim women, in the aftermath of 9/11 as Islam was recast from a religion to a political ideology, and people of the Muslim faith began to be thought of as political actors. This, Aziz argues, has justified discriminatory behavior against Muslims as "patriotic," among Islamophobes. Muslim women, especially those veiled, have become the subject of "intersectional discrimination," she contends—discrimination on the basis of multiple vectors, including gender, race, color, religion, and immigrant status (Aziz 2022).

The *Huffington Post* reported that Muslim women across the United States faced an increase in attacks following the election of Donald Trump in November 2016 (Hamze 2016). Similarly, Rana Elmir (2016) of the *Washington Post* reported that Muslim women in the United States have been bearing the brunt of Islamophobia. Sabrina Alimahomed-Wilson argues that violence against Muslim women gains attention in the United States only when the perpetrators of violence are foreign men. She found 85 percent of the Muslim women she interviewed in her study had been targeted with verbal assaults or threats and 25 percent experienced physical violence. Violence against Muslim women in the United States, she finds, is invisible, hidden (Alimahomed-Wilson 2017). The representation of Muslim women in the news media, under these conditions, is a vehicle for the representation of Islam. In terms of representation and in terms of vulnerability to harassment, Muslim women are in the eye of the storm (Perry 2014).

A disproportionate number of the attacks on Muslim have been on Muslim women in other countries as well. In the UK, Wright found that "Most victims of the U.K. hate crimes were Muslim girls and women aged from 14 to 45 in traditional Islamic dress. The perpetrators were mainly white males aged from 15 to 35" (Wright 2015). Another report, during the same time period, argued that Brexit had triggered the increase in attacks on Muslims in England, with Muslim women being their prime victims (Ullah 2016). Peter Hopkins argues that the racially and religiously motivated violence against Muslims in the UK is a form of gendered violence, linked particularly to the far right. He finds that most of this Islamophobic violence targets Muslim women (Hopkins 2016).

The *Edmonton Journal* (Canada) reported a "rash" of hate attacks in 2021, directed mostly at Muslim women (Wakefield 2021). As Hannan Mohamud observed, in reference to Canada, despite the increased awareness of gender-based violence, the violence against Muslim women is being ignored, particularly the violence against Black Muslim women. Those wearing hijab are most vulnerable (Mohamud 2021). In India, Islamophobic attacks in 2022 took the form of "auctioning" Muslim women on social media (Nabi 2022).

Categorical Strategies of Islamophobia

Islamophobia is a form of categorical thinking (Joseph 2019, 2021b, 2022). Categorical thinking, the grouping of people or things on the basis of presumed shared characteristics, is built into language, and perhaps built into the operations of the human brain. It is when categorical thinking homogenizes and essentializes differences within a group that it becomes problematic. It is when categorical thinking presumes or asserts that those differences are "natural," given in the peoples themselves, that it drives hate. It is when categorical thinking ranks groupings and judges the people in these groupings on a preassigned hierarchy of value or morality or status or trust that it becomes dangerous. It is when categorical thinking justifies discrimination that it becomes a form of racism. Categorical thinking undergirds the racialization of Islam. The problematics of categorical thinking have begun to be realized, even within the pages of the NYT (Solnit 2022).

A structural outcome of Islamophobia is that highly differentiated peoples have been collapsed into a racialized category on the basis of their presumed commonality of religion. A cultural outcome of this racialization is the production of figures of fear (the "terrorist"), resulting in what some scholars have called "moral panic" (Poole and Richardson 2006; Rana 2011; Salaita 2006). Racialization produces structural outcomes that create hierarchies of difference imbued with power, a "racial formation" to use the term of Omni and Winant (1994), on the global, as well as the national, stage (Balibar 1991).

Kumar argues that Islamophobia needs to be understood as about racism and not about religious intolerance (2021, 15). Racism, he argues, is integral to the dynamics of empire, reinforced by both liberal Islamophobia (liberal Islamophobia accepts "good" Muslims who accept the terms of empire) and conservative Islamophobia (conservative Islamophobia rejects "bad" Muslims who reject the terms of empire) (Kumar 2021, 12, 15). It is the recognition that Islamophobia is not about Islam as theology but rather about transforming disparate peoples into a racialized category as part of the dynamics of empire and the geopolitical dynamics of power, race, class, and gender that informs the analysis of Islamophobia of this book (Memmi 1991; Rana 2011; Salaita 2006).

Islamophobia in Print News Media

How has Islamophobia captured so much of the American political landscape? While film, television, radio, literature, social media, and other representational platforms are powerful vehicles of Islamophobia (Khatib 2006; Shaheen 1984), the role of professional print news media is particularly concerning (Friel and Falk 2007; Poole and Richardson 2006). American journalists who write misrepresentative articles or convey distorted images have become propagators of discriminatory racializing discourse directed at Muslims (often elided with Arabs and South Asians, especially Sikh South Asians) (Dabashi 2011; Hagopian 2004; Said 1997). Islamophobic representation by journalists did not begin with the 2016 elections, however. Journalistic misrepresentation of Islam, Muslims, and Muslim women has a long history in the United States and other places (Iskandar and Haddad 2013; Rana 2011). As Edward Said noted decades earlier, "covering Islam" is a political project of empire (1997). This book emerges from a 150-year analysis of the representation of Islam and Muslims in the NYT, from its establishment in 1851 to the present. The Media Analysis project began in 2001, following the events of 9/11, and has continued for over 20 years.

The Middle East and South Asia became the regional focus of the book for several reasons. The Middle East (we use the term Middle East for the Middle East and North Africa) is the historic regional origin and home of Islam. It is also the region for which most articles in the NYT discuss Islam and Muslim women. South Asia became important as it is the geographic center of Islam in the contemporary world. India and Pakistan together have more Muslims than the whole of the Middle East. India, Pakistan, Bangladesh, and Afghanistan together account for the single largest concentrations of Muslims in the world (Desilver and Masci 2017). Given their contiguity and historical relations, the Middle East and South Asia raise important comparisons for the study of the representation of Islam. As the chapters in the book demonstrate, US foreign policy toward the Middle East and South Asia is often connected in ways that appear to be reflected in the representations of Muslim women of those regions.

The NYT became the focus of the Media Analysis project following a project intensively comparing the representation of Islam, Muslims, Arab and Muslim Americans, and Muslim women, and the Middle East focusing on the Middle East, between 2000 and 2004 in the NYT and the *Wall Street Journal* (WSJ). The research found little difference between the leading national liberal newspaper and the leading national conservative newspaper in their coverage of Islam, Muslims, Arab and Muslim Americans, Muslim women, and the Middle East (Joseph 2006, 2008, 2021a; Joseph and D'Harlingue 2007, 2012). Both NYT and WSJ, in the period immediately before the 9/11 events and the period immediately after, depicted the Middle East region overwhelmingly in terms asserting or implying that hatred and violence in that region are hundreds or thousands of years old. Both depicted the region as backward and unchanging in foundational values and attributes. Both defined the region in religious terms. When conflict in the region led to the deaths of Palestinians, Lebanese, Syrians, and Israelis, both papers rarely identified the Palestinian, Lebanese, or Syrian persons who had died or those who grieved them. Both used a similar vocabulary of "violence" related to not only the region but to Arab and Muslim American citizens. Both depicted Muslim women as oppressed, voiceless, and lacking agency, and Muslim men as their oppressors. Given the similarities in the patterns of representation in the NYT and the WSJ, the Media Analysis project elected to focus on the NYT, with the thought that journalist standards of coverage might be found in the leading liberal newspaper of perhaps the world.

Media Analysis Project Methods

The long-term Media Analysis project is based on in-depth content analysis of thousands of articles from the NYT database, using ProQuest as the search tool. Over the two decades working on this project, nearly 100 undergraduate interns and graduate students have participated.[1] The project began by identifying a list of key words to search in the NYT database. Each intern was assigned specific terms to search within specific decades. The team met weekly, brought the articles from the searches, and engaged in discussions about their meanings. The Media Analysis results referenced above comparing the WSJ and the NYT also undertook a quantitative analysis of frequency of words associated with violence, policing, and other terms negatively associated with Muslims and Arabs (Joseph and D'Harlingue 2007, 2008, 2012). In addition, the Media Project spent over a year working with engineering/computer science colleagues developing programs for word counts (see endnote 1). Ultimately, we found the qualitative content analysis more revealing.

The project has been at times called the "Genealogy of Terminology" project, as we tried to identify what terms were used, when they were used, when they stopped being used, and the historical context in which they were used. For example, in the mid- to late nineteenth century, the NYT tended to use the term "Musliman" or variations thereof. It rarely used the term "Arab" until the end of the first half of the twentieth century. Many of the changes in terminology represented geopolitical changes over the 170 years. For example, references to "Jordan" in the nineteenth century are about the river, as the country did not come into existence until after World War I.

The work leading to this book took the same approach, as discussed above. Interns carried out searches of specific terms related to Muslim women, the veil, Islam, and the specific countries covered in the following chapters. Interns and graduate students met with me weekly to discuss articles and to carry out analysis. As patterns began to emerge, frameworks were developed to make sense of the patterns that emerged. As the frameworks crystalized, the team tested hypotheses against ongoing searches and findings. Eventually the arguments that comprise the chapters of this book were developed, supported by content analysis of the NYT articles.

The long-term Media Analysis project analyzing the representation of Islam, Muslims, Muslim women, Arabs, and Arab and Muslim Americans in the NYT, from 1851 to the present, reveals a very long history of misrepresentation of Islam, Muslims, Muslim women, Arab women (Arab and Muslim are often conflated in the NYT), the Middle East, and South Asia. It is important to observe that there is not a consistent or singular pattern of representation over the 170 years. There are a variety of representations of the region, of the religion, and of the men and women of the region. At times, reporting offers rather "ethnographic," descriptive accounts. There are exoticized and romanticized accounts. In the early twentieth century, for example, Arab women immigrants in New York City (most were Christian at that time) were often represented favorably in comparison to Arab men. They were often seen as hardworking, clever, beautiful. Their customs, while represented as peculiar, were often not demeaned (Joseph 2021a).

An undercurrent of misrepresentation, however, remained and began to consolidate into a more consistent discriminatory pattern in the 1950s following the formation of the state of Israel. This pattern crystalized particularly after the 1967 Arab-Israeli war. As a number of the chapters in this book document, the consolidation of a pattern of discriminatory representation of the Middle East and South Asia, Islam, and Muslim women often appears to parallel consolidation of US foreign policies or relations with the two regions or with specific countries in these regions.

After the 1967 war in the Middle East, for example, there were a number of US government operations targeting Arab Americans for surveillance and harassment. The FBI monitored Arab American citizens and residents, under Operation Boulder, among a number of other operations and programs. Those operations paralleled the increasing misrepresentation in the NYT and other news media of Arabs, Muslims, the Middle East, and Muslim women (Pennock 2018). The dynamics of colonialism, neocolonialism, orientalism, neo-orientalism, geopolitics, national security, and the matrices of power during the Cold War and its aftermath provided the soil in which state policies and NYT reporting often appear to be rooted. While the longer Media Analysis project considers historical shifts and patterns in representation in the NYT from 1851 to the present, this book focuses on the transformative period of 1980–2011.

US Engagement with Muslims, Middle East, and South Asia: 1979–2011

The period of 1979–2011 significantly shaped US political and strategic interests in the Middle East and South Asia. The three decades became a critical period of consolidation of misinformation and misrepresentation of Muslims, the Middle East and South Asia, and specific Muslim majority countries in the NYT. Representations of Muslim women in the NYT, during these decades, the authors in this book argue, appear to often resonate with US government policies toward these regions or specific countries in these regions.

Dramatic global and regional events make the decades of 1979–2011 key to analyzing the NYT's coverage of Islam, Muslims, and Muslim women in the Middle East and South Asia: The Islamic Revolution of Iran in 1979 overthrew one of the closest allies of the United States in the Middle East and set the stage for a number of regional and global events and developments. The Iran–Iraq war (1980–88) embroiled the region and a good part of the world, for a decade, taking a half million or more casualties. The Civil War in Lebanon (1975–90) saw a new phase as Israel invaded and occupied Southern Lebanon from 1982 to 2000—while Syria took control of the Beka'a area, initially at the invitation of the Lebanese government. Israel's occupation of South Lebanon triggered the founding of Hezbollah in 1982, the Lebanese Shi'i resistance movement backed by Iran that the United States labeled as a "terrorist" organization. Hamas, the Palestinian Islamic Resistance Movement, was launched in 1987 as the Palestinian First Intifada against Israeli occupation broke out—another organization the United States labeled as "terrorist." The First Gulf War (1990–91) against Iraq intensified American military engagement in the region and spawned further resistance movements, Islamic and non-Islamic. The Palestinian Second Intifada (2000–2005) eventually led to Israeli withdrawal from Palestinian Gaza and Hamas control of Gaza. The 11 September 2001 (9/11) attack on the United States was quickly followed by the Second Gulf War, the War on Afghanistan (2001–21), and the War on Iraq (2003–11) by the United States and some of its allies. As the three-decade period concludes, the Arab Uprisings, also called the Arab Spring, sparked in Tunisia in December 2010, saw the downfall of numerous autocratic leaders only to be followed by the rise again of new autocracies in the region, with the United States involved in a number of those transitions (Zayani 2015).

In South Asia, the 1979–2011 period started in the aftermath of the war between East and West Pakistan and the founding of the separate state of Bangladesh in 1971. While the Pakistan military coup in 1977 moved Pakistan toward Islamization policies, the United States continued to consider Pakistan an ally in the region, given Soviet proximity. Through numerous military and nonmilitary regimes, the United States maintained an awkward/ambivalent connection to Pakistan (Rana 2011). The Soviet Union invaded Afghanistan in 1979 and the United States began arming and training the Mujahideen Freedom Fighters (among whom was Osama bin Laden), many of whom were from Saudi Arabia. The United States launched its own war on Afghanistan in 2001 lasting through 2021. In India, Indira Gandhi came back to power in 1980 only to be assassinated by 1984. Her son Rajiv Gandhi, who also became prime minster, also was assassinated in 1991. The Bharatiya Janta Party (BJP) was established also in 1980 and slowly built its right-wing rise to power until it won elections in 2014. Throughout the period, internal tensions heightened as the rise of the BJP escalated tensions between Muslims and Hindus to the level of violent clashes and massacres. Intermittent clashes between India and Pakistan and Indian military engagement in Sri Lanka dot the landscape, as well as the BJP's close ties with Russia and China.

These highlights touch only on the large events that make this three-decade period critical to the study of news media's representation of Islam, Muslims, and Muslim women in the Middle East and South Asia. As authors in this book document, US policy toward the Middle East and South Asia shifted in some ways over the three decades. The three decades, in the United States, witnessed a variety of Republican and Democratic administrations. Policies toward specific countries varied at times, related to US shifts in national strategic interests as well as shifts in the politics of those specific regional countries. Yet, there are broad patterns that seem to connect the decades, with different US administrations reweaving the central threads of engagement. In general, US policy toward the Middle East, and to varying degrees, South Asia, was filtered through the geopolitics of oil and gas and other strategic resources. Given that these three decades emerged in the shadow of the 1973 Arab oil embargo, the various US administrations steered US policy toward efforts to control production, prices, and delivery of oil and other key resources from these regions.

A key threat to US control emerged as various resistance movements rose up, especially Palestinian, but later both Islamic and non-Islamic resistance to what was often regionally perceived as US imperial interests in the regions. The Islamic Revolution in Iran and the rise of Islamic resistance movements, many of which saw the United States as primarily responsible for deteriorations and corruptions of their societies, registered in US foreign policy. Viewing the two regions generally as fraught with violence, US foreign policy increasingly saw the two regions through the lens of religion, and for the Middle East, specifically Islam. Islam came to be defined as a threat to US foreign interests and the definition "war" became the "War Against Terror." Terror, however, was registered as largely religious, and largely Islamic.

US policy was directed at bolstering key allies for various national interests. No ally was more central than Israel. Much of US policy, in the Middle East region specifically, emerged from the priority of protecting and supporting Israel. Other key allies shifted over the three decades, as the authors of this book report. Egypt, Saudi Arabia, United Arab Emirates, Bahrain, Qatar, Lebanon, Iran, Turkey, Pakistan, and Afghanistan went in and out of favor in subtle and not so subtle ways. As some of the US allies were not allies of each other, the balancing act engaged the United States deeper, diplomatically and militarily, to manage regional changes as well as the power plays of other global powers. The rhetoric of democracy and human rights often appeared in US reports; yet, the United States regularly supported authoritarian regimes, both military and civilian. The representation of Muslim women in the NYT varied through these three decades as well. As the authors in this book document, often the variance in representation resonated with the shifts in US foreign policy toward the regions or toward specific countries in the region. The case can be made that the region continued to be viewed through the lens of gender, even as the lens shifted (Said 1978).

The Gendering of Lebanon: From Lady to Rescue to Terrorist Masculinity to Control

How reporting in the NYT shifted over time and how the representation was gendered can be seen in a condensation of the representation of Lebanon in the NYT from 1950 onward.[2] In Lebanon's "Golden Era," 1950–70, Lebanon was seen by the United States, by much of Europe, and represented in the NYT as the most Western, Western-friendly, and capitalist friendly of the Arab countries of the Middle East. It was dubbed the "Switzerland" of the Middle East, and its capital, Beirut, as the "Paris" of the Middle East. Yet there is an ambivalence, both in US and European views, and in NYT representation. A tiny country, seen as relatively democratic, relatively educated, and with a slight majority of Christians in those Golden days, Lebanon was depicted as needing protection. Its appealing attributes situated it as an "exception" in a sea of dictatorships, Arab nationalism, and anti-Western movements. Lebanon, especially Lebanese Christians, were depicted as needing rescue from Islamization. The motif of an attractive, even alluring, country needing rescue feminized Lebanon in subtle and not so subtle representations (Joseph *Submitted*).

In 1950, the NYT wrote,

> Half Christian and Half Moslem, half Western and half Oriental, Lebanon has the advantage of being in many ways neutral ground, too small to develop a preponderant mentality of her own, and with a very considerable portion of her educated population eager to see her become a Switzerland of

the Orient, maintain both political and intellectual neutrality. ("Wider Arab Study Sought to Aid U.S." 1950)

This positioning of Lebanon pulls "her" into the role of a lady removed from the fanatical politics of men. Lebanon is positioned as opposed to the "more fanatically nationalistic quarters of the Arab world" (Ross 1951). It is also positioned as opposed to Islamization. "Lebanon, according to published and other information here today, definitely has placed herself in opposition to efforts to link the Arab League states to a future pan-Islamic bloc" ("Lebanon Is Opposing Role in Islamic Bloc" 1952). Not only is Lebanon represented as a country with a slight Christian majority ("Lebanon Is Opposing Role in Islamic Bloc" 1952), but it is positioned as a bulwark against Communism, just at the height of the "Red Scare" in the United States. As the NYT reports, "Informed Lebanese show uneasy awareness that the Soviet Union's willingness to arm the Arab states might deliver the Middle East into the hands of the Communists" (Gilroy 1955).

This representation of Lebanon as friendly but fragile (and in need of protection or rescue) emerges especially in the depiction of President Camille Chamoun and his wife ("Beleaguered Lebanese, Camille Chamoun" 1958):

> The storm signals have been out for Camille Chamoun, President of tiny Lebanon, since the merger that made Syria a part of the United Arab Republic last February under President Gamal Abdel Nasser of Egypt. For the Moslems among Lebanon's 1,500,000 inhabitants tend to look to President Nasser for leadership while, among the Christians, many take an extremely apprehensive view of President Nasser's expanding "positive neutralism." The Christians are said to outnumber the Moslems, but their numerical advantage is slight at best.
>
> Long Friend of the West
>
> President Chamoun long hoped to draw the Arab States away from neutralism and to persuade them to adopt a unified policy in friendship with the West. He welcomed the 1957 Eisenhower Doctrine, designed to assist Arab States against possible Communist aggression.
>
> Cultivated and urban, perfectly at ease in English, French and Arabic, President Chamoun has always sought to make Lebanon an "invaluable transmission belt" for putting Western ideas into Middle Eastern terms. His sliver-gray hair and erect stature have come to be associated in the popular mind with the dignity of the State.

President Chamoun's wife, Zulfa, whose mother was English, is a Presbyterian and an accomplished hostess. They have two grown sons. ("Beleaguered Lebanese, Camille Chamoun" 1958)

This luxurious NYT depiction of Chamoun and his wife paints a picture of the perfect Western-friendly political couple. His half-English Presbyterian wife codifies their representation as people with whom the West can identify and whom the West can trust.

However, with the 1967 Arab-Israeli war, the representation of Lebanon becomes troubled. The Palestinian resistance movement, largely headquartered in Lebanon, was fighting an active war against Israel through South Lebanon in this period. Lebanon recalled its ambassador to the United States during the war and later asked the United States to resume ambassadorial relations ("U.S. Reports Thaw in Ties with Arabs" 1967). The Palestinians were represented as threat to the small Lebanese army and its Major General Emile Girges Bustani. Bustani was represented as a skilled diplomat who must guard against the "many Moslems, and even Christians, in the army who sympathize with the guerrillas and their leftist friends" ("Diplomatic Soldier, Emile Girges Bustani" 1969). Lebanon's weakness came through again, and its uncertain status as an ally. Yet it is enough of an ally that friendship and protection and rescue are in order, especially since the Lebanese are so cosmopolitan and understand both money and having fun (Hijai 1972).

As the Lebanese Civil War (1975–91) broke out and progressed, US involvement in Lebanon increased (including a peacekeeping mission in July 1982). Both Israel and Syria had occupied parts of Lebanon by this point. The US embassy was bombed in April 1983 and the US marine barracks were attacked in October of 1983. The United States joined the conflict by bombing Syrian positions in Lebanon. The Palestinian leadership was pushed out of Lebanon to Tunisia, and Hezbollah was born to fight Israeli occupation. In representational terms, now Lebanon appears in the NYT as no longer the Switzerland of the Middle East and Beirut is no longer its Paris. Lebanon becomes an adjective meaning fear, terror, danger, and despair. It is now the land of religion, religious conflict, of Muslim terrorists. It is the land of kidnappings by anti-Western Muslims. It is a land of leftist politics and rising Islamic movements that are elided as all anti-American. It is a country that now has a Muslim majority, rife with "gangsterism and machismo." It is Muslim and male. It is a country one can cry over (Markham 1975).

> Indeed, Why Lebanon? Is now the issue as the Moslem majority hauls down Christian privilege while Syria and Israel ponder intervention.
>
> Beirut, Lebanon is destroying itself. An improbable state since it was carved out of Syria by the French, who wanted to give a homeland to Levantine Christians and maintain a reliable foothold for their own mission civilisatrice, Lebanon is locked in a hopeless, open-ended cycle of communal violence and vendetta that has claimed at least 4,000 lives this year and left many more maimed and wounded. The Switzerland of the Middle East has swiftly degenerated into the region's Northern Ireland. Beirut, once a glittering, thinly sophisticated playground for the Arab rich, has changed masks: It is now one of this century's nastiest urban battlegrounds. Anonymous gunmen crouch behind sand-bagged barricades firing machine guns, grenade launchers, mortars, rockets and recoilless rifles at barely sighted targets; dazed women and children cower in shaking hallways; men are yanked out of automobiles in the bright glare of the Mediterranean sun, dragged away and shot if their Lebanese identity cards list a rival faith; rotting bodies, genitals horribly mutilated and hands roped behind backs, are dumped in no man's lands between warring neighborhoods; office buildings.
>
> Gangsterism and machismo, which is rife in Lebanon, do not explain the country's near civil war, however. The root clash is between the country's Maronite Christian community, which holds a disproportionate share of political power and wealth, and Moslem and leftist groups that are demanding a reordering and secularization of Lebanon's creaky polity. (Markam 1975)

Increasingly, the NYT prints letters and articles representing the Christians of Lebanon, not only at risk from Arab nationalism (Sahady 1978) but also needing US protection from the rising Muslim majority and even from being "systematically" "exterminated" (Wohl 1978). Lebanese are represented as "exhausted," as not able to bounce back as they previously always had, as in despair. The days when Beirut could rejuvenate itself are over, Thomas Friedman pronounced (Friedman 1983). By 1989, Friedman reports,

> Arab diplomats and Lebanese in Washington noted that after so many years of efforts by pro-Iranian Muslims to drive the United States out of Beirut—including car bomb attacks on the American Embassy and the Marine

headquarters—it was actions by the pro-Western Christians that finally prompted the Bush Administration to remove its diplomats altogether. (Friedman 1989)

As US interests and policies toward Lebanon shifted, and as Lebanese dynamics shifted, the representation of Lebanon in the NYT transformed in a rather gendered manner.

While representations of Lebanon and Beirut in the NYT continue to shift and evolve, in general, by the late 1980s and 1990s, it was no longer a lovely lady that needed to be and could be rescued. Rather, it was a terrifying male, Muslim, armed with Kalashnikovs and the Qur'an, that needed to be controlled. The matrices of power, geopolitics, colonialism and neocolonialism, capitalism, and US strategic national interests drove the changes in US policies toward Lebanon. A resonant shift in the representation of Lebanon in the NYT paralleled those driving factors. As the authors document in the chapters, there are many other resonances in policies and representation from 1980 to 2011 between US interests and NYT representation.

Patterns of Representation in the NYT of Muslim Countries and Muslim Women: 1979–2011

The authors of this book focus on different countries and different patterns of representation of Muslims and Muslim women in the NYT over the three decades of 1979–2011. Caroline McKusick's chapter, "Maturing Islam: Turkey as the Site of Islamic Liberalization in the *New York Times*, 1980–2011," follows the changes in the representation of Muslim women in Turkey, in the NYT as US policies toward Turkey shifted. Covering the period from the Turkish military coup in 1980 to the 2000s with the coming to power of the Justice and Development Party (AKP), she argues that following the 9/11 attack on the United States, the dynamics of the region and US government foreign policy toward the region transformed. With the launching of the "War on Terror," she contends, US foreign policy now needed a "moderate" Muslim country as an ally in the Middle East. As Turkey had begun its implementation of neoliberal economic policies, Turkey seemed poised to become that "moderate" Muslim ally for the United States in the region in the early 2000s. Turkey's dual status as a European (and member of NATO) and a Middle Eastern country (the fountain head of the Ottoman Empire that dominated the region from 1300 to 1922) lubricated its mediating role. Turkish Muslim women, she found, came to symbolize the country, modernizing and integrating into the global capitalist markets.

While the NYT continued to view Turkey through the "clash of civilizations" lens (Huntington 1993, 1996), Turkey, in the 2000s, was no longer seen as "stuck in the past," as it had been represented in the earlier decades. Rather, McKusick finds that the clash of civilizations (between Western/modern and Oriental/traditional) is presented in the NYT in the 2000s as a productive engagement. Turkey is seen as embattled with itself, moving toward progress by taking on the old Oriental traditions. Women, in this narrative line, come to be represented in the NYT as active agents of this push to modernity and civility. Muslim Turkish women emerge from the representation in the "collective" to being portrayed as individuals. The representation shifts from one that paints Turkish Muslim women as silent, invisible, backward, oppressed, objects of observation to stories of Turkish Muslim women as agents, having personal concerns, youthful and rebellious, outspoken, headstrong, and entrepreneurial (capitalist friendly). The contradictions in the "clash of civilizations" shift from being a burden or dead-end trap for the Turkish Muslim women to being the very process through which they help the nation transform to modernity, even being the handmaidens for the reconciliation of Islam and capitalism. This familiar figure of the modern Turkish Muslim woman offered by the NYT in the early 2000s, McKusick contends, requires as much rigorous critical analysis and contextualization as the figure of the silent, oppressed, backward Turkish Muslim woman of the 1980s.

Lena Meari, "The Material Life of Representation: 'Veiled Muslim Women' in the *New York Times*, 1980–2011," traces the gendering of Islamophobia. She analyzes the transformations in the representation of veiled Muslim women in the NYT over the three-decade period, finding in each decade a shifting narration corresponding to structural and political shifts in the United States. The representations change over time, she finds. Through those transformations, she argues there is an embedded thread, reproducing colonialist, racist, and Orientalist discourses, while mystifying US political–economic investments in the Middle East. She maps the three decades of representations to identify the images, the shifts, the narratives, and the political work undertaken by the images, in relation to US foreign policy in the region. This mapping, she contends, offers a genealogy of the racial formation of Islam and its gendering in the representations in the NYT, and the changing US interests in the region.

In the 1980s Meari finds that the NYT articles on Muslim women tended to focus on Saudi Arabia, Iran, and Afghanistan, three countries that were of vital interest to the United States at the time, for their oil or their dynamic in regional/global politics. During this decade, NYT articles featured the veil as an object of oppression, the veil symbolizing the subordination of Muslim women in these countries. While the diverse meanings of the veil often appear in NYT articles (an item of faith, devotion, self-protection, and a status equalizer), a negative frame about the veil as oppressive modulates the stories. The frame emerges as a discourse on discrimination against Muslim women in a repressive and hierarchical society in which the veil, or the figure of the veiled Muslim woman, is a stand-in for what is wrong and backward about the society. In the specific context of the post-1979 Iranian Revolution, the veil also stands in for anti-Western sentiments. The Islamic Revolution, represented as anti-Western, is seen as repressive and the veiled Muslim woman is seen as symbolic of the oppressive character of anti-Western Iran post-Islamic Revolution. It is in the case of the Iran Islamic Revolution and Afghanistan under the Russian invasion in the 1980s that the narrative of the veiled Muslim woman as victim needing rescue by the West takes is expansive form in the NYT (Abu Lughod 2013).

By the 1990s, with the Islamic regime fully installed in Iran, and Afghanistan turning to Taliban control, the veil becomes a consolidated sign of Muslim women's oppression and the oppressiveness and backwardness of a country, according to Meari's reading of the NYT in this period. During this time, Iran and Afghanistan are positioned as regimes hostile to the United States and Islamic movements are gaining momentum in the Middle East, including Algeria, Sudan, and Egypt. The term "Islamic fundamentalism" drives a discourse about Islam as a political ideology hostile to the West. Political movements are often seen through the singular lens of religion (such as Hamas in Palestine and Hezbollah in Lebanon). Again, the clash of civilizations lens frames the discussion in the NYT with articles representing the region as needing Western help to modernize and Muslim women their prominent object of liberation. The diverse meanings of the veil for Muslim women, in the 1990s, Meari finds, crystalize into one meaning: oppression. In the 1990s, Meari argues, the focus is on the ethical responsibility of the West to rescue veiled Muslim women from their societies.

The 2000s representation in the NYT are dramatically impacted by the 9/11 events, including the war on Afghanistan, the war on Iraq, and the "War on Terror." Veiled Muslim women come to be seen as part of Islamic terrorism, rather than oppressed subjects needing rescue. The 2000s articles in the NYT turn their attention to the "enemy" at home, with Muslim Americans being tracked, searched, and imprisoned. Securitization of the home front leads to surveillance of domestic communities. Veiled Muslim women become their most visible object. A considerable number of articles in the NYT in this period group Muslim women into "good" Muslim women ("modern," oppose the veil, support the West) and "bad" Muslim women (conservative, support the veil, critical of the West). The three-decade survey Meari undertakes produces a map of changing political alignments in the United States that appear to parallel changing representational narratives in the NYT.

Tanzeen Doha, "Specters of Islam: Anti-Islamist (Re)Presentations in the *New York Times* and Academic Feminism, 1979–2011," traces a different kind of genealogy: the parallels in the representation of Muslim women in the NYT and academic feminist understandings of Muslim women during the same period of time. His periodization of the three decades focuses on signature Islamic events. The analysis produces a mapping of anti-Islamist moves in feminism and the academy. He moves away from the conceptualizations of Islamophobia as either a set of misinformation that produces a behavioral–psychological disposition or as anti-Muslim racism. For Doha, Islamophobia entails a systematic process of negating and undermining the world-making aspirations of Islam. Insofar as Muslim women have become iconic representatives of Islam in Western discourse, he examines the parallel moves he finds in academic feminism and media representation of Muslim women, both of which, he contends, promote anti-Islamism. He argues that anti-Islamism is found in a wide spectrum of academic feminist thinking—liberal, Marxist, post-structural—despite the many critiques of hegemonic feminist discourses in postcolonial and transnational feminist theory. While not undertaking a comprehensive critique of feminist thinking, Doha's concern is the notion that feminist discourse is largely grounded in secularity and that modern secularity turns Islam into culture by decentering Sharia.

Doha reviews signature Islamic events from the 1979 Islamic Revolution in Iran, the 1980s consolidation of Islam, the 1991–2001 period of Islamic reconfiguration and US hegemony post-Cold War, and the 2001–11 period. The killing of Osama bin Laden, during the height of the Arab protests in 2011, is represented as the end of the "Islamist Winter" in the face of the "Arab Spring." Doha finds significant parallels between media representation of Muslim women and feminist discourse in each of these periods. With some exceptions, he argues that modern academic feminism and Islamism are incompatible, in their visions of the world.

Hakeem Naim, "Friends and Foes: The Pragmatic Liberal Biases in Representation of Saudi Women vs. Iranian Women in the *New York Times*, 1980–2011," compares the representation of Saudi Arabian women and Iranian women over a three-decade period of US relations with those two countries. Women of both Saudi Arabia and Iran were represented as oppressed in the NYT, he finds, consistent with the findings of other scholars in this book. He comes to an intriguing additional finding. During the period under review, in general, the oppression of Iranian women was attributed to the Iranian state. The oppression of Saudi women, however, he argues, was attributed, in the NYT, to religion, culture, and tradition. The period under review is the period immediately after the Islamic Revolution in Iran, and after the year-long taking of American hostages in the American embassy in Tehran. Sentiment against Iran was running high not only in the American public but also in the American government.

Iran had turned from close ally in the Middle East under the Shah, to fierce enemy under the ayatollahs. The US government withheld Iranian deposits in American banks, sanctioned Iranian goods, and treated Iran as a terrorist pariah state. The NYT, Naim reports, represented Iran during this period of time as a country ruled by Islamic tyranny. The Iranian government was represented as a state governed by irrational religion and irrational men of religion.

Saudi Arabia remained a close ally of the United States and became a fierce enemy of the Iranian state during this review period. While the NYT represented Saudi women as oppressed, their oppression was not represented as a condition of their state, their government, despite the fact that it was the Saudi state that imposed shari'a (Islamic law) and controlled the religious courts and created secular laws that were oppressive to women (women were not allowed to drive, could not pass citizenship on to their children, could travel only with their male kin's permission, and so forth). Rather, the state was absolved of responsibility for the condition of Saudi women. The oppression of Saudi women, in the NYT, was attributed to Islam, to culture, and to centuries old traditions. Naim argues that the difference in attribution of the causes of women's oppression in the NYT parallel the difference in US foreign policy toward Saudi Arabia versus Iran. He suggests that representation of Muslim women in the NYT be understood in the context of US economic and political interests in the Middle East, US national security, the matrices of power, American-centric values, and American centrism.

Rajbir Judge, "The Islamic World Is Flat(tened)": Contesting Islam in South Asia in the *New York Times*, 1980–2011," focuses on the representation of Muslim women of South Asia in the NYT, particularly on Pakistan and Bangladesh. He argues that the NYT flattened the dynamism of Islamic tradition in South Asia. Tracing shifts in the three-decade period, he finds a pattern of representation condensed into the binary of the Good Muslim/Bad Muslim. Bangladesh emerged as embodying Good Islam with efforts at liberal secularism. Bangladesh experimented with neoliberal economic policies, shifted its policies in favor of the United States, took on the mantle of the "civilizational war" against Islamic terrorism by attacking Islamic "radicals" in its own country, and made advances for women. Its face was the face of a "gentler" Islam, in the NYT's representation of Bangladesh.

Pakistan emerged as embodying "Bad Islam." It sported ties that were too close to post-Islamic Revolution Iran, and was accused of emulating Iran. The pre-1978 period had seemed hopeful in liberalization of Pakistan, but by 1979, NYT declared Pakistan as having struck against freedom, derailing the progress that had been made earlier under a regime friendly to liberalism and friendly to the United States. The specter of Islamic Pakistan forcing Islamization upon its women filled many pages in the NYT. Yet, Pakistan was a US ally. As an ally of the US government during the Cold War, Pakistan received a soft critique. The hope that it would right itself was proposed often in the NYT. It was claimed to have the civilizational capacity to slow down the decivilizing aspects of Islamic religion.

As Pakistani regimes changed, the representation of its treatment of women and the threat of Islam shifted. As Bangladeshi regimes changed, representation of its treatment of its women and the threat of Islam shifted. The changes in the representation of Pakistan, Islam in Pakistan, and Muslim women in Pakistan, Judge argues, paralleled shifts in US foreign policy toward Pakistan. The changes in the representation of Bangladesh, Islam in Bangladesh, and Muslim women in Bangladesh had a remarkable parallel to US foreign policy toward Bangladesh. In both cases, regional geopolitics came to be written on the bodies of the women of these countries. Judge argues that women were the ground on which the debates of the colonial order played out. The women were not the subject of the debates but a site, a location, a set of bodies on which could be inscribed the terms of colonial contestation.

Decolonizing the Representation of Muslim Women in the News Media

What is the reality of Muslim women? The expansive history of creativity, arts, literature, language, politics, technology, science, philosophies, mathematics, social movements, and social change in which Muslim women (and non-Muslim women of the regions) have played roles in the Middle East and South Asia is not the subject of this book. The newly published *Handbook of Middle East Women* (Joseph and Zaatari 2022) documents histories of civilization after civilization, of invention and innovation, of dynamic societies with robust populations. The 100-page article by Hatoon Al Fassi (divided into two chapters) details period after period in which women played critical political and social roles in both pre-Islamic and post-Islamic Middle East and South Asia. The 46 chapters written by 50 scholars offer in-depth and comprehensive reviews of research on history, literature, arts, culture, social dynamics, politics, and economies covering 2,000 years of history.

While this book is not a history of Islam, Islamic civilizations and cultures, or Muslim women, it calls out the misrepresentation of Islam and Muslim women in the NYT or other news media. Yet, it suggests more. It is an invitation to readers to seek out information and to counter the misrepresentation, the racialization, and the discrimination. It is an invitation to learn about Islam and Muslim women. It is an invitation to situate them in their cultural and historical context; in the context of history of racialization; and in the history of colonialism, neocolonialism, capitalism, and empire. It is an invitation to decolonize the production of knowledge about Islam and Muslim women, to decolonize the production of knowledge on women and gender globally (Mignolo and Walsh 2018; Santos 2007, 2014, 2018), and to decolonize the journalism.[3]

While it is not the purview of this book to detail the history of Muslim women of the Middle East and South Asia, it is also not the claim of this book that NYT has offered only one singular representation of these regions and of Muslim women in these regions. It is the claim that there have been critical patterns and that these patterns have a noticeable parallel to US foreign policy to these regions and to specific countries in these regions. It is also the case that there has been noticeable shifting in the past five years or so in the NYT. Muslims are more often identified as persons with lives that are loved and mourned. More articles seem to report understanding of the oppression of the Palestinians. An article on Sunday, 17 April 2022, for example, not only lists the Palestinians who died under Israeli gunfire but also names them, their ages, and their professions or social roles (Abulrahim 2022).

The critical intervention of this book is that Islamophobia and misrepresentation of Muslim women is not just about Islam or about Muslim women (Kumar 2021). It is about empire, it is about race, class, gender, and the matrices of power (Rana 2011; Said 1997; Salaita 2006). Muslims (and Muslim women as their iconic representatives) are not necessarily exceptional in being misrepresented in leading US print news media. Misrepresentation of racialized groups has been historic. It has been the Jews; it has been the Irish; it has been the Italians; it has been the Japanese; it has been the Chinese; it has been the Mexicans. Similar representations have been used again and again. "They" are backward, they are slovenly and lazy, they are rich, they are after our riches, their women are oppressed by their men, their men are after "our" women. They are an enemy within and an enemy without. One only needs to be reminded that the United States put Japanese Americans into internment camps and incarceration sites during World War II. What is less well known is that, in 1987, the FBI had a contingency plan to put Arab Americans in internment camps in Oakdale,

LA, if war with certain countries broke out. That information was revealed by California representative Robert Matsui to the Sacramento Bee in 1991 and was covered by very few national newspapers (Joseph 1999; Mecoy 1991).

Misrepresentation of Muslim women is about rationalizing hierarchy and inequality through the manipulated representation of the bodies of women. It is a way of dividing populations and creating enemies, internally and externally. All forms of discrimination have to be challenged, because phobia is not about religion or any one religion, it is not about specific "races"—it is about institutionalizing matrices of power. Muslims are the fear object of the historical moment. Much of Islamophobia is about creating an "other." It is about consolidating selected internal class, race, and gender loyalties. It is about constructing women as iconic representatives of what is wrong or unjust or "bad" in other societies in order to justify strategic interventions toward their countries, often with the elites of those regions working hand in hand with empire for the extraction of labor and resources from their own peoples. The representation of Islam and Muslim women must be understood not just in the context of Islam and Muslim women but in the context of global history, in the context of colonialism, neocolonialism, race, class, and gender globally. It needs to put into the context of how religions and genders are understood, represented, and materially treated in the context of the history of empire.

News media play a significant role in representation and misrepresentation. They are called upon to tell the stories of peoples, nations, and worlds. They are called upon to explain the past and document the present. They are called upon to be truth tellers to power. As the leading liberal newspaper of the United States and perhaps the world, the NYT holds itself responsible for setting a journalist standard for ethical reporting and representation ("Ethical Journalism: A Handbook of Values and Practices for the News and Opinion Departments" 2022). This book documents some of the failures of the NYT to achieve its own standard of reporting, representation, and journalism.

Notes

1   I would like to acknowledge the work of the following University of California, Davis undergraduate interns in the Joseph Lab for this project: Abdul Majid Aziz, Abigail Turner, Abir Sabbagh, Alex Chavez, Ambika Kandasamy, Amira Elmallah,

Anna Hamilton, Azka Fayyaz, Azza Malik, Brandon Rapoza, Brittany Kingman, Brittney Tapia-Nunez, Carina Alexandra Mkrtchiyan, Chelsea Snow, Christopher Alam, Nour Taha, Dalal Audesh-Scarbrough, Elise Boyle, Elham Bakhtary, Eman Ateyeh, Emily Abraham, Erik Kennedy, Faisal Alghassab, Gheed Saeed, Gizem Basar, Hanna Khalil, Hannah Phillips, Imran Ahmad, Jazzmin Fragiacomo, Jessica Babaknia, Jessica Bray, Jonathan Pan, Josh Wizman, Julia Bagget, Juliet Bost, Ka Hin Wong, Karla Marquez, Karina Piser, Kavika Kapoor, Karissa Oliver, Kevin Woldhagen, Kimia Akhbari, Krystina Baudrey, Kymberley Chu, Lara Kiswani, Layla Mustafa, Luana Coberg, Layla Mustafa, Madina Stanackzai, Majid Aziz, Manpreet Singh, Marion Everidge, Marjan Ansari, Nancy Juarez, Natalie Hovsepian, Nia Robertson, Noor Halabi, Noor Adilla Jamaludin, Nour Taha, Othman Elgarguri, Puja Prathi, Rachel Diamond, Rima Akras, Maahum Shahab, Raheel Hayat, Reem Suleiman, Rita Maalouf, Sabrina Shupp, Saliem Shehadeh, Samir Halteh, Sandy Hage, Sara AlJassar, Sarah Couvalt, Sarah Sharif, Saranjit Uppal, Serena Stashak, Shana Khan, Sheeba Desai, Sohail Morar, Sophia Luskin, Soulaima Dennawi, Tara Saghir, Taylor Ward, William Northrup, Yara Kaadan, Yasaman Nourkhalaj, and Yasmine Orangi. In addition, graduate students who helped with formatting, editing, and background work include: Aleksandra Taranov, Elise Boyle, Justin Malachowski, Karin Root, Meghan Klasic, Rachel Feldman, Kevin Smith, Suzanne Guiod, Tarecq Amer, Tory Brykalski, and Zuzanna Turowska. Several early articles from the media project were coauthored with Benjamin D'Harlingue. I also thank UC Davis librarian Adam Siegel who helped train students and guide our utilization of ProQuest. The project collaborated with Profs. Laurent El Ghaoui and Babak Ayazifar's engineering Lab at the University of California, Berkeley for several years developing tools to quantify key word searches, funded by a UC Berkeley CITRIS grant. It was during this period of working with El Ghaoui and Ayazifar's Lab that Lena Meari, Tanzeen Doha, Hakeem Naim, Rajbir Judge, Caroline McKusick, and Kevin Smith (Smith was part of this project in the early days, before he redirected his research away from anthropology) met weekly with me and the interns to discuss the findings, patterns, and approaches to the three-decade representation of Muslim women in the NYT. There were others involved over the 20 years of this project. For names missed, I offer apologies.

2   This section is summarized from a larger Joseph paper "How Switzerland Was Lost" that is in progress. Jessica Bray, UC Davis undergraduate intern, searched the NYT database for articles from 2000 to 2010. Lena Meari, at that time UC Davis graduate student, searched and evaluated the NYT articles for patterns that I had hypothesized for the 1950–90 period. Nour Taha, UC Davis undergraduate intern, assisted with searching for the full references. The final analysis is mine and I take responsibility for any shortcomings.

3 A critical site to address the representation of Muslim women, Islam, and Islamic histories and cultures is the training of future journalists. There is a present and urgent need to train early career journalists and communication experts in the histories, cultures, and global diversities of Islam and Muslim women. Journalism students are the future of journalism. Work that is done with them will impact the understandings of Islam, Islamic culture, and Muslim women around the world. To learn about training institutes for journalists see: sjoseph.ucdavis.edu/muslim-women-and-media-training-institute; acls.org/programs/luce-acls-program-in-religion-journalism-international-affairs/; www.hluce.org/programs/theology/.

References

Abdulrahim, Raja. 2022. "'We're Exhausted': Palestinians Decry Israeli Raids." *New York Times*, 17 April 2022: 1.13.

Abu Lughod, Lila. 2013. *Do Muslim Women Need Saving?* Cambridge, MA: Harvard University Press.

Alfonseca, Kiara. 2021. "20 Years after 9/11, Islamophobia Continues to Haunt Muslims. Anti-Muslim Hate Crimes Spiked after 9/11 and during the Trump Administration." *ABC News*, 11 September 2021. https://abcnews.go.com/US/20-years-911-islamophobia-continues-haunt-muslims/story?id=79732049 (accessed on January 2022).

Alimahomed-Wilson, Sabrina. 2017. "Invisible Violence: Gender, Islamophobia, and the Hidden Assault on U.S. Muslim Women." *Women, Gender, and Families of Color* 5 (1): 73–97.

Aziz, Sahar 2022. "Terrorism and the Muslim 'Veil.'" *Oxford Islamic Studies Online*. http://www.oxfordislamicstudies.com/Public/focus/essay1009_terrorism_and_the_muslim_veil.html (accessed on January 2022).

Balibar, Etienne. 1991. "Is There a Neo-Racism?" In *Race, Nation, Class: Ambiguous Identities*, edited by Etienne Balibar and Immanuel Wallerstein, 17–28. London: Verso.

Bayoumi, Moustafa. 2006. "Racing Religion." *New Centennial Review* 6 (2): 267–93.

Bayrakli, Enes, and Farid Hafez, eds. 2020. "European Islamophobia Report 2020." Andalou Agency. https://www.aa.com.tr/en/world/islamophobia-in-europe-has-worsened-in-2020-report/2460785 (accessed on January 2022).

"Beleaguered Lebanese, Camille Chamoun." 1958. *New York Times*, 12 April 1958: 6.6.

Breitbart 2015, http://www.breitbart.com/big-government/2015/12/02/poll-strong-majority-including-63-of-hispanics-believe-u-s-should-not-accept-muslim-refugees/ (accessed on January 2022).

Bobic, Igor. 2015. "Donald Trump Calls for 'Complete Shutdown' of Muslims Entering U.S." *Huffington Post*, 8 December 2015.

Cohen, Roger. 2022. "In France, Macron Defeats Le Pen for Presidency." *New York Times*, 25 April 2022: A1, A6.

Dabashi, Hamid 2011. *Brown Skin, White Masks*. London: Pluto Press.

Desilver, Drew, and David Masci. 2017. "World's Muslim Population More Widespread Than You Might Think." Pew Research Center. https://www.pewresearch.org/fact-tank/2017/01/31/worlds-muslim-population-more-widespread-than-you-might-think/ (accessed on January 2022).

"Diplomatic Soldier, Emile Girges Bustani," 1969. *New York Times*, 1 November 1969: 3.3.

Ellison, Keith. 2016. "I'm the First Muslim in Congress: I Believe American Can Beat Islamophobia." *Washington Post*, 10 September 2016.

Elmir, Rana. 2016. "How Muslim Women Bear the Brunt of Islamophobia. We're Treated as Both Villains and Victims." *Washington Post*, 16 September 2016.

"Ethical Journalism: A Handbook of Values and Practices for the News and Opinion Departments." 2022. *New York Times*. https://www.nytimes.com/editorial-standards/ethical-journalism.html (accessed on January 2022).

European Union. 2017. "Second European Union Minorities and Discrimination Survey: Main Results." *European Union Agency for Fundamental Rights*. https://fra.europa.eu/sites/default/files/fra_uploads/fra-2017-eu-midis-ii-main-results_en.pdf.

Federal Bureau of Investigation. 2020. "FY 2019 Hate Crimes Statistics Report." FBI. https://www.justice.gov/crs/highlights/FY-2019-Hate-Crimes.

Friedman, Thomas L. 1983. "Beirut, the City of Despair." *New York Times*, 28 November 1983: A1.

Friedman, Thomas L. 1989. "Americans at Lebanon Embassy Pull Out Amid Christian Threats." 7 September 1989: 1.1.

Friel, Howard, and Richard Falk. 2007. *Israel-Palestine on Record. How the New York Times Misreports Conflict in the Middle East*. London: Verso.

Gilroy, Harry. 1955. "Lebanese Uneasy at Red Arms Bids." *New York Times*, 2 October 1955: 10.

Glasser, Anne 2016. "New French Report Shows Rise in Attacks on Muslims, Sustained Targeting of Jews." *Human Rights First*. http://www.humanrightsfi

rst.org/blog/new-french-report-shows-rise-attacks-muslims-sustained-targeting-jews (accessed on January 2022).

Hagopian, Elaine, ed. 2004. *Civil Rights in Peril: The Targeting of Arabs and Muslims*. London: Pluto Press.

Hamze, Adam. 2016. "Muslim Women in America Face Attacks in the Face of Donald Trump's Win." *Huffington Post*, 11 November 2016.

Hastings, Dorothy. 2021. "20 Years on, Muslim Journalists Reflect on Reporting in a post-9//11 World." *Nation*, 7 September 2021.

Hijazi, Ihsan A. 1972. "In Beirut: Exiles, Intrigue and Money, by Ihsan A. Hijazi." *New York Times*, 21 January 1972.

Hopkins, Peter. 2016. "Gendering Islamophobia, Racism and White Supremacy." *Dialogues in Human Geography* 6 (2): 186–89.

Huntington, Samuel. 1993. "The Clash of Civilizations?" *Foreign Affairs*. https://www.foreignaffairs.com (accessed on January 2022).

Huntington, Samuel. 1996. *The Clash of Civilizations and the Remaking of World Order*. New York: Simon & Schuster.

Iskandar, Adel, and Bassam Haddad, eds. 2013. *Mediating the Arab Uprising*. Washington, DC: Tadween.

Jamal, Amaney, and Nadine Naber, eds. 2008. *Race and Arab Americans before and after 9/11: From Invisible Citizens to Visible Subjects*. Syracuse, NY: Syracuse University Press.

Jeory, Ted. 2016. "UK Entering 'Uncharted Territory' of Islamophobia after Brexit Vote." *Independent*, 27 June 2016.

Joseph, Suad. 1999. "Against the Grain of the Nation-The Arab." In *Arabs in America: Building a New Future*, edited by Michael W. Suleiman, 257–71. Philadelphia, PA: Temple University Press.

Joseph, Suad. 2006. "(Mis)Representing Arab and Muslim American: Recurring Patterns in U.S. Print Media." *Arab-US Media Forum*. Queenstown, MD: Aspen Institute (Autumn): 2–3.

Joseph, Suad. 2019. "Categorical Thinking." In *Economic and Social Commission for West Africa*. Beirut: United Nations.

Joseph, Suad. 2021a. "Arab American Gender Representations in the *New York Times*: 1851–1919." In *Arab American Women: Representation and Refusal*, edited by Michael W. Suleiman, Suad Joseph, and Louise Cainkar, 329–64. Syracuse, NY: Syracuse University Press.

Joseph, Suad. 2021b. "Brothers and Sisters, Husbands and Wives: Love, Power, and Being an In-Law." In *Brothers and Sisters. Sibling Relationships Across the Life*

Course, edited by Ann Buchanan and Anna Rotkirch, 105–21. Cham: Palgrave Macmillan.

Joseph, Suad. 2022. "The Politics of Engaged Gender Research." In *The Politics of Engaged Gender Research in the Arab Region: Feminist Fieldwork and the Production of Knowledge*, edited by Suad Joseph, Lena Meari, and Zeina Zaatari, 33–50. London: I.B. Tauris.

Joseph, Suad. *Submitted*. "How Switzerland Was Lost to the West: The Orientalization of Lebanon in the *New York Times*." *Islamophobia Studies Journal*.

Joseph, Suad, and Benjamin D'Harlingue. 2007. "Media Representations and the Criminalization of Arab Americans and Muslim Americans." In *Women's Lives: Multicultural Perspectives*, edited by Gwyn Kirk and Margo Okazawa-Rey, 464–68. Syracuse, NY: Syracuse University Press.

Joseph, Suad and Benjamin D'Harlinque. 2012. "The Wall Street Journal's Muslims: Representing Islam in American Print News Media." *Islamophobia Studies Journal* 1(1) (Spring): 132–64. Center for Race and Gender. University of California, Berkeley.

Joseph, Suad, Benjamin D'Harlingue, and Ka Hin Wong. 2008. "Arab Americans and Muslim Americans in the New York Times, Before and After 9/11." In *From Invisible Citizens to Visible Subjects: Arab American Identities before and after 9/11*, edited by Amaney Jamal and Nadine Naber, 229–75. Syracuse, NY: Syracuse University Press.

Joseph, Suad, and Zeina Zaatari, eds. 2022. *Handbook of Middle East Women*. London: Routledge.

Khatib, Lina. 2006. *Filming the Middle East: Politics in the Cinemas of Hollywood and the Arab World*. London: I.B. Tauris.

Kumar, Deepa 2021. *Islamophobia and the Politics of Empire. 20 Years after 9/11*. New York: Verso.

"Lebanon Is Opposing Role in Islamic Bloc." 1952. *New York Times*, 7 April 1952: 3.3.

Lee, Tony. 2015. "Poll: Strong Majority–Including 63% of Hispanics–Believe U.S. Should Not Accept Muslim Refugees." *Breitbart*, 2 December 2015.

Leetaru, Kalev. 2015. "How Donald Trump Attacks on Muslim Brought Him More Media Coverage Than Ever." *Washington Post*, 13 December 2015.

Lichtbau, Eric. 2016. "US Hate Crimes Surge Fueled by Attacks on Muslims." *New York Times*, 15 November 2016.

Markham, James M. 1975. "Cry Lebanon." *New York Times*, 9 November 1975: P264, section 264, vol. CXXV, no. 42,023.

Massoumi, Narzanin. 2020. "Why Is Europe So Islamophobic?" *New York Times*, 6 March 2020.

Mecoy, Laura. 1991. "Questioning of Arab-Americans Protested." *Sacramento Bee*, 24 January 1991: A9.

Memmi, Albert. 1991. *The Colonizer and the Colonized*. Boston, MA: Beacon Press.

Mignolo, Walter D., and Catherine E. Walsh. 2018. *On Decoloniality. Concepts, Analytics, Praxis*. Durham, NC: Duke University Press.

Mohamed, Besheer, 2018. "New Estimates Show U.S. Muslim Population Continues to Grow." Pew Research Center. https://bible-quran.com/wp-content/uploads/2018/10/2018-A-new-estimate-of-U.S.-Muslim-population-Pew-Research.pdf.

Mohamed, Besheer. 2021. "Muslims Are a Growing Presence in the U.S., But Still Face Negative Views From the Public." Pew Research Center. https://www.pewresearch.org/fact-tank/2021/09/01/muslims-are-a-growing-presence-in-u-s-but-still-face-negative-views-from-the-public/ (accessed on January 2022).

Mohamud, Hannan. 2021. "Hate Crimes against Black Muslim Women Are Skyrocketing—Why Is No One Paying Attention?" *Refinery 29*, July 2021.

Moody, Chris, and Kristen Holmes. 2015. "Donald Trump's History of Suggesting Obama Is a Muslim." *CNN*, 18 September 2015.

Naber, Nadine. 2008. "'Look, Mohammed the Terrorist is Coming!' Cultural Racism, Nation-Based Racism, and Intersectionality of Oppressions after 9/11." In *Race and Arab Americans before and after 9/11: From Invisible Citizens to Visible Subjects,* edited by A. Jamal and N. Naber, 276–304. Syracuse, NY: Syracuse University Press.

Nabi, Safina. 2022. "Online 'Auctions' of Women Are Just the Latest Attacks on Muslim in India." *MIT Technology Review*, 21 February 2022.

National Press Club. 2016. "U.S. Reps Andre Carson and Keith Ellison on Islamophobia Election." YouTube. https://www.youtube.com/watch?v=DEIbptZFKjA.

Omar, Ilham. 2021. "Rep. Omar Remarks on Islamophobia." *Minnesota 5th District Press Release*, 1 December 2021. https://omar.house.gov/media/press-releases/rep-omar-remarks-islamophobia (accessed on January 2022).

Omni, Michael, and Howard Winant. 1994. *Racial Formation in the United States: From the 1960s to the 1990s*. New York: Routledge.

Pennock, Pamela E. 2018. "From 1967 to Operation Boulder: The Erosion of Arab Americans Civil Liberties in the 1970s." *Arab Studies Quarterly* 40 (1): 41–52.

Perry, Barbara. 2014. "Gendered Islamophobia: Hate Crime against Muslim Women." *Social Identities: Journal for the Study of Race, Nation and Culture* 20 (1): 74–89.

Pew Research Center. 2017a. "Europe's Growing Muslim Population." https://www.pewresearch.org/religion/2017/11/29/europes-growing-muslim-population/ (accessed on January 2022).

Pew Research Center. 2017b. "Assaults against Muslims in US Surpass 2001 Level." https://www.pewresearch.org/fact-tank/2017/11/15/assaults-against-muslims-in-u-s-surpass-2001-level/ (accessed on January 2022).

Poole, Elizabeth, and John E. Richardson, eds. 2006. *Muslims and the News Media*. London: I.B. Tauris.

Ramadan, Janna. 2021. "Perpetuating Islamophobic Discrimination in the United States: Examining the Relationship between News, Social Media, and Hate Crimes." *Harvard Human Rights Journal*. https://harvardhrj.com/2021/05/perpetuating-islamophobic-discrimination-in-the-united-states-examining-the-relationship-between-news-social-media-and-hate-crimes/ (accessed on January 2022).

Rana, Junaid. 2011. *Terrifying Muslims: Race and Labor in the South Asian Diaspora*. Durham, NC: Duke University Press.

Ross, Albion. 1951. "Town in Lebanon to Stress U.S. Ways." *New York Times*, 7 October 1951: 30.30.

Sahady, Michael S. 1978. "Letters: 'The Lebanese Ask That They Be Left Alone.'" *New York Times*, 13 July 1978: 20.20.

Said, Edward. 1978. *Orientalism*. New York: Pantheon Books.

Said, Edward. 1997. *Covering Islam*. New York: Knopf Doubleday.

Salaita, Steven. *2006. Anti-Arab Racism in the USA: Where It Comes from and What It Means for Politics Today*. London: Pluto Press.

Santos, Boaventura de Sousa, ed. 2007. *Another Knowledge Is Possible: Beyond Northern Epistemologies*. London: Verso.

Santos, Boaventura de Sousa. 2014. *Epistemologies of the South: Justice against Epistemicide*. London: Routledge.

Santos, Boaventura de Sousa. 2018. *The End of the Cognitive Empire: The Coming of Age of Epistemologies of the South*. Durham, NC: Duke University Press.

Shaheen, Jack G. 1984. *The TV Arab*. Bowling Green, OH: Bowling Green University Popular Press.

Shyrock, Andrew, ed. 2010. *Islamophobia/Islamophilia: Beyond Politics of Enemy and Friend*. Bloomington: Indiana University Press.

Siemaszko, Corky. 2015. "Hate Attacks on Muslims in U.S. Spike after Recent Acts of Terrorism." *NBC News*, 20 December 2015. http://www.nbcnews.com/news/us-news/hate-attacks-muslims-u-s-spike-after-recent-acts-terrorism-n482456 (accessed on January 2022).

Smith, David, McGowan, Michael, Knaus, Christopher, and Nick Evershed. 2019. "Revealed: Ilhan Omar and Rashida Tlaib Targeted in Far-Right Fake News Operation." *The Guardian*, 5 December 2019.

Solnit, Rebecca. 2022. "Don't Stop Believing That People Can Change." *New York Times*, 24 April 2022: 4.4.

Soltani, Anoosh. 2016. "Confronting Prejudice against Muslim Women in the West." *Our World*. United Nations University. https://ourworld.unu.edu/en/confronting-prejudice-against-muslim-women-in-the-west (accessed on January 2022).

Stack, Liam. 2015. "American Muslims under Attack after San Bernardino and Paris Terror." *New York Times*, 22 December 2015.

Ullah, Par Areeb. 2016. "Muslim Women 'More Likely' to Be Victims of Islamophobia: Report." *Middle East Eye*. https://www.middleeasteye.net/fr/news/muslim-women-more-likely-be-victim-islamophobia-report-452800693 (accessed on January 2022).

"U.S. Reports Thaw in Ties with Arabs," 1967. *New York Times*, 8 September 1967: 11.11.

Wakefield, Johnny. 2021. "Why Are Muslim Women in Edmonton Being Attacked? Details Reveal a Complicated History." *Edmonton Journal*, 28 October 2021. https://edmontonjournal.com/news/local-news/a-string-of-hate-motivated-attacks-muslim-women-in-edmonton-reveals-a-complicated (accessed on January 2022).

"Wider Arab Study Sought to Aid U.S," 1950. *New York Times*, 11 June 1950: 1.24.

Wohl, Amiel. 1978. "Letter: 'Of Lebanon and a Christian Silence.'" *New York Times*, 24 July 1978: A16.

World Population Review. 2022. "Muslim Population by Country 2022." https://worldpopulationreview.com/country-rankings/muslim-population-by-country (accessed on January 2022).

Wright, Oliver. 2015. "Attacks on British Muslims Have Gone Up 300% Since Paris." *Indy100*, 23 November 2015. https://www.indy100.com/news/attacks-on-british-muslims-have-gone-up-300-since-paris-7284721 (accessed on January 2022).

Zayani, Mohamed. 2015. *Networked Publics and Digital Contention: The Politics of Everyday Life in Tunisia*. New York: Oxford University Press.

2

Maturing Islam: Turkey as the Site of Islamic Liberalization in the *New York Times*, 1980–2011

Caroline McKusick

Introduction

This chapter follows the *New York Times*' articles on Turkey—beginning in 1980, the year of a major military coup in Turkey, and ending with the period of the rise to power by the AKP (Justice and Development Party), in the 2000s. For decades, the figure of the Muslim woman has been featured strongly in the *New York Times*' accounts of Turkey. However, this figure of the Muslim woman undergoes several key shifts. These shifts correspond with Turkey's implementation of neoliberal economic policies and with the need in US foreign policy for a "moderate Muslim" ally in the Middle East during the War on Terror. This chapter argues that the figure of the Muslim woman became the symbol and protagonist of the *New York Times*' image of Turkey as on the verge of change, productive, and able to be integrated into global capitalism.

The *New York Times*' journalistic representation of women, particularly women identified as Muslim, in Turkey shifted in several ways: from unknowable and part of a mass to individualistic; from unquoted, mediated, or viewed in public space to the subject of intimate personal profiles, viewed in personal space; from working class to middle class; from a conservative drone to a youthful rebel; from plagued by contradiction to animated by contradiction. While this shift began in the 1990s, it was fully realized by the 2000s across 13 articles analyzed here.

This shift also corresponds to a shift in the implicit temporal and historical framing of the *New York Times*' coverage of Turkey. The *New York Times* abandons its emphasis on the classically Orientalist scheme of steady linear progress—movement from a state of being "stuck in the past" toward a horizon of Western modernity. Instead, the *New York Times* emphasizes the present moment on the verge of change. The *New York Times* comes to position Turkey within the temporality of investment and neoliberal potentiality, rather than state-centered modernization.

Still, across all the articles explored, the *New York Times* consistently maintained a theme of the "clash of civilizations" and the civilizational contradiction of Turkey's position between the Islamic world and Europe. What changed in the *New York Times*' representations was that this clash came to be framed as productive and emergent, and Muslim women were seen as the protagonists of a changing Turkey. This corresponded to changes in US foreign policy position on and political–economic interest in Turkey.

Turkey, 1980–2010: Pro-system Islamism Emerges

The moment this analysis takes as its beginning, 1980, marks at once a period of silence in the *New York Times*' coverage of Turkey and a period of violent shifts in Turkey—for this was the year of a brutal military coup in the country. The repercussions of the coup and the postcoup period would restructure the political field in Turkey and echo visibly in later coverage by the *New York Times* of the 1990s and 2000s.

The 1980 coup in Turkey responded to a wave of social movements and political activity challenging the underpinnings of the state, coming from various political groups including Kurds, the Turkish left, and Islamic groups. The immediate postcoup period involved political suppression on a massive scale, including executions, torture, exile, arrests, and restrictions of basic civil rights throughout Turkey. What coverage the *New York Times* provides of this period is sparse, and much of it appears to have come from the Turkish government's own statements.

The immediate postcoup period in Turkey saw another development that was later reflected in the *New York Times*: the integration of a certain form of Islam into national institutions. The military junta became invested in a normative figure of the Turkish citizen that was more emphatically Sunni Muslim than ever before. The constitution implemented by the military junta in 1980 remains in place today.

The 1980 constitution ushered in increased judicial interference with political parties, with 37 political parties closed between 1980 and 2010. Parties of the Kurdish movement and oppositional Islamic parties have been major targets. In the early 2000s, the AKP emerged on the strength of Islamic parties' political base, but with a novel combination of religious conservatism and populist appeals. The AKP's rapid rise to power also coincided with the shift in US global foreign policy known as the War on Terror. Turkey had long been a major military, diplomatic, and economic partner of the United States in the region, but the election of a "moderate Muslim" party played into a US position that marshaled Turkey's Muslimness (now a resource for the United States) in support of new policies and wars in the Middle East.

Cihan Tuğal characterizes the AKP's success as an "absorption" by capital and the state system of the radical challenge posed by Islamic politics. This absorption of the challenge to capital, Tuğal argues, produced a moderate and pro-system Islamism (Tuğal 2009). While the *New York Times* follows the political success of pro-system Islamism with particular interest, it is important to remember that the *New York Times*' coverage does not necessarily directly reflect the history of this dramatic period in Turkey, which involved a protracted and brutal state war in the Kurdish region; sweeping economic restructuring; and dramatic struggles played out in the field of party politics.

The *New York Times* coverage works on and transforms certain moments in Turkey's political life throughout this period, filtering them through a set of ideas about the normative human subject that I argue is more or less consistent and can be related to US interests in the Middle East. I argue that from this process, the figure of the "Muslim woman" emerges as a key site for the *New York Times*' emergent understanding of Turkey in this period. US political economic interests in drawing on Turkey as a moderate Muslim ally in the Middle East during the War on Terror drove major shifts in the representation of Turkey.

Clashing Civilizations, Productive Contradictions

Between the 1990s and the AKP's rise in the 2000s, the representation of Turkish Muslim women in the *New York Times* begins to change dramatically. Toward the late 2000s, during the period of the expansion of the War on Terror as well as the AKP's intensification of neoliberal economic policies, Muslim women begin to be represented as headstrong, outspoken, and entrepreneurial rather than backward, oppressed, and obedient.

While the portrayal of Muslim women in Turkey clearly takes a turn for the sympathetic during the 2000s, one theme consistently guides representations throughout all three decades: the theme of contradiction. In almost every article on Turkey, the *New York Times* characterizes it as a "nation of contradictions" (Sengupta 2002, A22) and "clashing impulses" (Sengupta 2001, A4). The guiding assumption is that Europe and Islam (with which the *New York Times* largely identifies Turkey) are essentially distinct civilizations, which cannot coexist in one person or group without friction.

Recent scholars have identified Samuel Huntington's notion of world history as defined by a "clash of civilizations" (especially Islam and the West) as the central underlying ideology of the United States' War on Terror, now in its second decade. For Talal Asad, this constitution of Islam as European civilization's primary other is critical to maintaining the coherence of Western identity—one defined essentially by Europe's "productive elaboration" of other lands and cultures, and therefore unstable at its core (Asad 2003, 167). Islam, as the other of Europe, must be defined as a dead civilization incapable of this productive elaboration—and therefore as a civilizational identity that can be shed or incorporated as a subordinate identity in the West.

Turkey, as a predominantly Muslim country at the border of Europe, has been invested to various degrees in a state project of Westernization and/or modernization since the founding of the current Republic of Turkey—and before that, in the last centuries of the Ottoman Empire. The notion of Turkey as potentially European, able to shed Islam, long obsessed many Ottoman, Turkish nationalist, and Western thinkers. "Muslims," writes Asad, "as members of the abstract category 'human,' can be assimilated or (as some recent theorists have put it) 'translated' into a global ('European') civilization once they have divested themselves of what many of them regard (mistakenly) as essential to themselves" (Asad 2003, 169).

For the *New York Times*' viewpoint, the acceptable reconciliation and commensuration of Turkey with European civilization would require a transformation or reform of Islam (seen as the defining characteristic of Turkey) into a cultural identity compatible with a regime of consumerism and multiculturalism—in contrast to a <u>bad</u> Islam, which threatens to make dangerous demands on its subjects. Viewed through the lens of a global War on Terror for whom Muslim populations are anxiety-producing subjects, the narrative of Turkey's potential as a site for the domestication of that anxiety, and even the transformation of "Muslimness" into a productive resource, comes to dominate any other narrative for understanding the country in the mainstream media. This narrative precludes discussion of the ethnically, religiously, and linguistically diverse populations living in Turkey, subsumed and invisibilized in the category of "Muslim," and Turkey's record of human rights violations and massacres perpetrated against these populations.

Before the 1990s, special attention to women in Turkey qua Muslims is peripheral in the *New York Times*' articles on Turkey. Searches for articles mentioning Islam and women produced few results in the 1980s. In the 1990s, however, the condition of women in relation to religion and secularism comes to be the *New York Times*' central explanatory analytic for Turkish political change and historical development. The very increase in search results found over the course of this research indicates the new investment of the *New York Times* in the image of the Muslim woman. As the *New York Times* closely follows the rise of mainstream Islamic political parties in Turkey, especially through the ongoing controversies over headscarf during the 1990s, a coherence emerges in the *New York Times*' representations of women. The identity of women comes to stand in for nothing less than the <u>contradiction</u> at the heart of Turkish identity, positioned as a contradiction between Islam and the West. In this period, Muslim women are portrayed as distanced and confusing, and distanced especially by their headscarves. As Lena Meari (this volume) points out, the headscarf becomes obsessively overvalued as the ultimate marker of otherness for the *New York Times*.

Over the course of a decade between the late 1990s and the present, the valuation of the Turkish woman's inherent and assumed "contradiction" changes in line with the *New York Times*' vision of a reformed, liberal Islam with Turkey as its cradle. In the late 1990s, Muslim women are portrayed as grotesque or hypocritical products of an identity contradiction. But by the 2000s, they come to be portrayed as individualistic and dynamic.

In the 2000s, with the rise of the AKP as the ruling party of Turkey and the global figureheads of a neoliberal Islamism, there arrives a new Turkish Muslim woman in the *New York Times*. She possesses a kind of hybrid vigor attributed to the contradiction between East and West, often in explicit contrast with Muslim women in other countries. She is cheerful, hardworking, and modern. Islam is now an option for consumption and even (healthy, nonviolent) youth rebellion, and Turkey is the site where a new, more liberal Islam is being worked out. The headscarf takes on a new shade of meaning as the ultimate sign of liberating choice. This change tracks the *New York Times*' promotion of a notion of liberal Islam as an identity choice for individual Muslim women on a worldwide scale, from Southeast Asia (as traced by Rajbir Singh Judge (this volume)) to Anatolia.

The format of the articles themselves reflects a deep change in the *New York Times*' assumptions about what kind of subjects Turkish Muslim women are and what political potential they possess. Personal profiles of individual Turkish Muslim women, from average women to politicians, increasingly become the foci and predominant format of the *New York Times*' articles on women in Turkey. However, this trend should not be simply read as a progressive impulse designed to remedy the sidelining of women in past media coverage. The admission of these women to the category of individual not only reflects the *New York Times*' new optimism for Turkish Muslims' integration into the capitalist world system but at the same time allows for the maintenance and reconfiguration of the narrative of civilizational contradiction. The contradiction between Islam and the West is now revalued: it is no longer a societal conflict that threatens political stability but rather an interior aspect of individual identity. This contradictory position between East and West, now reframed as something eminently dynamic, makes the Turkish Muslim woman a valuable globally connected worker.

The *New York Times* did not construct this narrative of Turkish identity out of whole cloth. The *New York Times* discourse, through the lens of the global War on Terror that positions Turkey as a site of good, docile, feminine Islam in contrast to threatening masculine Islam identified with Arab countries, refracts an existing logic of the Turkish state itself. This narrative reproduces the obsession with gender in the Muslim world as originally problematic, which Tanzeen Doha demonstrates recur throughout Western liberal thought during this period (Doha, this volume). The postcoup normative subject in Turkey was an ethnically and linguistically Turkish, Sunni Muslim one, and the task of resolving the internal threats to that normative identity played out in policies targeting women as particularly problematic. For example, the "Father, Send Me to School" campaign urged families to send female children to public schools (which involve Turkish-only, Sunni Muslim–oriented education) in order to resolve the problematic backwardness and resistance seen as stemming from the condition of women and girls in the largely Kurdish southeastern part of Turkey (the Northern Kurdistan region).

The idea of the Turkish nation as one plagued by unresolved contradictions between East and West has justified the purifying of the nation through state violence, from the constitutive violence of the 1915 Armenian genocide to the brutal war and human rights violations in the Kurdish region from the 1980s to the present. This contradiction and its resolution into an imagined state of harmony have long been the ideological justification for violence within Turkey against any population deemed unruly. Through the figure of the Turkish Muslim woman, the *New York Times* empties this narrative of a history of struggles to posit the contradictions of identity in Turkey as potentially productive. History is reshaped in pursuit of a single underlying question that organizes the *New York Times* analysis of the Muslim world: how to develop and export a harmonious, liberal, and flexible Islam for the purpose of governing unruly Muslim peoples around the world.

The 1980s and 1990s: Progressive Secular Time

In the *New York Times* articles, secularist-nationalist Kemalists and Islamists are almost without exception positioned as the only two relevant forces of Turkish politics, a move that erases other axes of identity (ethnic, linguistic, or sectarian). In the move toward a new image of the Muslim woman, the relative values of these two poles change in the *New York Times*. In 1980s articles in the *New York Times*, Kemalists are the protagonists of modernization, with the Islamists as their backward, irrational Other. By the 2000s, the *New York Times* has switched these two groups' places in the drama of Turkish history. In the first narrative, Islamists are portrayed as dogmatic and irrational. They are under suspicion, as grotesque chimeric creatures produced by the traditional East's resentful reaction to modernity. They are incapable of tolerating the modern. In the second narrative, it is the secularists who the *New York Times* portrays as intolerant—intolerant of the new religious identity necessary for Turkey to thrive. This change represents a shift in the *New York Times*' attitude to the temporal narrative of history in Turkey that is often read through the status of women.

In either narrative, the dichotomy of these two political forces (secularists and Islamists) based on their relation to Islam turns Turkey into an arena for working out questions of secularism and Islam, enabling the *New York Times* to minimize other questions. The Kurdish problem, for instance, is treated as a problem internal to Turkey, and sited in a murky peripheral region. Women's struggles are minimized by the reminder that women are relatively privileged for the Middle East. Meanwhile, the question of Islam is seen as exemplary and exportable, and developments around Islam and secularism are followed with close interest. Turkey is positioned as a laboratory and a proving ground for making an Islamic country modern. The *New York Times*' representation consistently positions secularism as the defining existential problem of the Turkish state, folding other dimensions of life and politics in Turkey into questions of secularism and religion.

The 1980s and 1990s *New York Times*' representations of Turkey reproduce the secularist, nationalist historical narrative of what Turkey is and should be, with the narrative being reproduced more strongly in the years closest to the 1980 military coup. According to this narrative, the founding figure of the Turkish Republic, Mustafa Kemal (known as Atatürk), bequeathed a possibility of modernization on the blighted remains of the Ottoman state through his staunchly secular nationalism, but his modernizing project is incomplete. His political heirs must protect this fragile development from the retrograde forces of tradition. The *New York Times*' articles in this period repeat secularist fears of a modernizing project under threat, writing that "military and civilian leaders believe that the head scarf is being used as a symbol by fundamentalists whose goal is to pull Turkey away from the modern world" (Kinzer 1999, A7). Concerns with time and with movement toward or away from modernity are crucial in this framework. Words like "fundamentalist" and even "puritan" (Cowell 1994, A4) are more common in portrayals of Islamists during this period, as well. A 1995 article on the threat of "revolutionary Islam" in Turkey, for example, quotes Prime Minister Tansu Çiller:

> In this part of the world, there are two models. ... One is the Khomeini model of Iran and the forces of the uprising trend of radicalism. The other is Turkey, with the first woman Prime Minister, the only country among 52 Muslim countries that is secular and democratic. (Darnton 1995, A1)

Here, the meaning of "Turkey" is defined for the *New York Times*' readers in terms of its relation to Iran, a neighbor perceived as Islamic to an unruly degree. Turkey's own messy internal affairs at the time (such as the state's war in Kurdistan) are definitively not a subject of inquiry for the *New York Times*. Instead, Turkey is presented in comparison to other Muslim countries. As Hakeem Naim points out, this was also the period in the wake of the Iranian Revolution of 1979, when an overwhelming antipathy to Iran, and its repeated identification with the dangerously backward past, dominates the *New York Times* coverage of the Middle East (Naim, this volume). In this period, Turkey is often presented as faced with two futures, two directions in a historical time that is figured as a line in an implicitly spatial model of time—forward toward the future and the West, or backward toward the past and East (where Iran lies). Many articles on women in Turkey or other internal affairs in the country refer directly to Iran.

In another article, a politician argues that Turkey is simply working through the history Europe has already had:

> You have had hundreds of years to distance yourself from religious extremism, so now when your President puts his hand on the Bible to take the oath of office you don't see anything wrong. But in Turkey, our Renaissance began with Ataturk. We need time to let these ideas take hold. (Kinzer 1997, A1)

In the articles of the 1990s in particular, authors often mention the election of Tansu Çiller as prime minister in favorable terms (although the United States, among other countries, had never had a female head of state, and Çiller herself was no friend of women's movements) as the fruition of a century of pro-Western movement forward begun by Mustafa Kemal. For example, one article attributes the rise in the number of women in the professions, and finally the eventual election of Tansu Çiller, to a forward movement started by Mustafa Kemal.

> That (Mustafa Kemal's actions) helped build a core of professional women in fields like law, medicine, and higher education, whose influenced helped

to challenge Islamic conservatism and propel this land toward Western secularism. Indeed, Turkey has a woman as Prime Minister for the first time, Tansu Ciller, who has been in office since June. (Cowell 1994, A4)

In this article, the author presents Turkey as being propelled forward to the West and away from Islam, with the election of Tansu Çiller coming at the end of a century of this.

Still, this forward movement is usually portrayed as contingent and under threat. The article goes on to quote Istanbul University Professor Necla Arat as saying that "Seventy years is not enough for a real revolution. ... These are pioneer women" (Cowell 1994, A4). The author frames this quote describing women as "pioneers" alongside a description of Istanbul as "the wild West." The metaphor suggests a settler-colonial time frame in which secular women, like settler pioneers, are dragging Turkey forward and westward against the potential protestations of the natives (Islamists), who wish to live in the past.

The 2000s: Changing Turkey's Timeline

In the 2000s, the *New York Times*' representations of Turkey abandon this straightforward recitation of Kemalist pieties of forward movement in favor of a new narrative of Turkey. While the conflict over religion is still central for the *New York Times*, it is now seen as a generative engine for new prosperity rather than an attempt to drag Turkey backward and/or eastward. For the *New York Times* articles in the 2000s, Mustafa Kemal is cited less and less as the beginning of Turkish modernity. The attribution of Islam or secularism to particular moments on a timeline largely disappears. The constant invocation of the linear time of progress is replaced by a synchronic image of a present moment crowded with competing ideological elements, a moment on the verge of an unspecified but momentous change. In these articles, we are no longer in the long, arduous time of historical progress (anchored by the birth of the Republic) but the short time frame focused on the present moment and its immediate potential resolution.

Turkey's state of contradiction no longer means that it is threatened by its backward past, but that it is ripe for giving birth to a new model of a state under the AKP that is fundamentally Muslim and can therefore be exemplary for the rest of the Muslim world. To be sure, the *New York Times* maintains the crux of civilizational clash and internal contradiction in these stories. But this clash is now not a source of pain, friction, and ressentiment threatening a return to the past but a source of dynamism and energy in the form of a new "Islamic capitalism" (Bilefsky 2006, 4) and Islamic youth activism (Tavernise 2008b). As we will see, Muslim women come to stand for this dynamic present moment.

Kemalism ceases to appear as the standard bearer of the West, and by 2008, it is represented as suspect and even fanatical. For example, the ban on headscarves in public buildings is described as "a relic of the aggressive secularism enforced by modern Turkey's founder, Mustafa Kemal Ataturk" (Feldman 2008, A19). Secularists are no longer portrayed as the best hope for Turkey's Westernization; they are now the anachronistic elements of a moribund statist nationalism holding Turkey back. In these articles, it is secularists, not Islamists, who are the figures made grotesque by the contradiction between West and East, for they are overzealously committed to an idea of Western liberalism taken too far, while the new Islamists exemplify a harmonious, productive combination of East and West.

Alberto Toscano tracks the figure of the fanatic through the history of Western thought as one "outside the frame of political rationality" (Toscano 2010, xi). Fanaticism is a dangerous threat, involving "a refusal of compromise and a seemingly boundless drive to the universal" (Toscano 2010, xii). In the transition in the *New York Times*' representations of Turkish political groups, we see that Islam is not necessarily characterized for the *New York Times* through the "fanatical devotion to the abstract" that Western liberal thought inherits from Hegel. New representations, increasingly common in the 2000s, come to lean on the portrayal of Kemalism as devoted to an abstract ideal of secularism to an inappropriate degree—indeed, to a religious degree, complete with "relics." Narratives continue to emphasize the threat of Turkey being dragged <u>backward</u> in time, but now site this threat in statist projects.

Framing Atatürk in the New Time Frame

An analysis of articles on Muslim women in Turkey in the *New York Times* reveals a particular shift in the gendered dynamic of images not just of women themselves but also of the image of Mustafa Kemal Atatürk, positioned as a silent, male observer of debates around women's rights and the headscarf. As previously mentioned, many articles in the 1980s and 1990s described Mustafa Kemal as setting off the changes toward progress that would eventually (against backward opposition) bear fruit. It is almost obligatory for the *New York Times*' articles to run an image of Mustafa Kemal alongside articles on Turkey, especially when religious issues are involved (as in Haberman 1989). The appearance of such a picture makes the founding figure coeval with current political developments, but this representational tactic changes in terms of its valuation between the 1980s and 1990s and the 2000s.

An article on Turkey from 1982 makes explicit the position of Mustafa Kemal as protector of women's rights, characteristic of that period of the *New York Times*' coverage:

> Turkey is once again taking the lead on women's rights in the Islamic world with preparations for a new law to legalize abortion and permit voluntary sterilization. The generals' action is in line with policies of Mustafa Kemal Ataturk, the founder of modern Turkey, who ardently believed in the equality of the sexes. (Howe 1982, A19)

Although this postcoup period was a nightmarish time of intense political persecution in Turkey, the invocation of Mustafa Kemal helps the *New York Times* place Turkey in the progressive narrative of history characteristic of this period and authorized the rule of the junta through reference to women's rights (portrayed as Mustafa Kemal's invention).

A 2008 article demonstrates the change in orientation. Now, instead of the straightforward portrait of Mustafa Kemal that the *New York Times* sometimes ran alongside articles on Turkey, the article features an image of Mustafa Kemal's portrait on a city wall, with headscarf-wearing women walking beneath it—an image that wordlessly rebukes secularists as anachronistic and lifeless through a juxtaposition of the iconic portrait with the living Muslim women. Mustafa Kemal is repeatedly invoked in articles throughout the 2000s, no longer as the paragon of modernism but as an ominous and authoritarian shadow over Turkey's opening to the West, as in 2008: "Turkey's reigning ideology and law are strictly secular, dating from the authoritarian rule in the 1920s of Mustafa Kemal Ataturk" (Tavernise 2008b, A1). Whereas the older articles ran Mustafa

Kemal's image alongside the day's developments as though to place him in the modern day, now he is framed, bracketed, and relegated to the background as a moment in the past.

This change in the images used to accompany articles forms the inverse of another change from Muslim women as anonymous to individualized. Whereas in earlier 1980s and 1990s articles women were presented through reported speech and observed from a suspicious distance, now it is Mustafa Kemal who is framed, mediated, and held at a distance. Changing representational approaches of distancing or intimacy point to changing political approaches toward Turkey, as the next section will explore.

Women: From Anonymous Masses to Individuals

Ideas and anxieties around class and gender play a key part in the *New York Times*' evolving representations of Islam. Early articles on the Refah Party and other pre-AKP Islamist political parties ominously mention their outreach to the poor alongside fears about Turkey following in the path of Iran. Here, the poor are usually nongendered and portrayed as a mass, talked about in the abstract. Muslim or Islamists are rarely interviewed, and Muslim women even less. Frequent quotes from experts and "foreign residents" are used instead: "You find people with stronger beliefs in the big cities, where it used to be that you could be fired for going to the mosque," a longtime foreign resident said. "Some of this may be a reaction to secularism. But you also have Turks who have come back after working in West Germany, and who reacted to hostility there by falling back on what was familiar. And that was Islam" (Haberman 1989, 14).

In this article, the rise of Islam in Turkey is identified as a reactionary, irrational, working-class phenomenon, especially belonging to migrants. The *New York Times* purports that recent Islamic political mobilizations "have led many Turks to fear that the secular identity of their country is under threat. Many others—it is impossible to know how many—welcome the moves" (Kinzer 1997, A1). These quotes position the "others" as an unknowable element, an uncounted mass, who threaten the good "Turks" defending their national identity.

Later, in the early 2000s, an Orientalist fascination with Muslim women begins to appear in a number of articles. In line with the discourse of Muslims as mass, Muslim women are presented as anonymous and despecified. One article covers a new law that mandates marital equality for men and women. For the *New York Times*, the question of marriage and women is necessarily connected to Islam, and Islam is seen as the problem that will prevent the orderly implementation of this law (rather than patriarchy, which could be secular or religious). This article opens by setting up a relation of parity between the nation and the internal state of women:

> Just like Turkey itself—a majority Muslim country and a secular state—women here repeatedly tangle with the clashing impulses brought by tradition and greater Westernization. To the Western eye, the social mores on faith and sex here can sometimes seem like an inconsistent jumble. (Sengupta 2001, A4)

The article goes on to describe headscarf-wearing Muslim women as the visible embodiments of this contradiction. The clashing impulses of their interiority can seemingly be clearly read by the writer through their exteriority, especially through their mode of dress. The article represents Muslim women from a distance, through the ways they present themselves to the journalist's gaze in a stroll down the street:

> Among women who cover, some wear what is sometimes referred to here as "the uniform"—a bland combination of a long solid-colored coat and a scarf tied in the Islamic custom.
>
> But take a nighttime stroll along the Istiklal, the city's main party drag, and you will notice covered women with brightly painted lips, black leather boots as spiky as minarets, hip-hugging jeans. You can see covered women (and remember, to cover is a sign of modesty) making out with their boyfriends on the promenade. (Sengupta 2001, A4)

The writer juxtaposes an image of Muslim women as passive, uniformed, and anonymous (an idea lent credence by putting the idea of "the uniform" in the mouths of "locals") with an image of Muslim women as highly visible, sexualized, gaze-drawing signs of a contradiction between tradition/Islam and modernity/the West. The image of "boots as spiky as minarets" turns women's clothes into a national-religious landscape, which the *New York Times* interprets as a landscape mismatched and plagued by contradiction. Against this contradictory external appearance, their behavior is interpreted as a sign of their hypocrisy.

As the AKP rises in the 2000s, the *New York Times* starts to take pains to assure readers that Islamism appeals to the middle classes—especially by featuring quotes from women, professional women coded as modern and moderate, such as one "single woman and fashion stylist, who attended Mr. Erdoğan's rally in trousers with an uncovered head" (Fisher 2002, A3). Although we are in the space of a mass rally, we are now being presented with a portrait of an individual woman rather than descriptions of vague and angry masses or unknown elements. The *New York Times* quotes this woman at length, after framing her by describing her clothes. But rather than the sensationalizing "hip-hugging jeans" of earlier articles, she wears sensible-sounding "trousers." Her clothing overdetermines her politics, and functions to assure the reader that her opinions are politically acceptable. Her quote—"As long as he maintains a balance, as long as he doesn't stop over the line, he is the leader" (Fisher 2002, A3)—points to the change in the depictions of women, who now legitimize the narrative of the new Islamism as a phenomenon of balance and moderation between presumed contradictory impulses.

Women in Headscarves: From Drones to Rebels

These shifts in the historical narrative and composition that the *New York Times* assigns to Islamism track with the United States' increased reconciliation with Islamists and Muslims in Turkey throughout the 2000s, coinciding with the rise of the AKP. However, the *New York Times* does more than simply parrot the line of the Turkish ruling party; it continually reworks ideology into changing narratives of development, with a goal that is always just out of reach and seems to require Western intervention and protection. The figure of <u>youth</u>, appearing in the *New York Times* especially in its coverage of the 1990s debates on the wearing of the headscarf in universities, positions this development process as Islamic and feminized, but also immature and vulnerable.

The 1990s articles on Islam in Turkey focus on the ongoing debate about the wearing of headscarves in government buildings and universities, a practice outlawed since early in Turkey's history. The headscarf changes its significance from "a freestanding symbol that has the power to elicit negative and discriminatory associations" (Meari, this volume, p. 75) to a more ambiguous sign of Islam's potential (salutary) transformation into a matter of taste, choice, and fashion. I argue that this change requires the *New York Times* to enact a new temporal framing of Turkey through the metaphor of youth and maturation. This involves the feminized representation of <u>Islam on the verge of change</u> through a focus on young women.

In one 1980s article on the headscarf debates in Turkey, the *New York Times* (typical for the period) codes Islam as "eroding" modern advances in Turkey and insinuates that the Iranian regime will "exploit" debates about the headscarf to undermine the stability of the Turkish state. As mentioned, the *New York Times* in this period portrays Muslims as an unknowable mass and rarely interviews individual Muslim women. However, when they do, the woman quoted is portrayed as obedient, an unthinking slave of her religion. The portrayal of her clothes as monochromatic enforces this image of the woman as uniformed, anonymous, and drone-like: "My religion orders me to do this," said Huriye Alemdar, a 20-year-old student at Ankara University, who was dressed in a gray scarf and a long gray coat. "I am only following my beliefs" (Haberman 1989, 14).

A 1990s article following the controversy at Istanbul University over the headscarf interviews a similar woman: a young student. But the change between 1989 and 1998 is evident. Now, the *New York Times* describes a student defying the headscarf ban in more sympathetic detail, presenting her as a "bright-eyed medical student." The following quote from the woman puts in her mouth the idea that the *New York Times* increasingly moves toward: that unnecessary resistance (irrational secularist fanaticism) to moderate, potentially liberal Muslims such as "bright-eyed medical students" is the true source of dangerous "fanaticism" in the Islamic world. "We love God, we read our Koran, we believe in our religion, and we want to apply this religion in our lives," Ms. Erdoğan said. "What has happened in the last few weeks makes me very angry. I am protesting as much as possible because I really want to become a doctor. It's bad to become a fanatic, but they are pushing us towards fanaticism" (Kinzer 1998, A4).

The contrast between these two articles is striking because they both portray ostensibly comparable subjects—female Muslim students disobeying the headscarf ban in universities—in very different ways. In the first article, the student's only desire is to "follow her belief." In the second, the *New York Times* foregrounds her desire to be a doctor (i.e., modern, professional, and emancipated) and positions it in implicit contradiction to her headscarf. But this contradiction poses the possibility of being resolved productively. Unlike the first student who seems to be obeying an abstract desire to submit, this student is portrayed as heroically defiant of orders. Her defiance is presented to the reader as a reassuringly normal characteristic of <u>youth</u>, a category with a history in Western thought, which ascribes to youth a tendency to crisis that must be managed and made productive for society (El Shakry 2011, 591–610). This young woman's crisis tends toward a productive resolution of what *New York Times* articles repeatedly position as the central contradiction of Turkish identity (the contradiction between East and West) if her rights can be guaranteed. At the same time, she is in danger of losing control of herself and becoming a fanatic ("they are pushing us towards fanaticism") if no one can guarantee an environment for <u>moderation</u>.

The *New York Times*' portrayal of the struggle for the headscarf changes even more dramatically within the next decade of the 2000s. The year 2008's "Youthful Voice Stirs Challenge to Secular Turks" profiles a young activist working to pass the bill that would overturn the headscarf ban. Unlike the earlier representation of Muslim women as uniformed and obedient, the activist is now defined not by her <u>conservatism</u> but by her rebellion. The change is evident in the very first paragraph:

> High school hurt for Havva Yilmaz. She tried out several selves. She ran away. Nothing felt right.
>
> "There was no sincerity," she said. "It was shallow."
>
> So, at 16, she did something none of her friends had done: She put on an Islamic head scarf. (Tavernise 2008b, A1)

Here even more than before, Islam is portrayed as a matter of individual identity. The *New York Times* stresses that this was a choice she made, and that she was not <u>raised</u> to wear the headscarf. The writer goes on to say that "her personal choices are part of a paradox at the heart of the country's modern identity," maintaining the tropes of contradiction and the familiar representation of women as stand-ins for the nation.

By dropping out of the education system, she found her way into Turkey's growing, lively culture of young activists.

She attended a political philosophy reading group, studying Hegel, St. Augustine and Machiavelli. She took sociology classes from a free learning center. She met other activists, many of them students trying to redefine words like "modern," which has meant secular and Western-looking for decades. She made new friends, like Hilal Kaplan, whose scarf sometimes had a map of the world on it. (Tavernise 2008b, A1)

While still defined by the headscarf, this Muslim woman is portrayed as valuable because she is open to the West—which is defined in terms of a liberal philosophical heritage and practices of consumption. The symbol of Yilmaz's activist group, the *New York Times* reports, is a Converse sneaker. Again, clothing overdetermines politics, but now the headscarf (notably portrayed as a "map of the world" in the case of Hilal Kaplan, a famous media figure associated with the AKP) is juxtaposed carefully with the Converse sneaker. Both the headscarf and the sneaker read as symbols that are legible on the surface and that function like commodities and symbols of consumerist identity. Islamic politics itself is now portrayed as facing toward a global (i.e., Western) capitalist civilization, not toward Iran, the East, or the past.

The article explicitly positions Yilmaz, a young Muslim woman, as the figure of the nation itself. I argue that this represents a shift not just in the *New York Times*' sympathy to Islam in politics but in the temporal framing of the *New York Times*' articles on Turkey. The *New York Times* follows its evocative description of Yilmaz's teenage identity crisis with an evocation of the present moment, which it calls "a moment of religious revival across the Muslim world" (Tavernise 2008b, A1). The article is itself part of a comparative series on this "moment" that the *New York Times* has identified, focusing on "the lives of the young across the Muslim world" (Tavernise 2008b, A1).

This moment is not the historical time of a march of progress seen in the articles analyzed earlier that framed Kemalist secularism more approvingly. The *New York Times* focuses on a moment on the cusp of productive change and emergence—understood in these articles through the metaphor of youth experience as a naturalized category—a temporality of prediction, shifting capital, investment, and potential yields from uncertain situations. Yilmaz's experience of youth rebellion, framed as a universal human experience, is implicitly the metaphor for the impending, potentially productive crisis of the Muslim world at large.

In another 2008 article profiling an individual woman wearing the headscarf, Tavernise describes lawyer Fatma Benli's battle for the headscarf as deeply personal. Again, Muslim women are no longer portrayed as anonymous drones but as individuals in interiority. Benli describes crying when she was forbidden from attending her master's defense at university. This description of emotion and interiority would be unthinkable in 1980s and 1990s depictions of Muslim women as anonymous masses. Tavernise goes on to describe Benli's reasons for wearing the headscarf specifically in terms of her individual interiority, which she maintains against pressure from violent, even authoritarian, secularists:

> She says the reasons, deeply personal and hard to put into words, are a combination of her relationship to God and her aversion to accepting what she sees as misplaced authority.
> "This is related to my private life," she said. "It's my personality. My wholeness." (Tavernise 2008a, A4)

The article goes on to describe how "young women have used computer graphics programs to draw hair over their scarves" (Tavernise 2008a, A4) in order to get past the ban on headscarves at public universities. This detail portrays Muslim women as ingenuous, antiauthoritarian, and skilled in the technologies of global capitalism. The article personalizes a group who had been formerly portrayed as an anonymous mass by connecting them with signifiers of a more normal youth from a Western perspective: rebellion and technology.

The *New York Times*' discourse about individual Muslim women condenses the Muslim world in the figure of the immature and female subject (recalling colonial discourses of non-Europeans and Middle Eastern women in particular as child-like) defined by tension and contradiction, emotion and interiority. The *New York Times* positions this existential identity crisis as one that, like the crises of youth, is on the cusp of productive, positive resolution—but in a state of immaturity that implicitly requires intervention and guidance.

Linking Turkey and the United States through Women

Several articles point approvingly to one route that will ensure that the crisis impending in Turkey is productively resolved to produce a liberal Islam: through Turkey's link to the United States. The young woman in particular stands in for Turkey as a whole, and her learning in the United States and from the West promises to convert her potential into value. Women's travels to the United States reappear in the *New York Times* throughout the 2000s.

In one editorial, the author recalls an anecdote that sums up the change in attitude in the *New York Times*: "I met a daughter of (AKP) Prime Minister Recep Tayyip Erdoğan—not in Istanbul, but at Indiana University, which she was attending at least in part so she could cover her head while getting an education" (Feldman 2008, A19). The United States is now positioned as the special guarantor of freedom for young Muslim women, not by unveiling them but by allowing them to veil. The daughter of then-Prime Minister Erdoğan is presented as something of an everywoman whose problems are identified with the problems of all Turkish women. And here, the struggle over the headscarf appears as only resolvable through Turkey's emulation of America.

The *New York Times*' profile of the Islamist politician Merve Kavakci, which represents the shift to individualism and the personal profile, draws this United States–Turkish connection as well, focusing on how Kavakci is ultimately driven not so much by Islam but by "ideas of freedom she developed while living in Texas."

> "In the United States I was accepted, not discriminated against," she said. "People in America smile at everything and tolerate everything. They accept you even if you have a different background or culture or religion. They take it easy."
>
> "Things are different here. In our Parliament, if you think, if you're smart, that's trouble. I am what I am, and they don't like that." (Kinzer 1999, A4)

Here, an idealized American multiculturalism and tolerance of all is presented as the ultimate model for Turkey. America is seen as the guarantor of a fragile (young and/or feminized) Islam personified in people like Ms. Erdoğan and Merve Kavakci, an Islam whose fraught identity crisis can be resolved productively through Western guidance.

From Mediated Suspicion to Intimate Individualism

The *New York Times*' close attention to the politician above, Merve Kavakci, an MP for the Islamist Virtue Party (later closed), provides a case that illustrates the representational shift taking place in the *New York Times*. A controversy erupted when Kavakci became the first woman to enter the parliamentary chamber wearing a headscarf. Shouted down by opposition MPs, Kavakci was never sworn in. Over the course of a series of articles on Kavakci, the *New York Times* switches from the rhetoric of distancing (as in portrayals of Muslims as masses or anonymous) to the rhetoric of intimacy that positions Turkey (in the figure of the Muslim woman) as a trustworthy, productive site for resolving the problem of Islam.

In its first article on Kavakci, the *New York Times* presents her from the beginning through her mediated image in the Turkish press. The article describes how "front pages of today's newspapers were dominated by photos of Ms. Kavakci in Parliament, where her appearance with a headscarf on Sunday sparked pandemonium. Television stations endlessly rebroadcast tape showing legislators shouting insults at her" (Kinzer 1999, A7). The article also cites Kavakci's press statement on the incident with the note that it was "read before journalists," precluding any sense of personal connection with her words. Kavakci is perpetually mediated by screens, newspapers, and press statements, and not quoted directly.

The article represents this eruption of interest and scandal as a sign that the Islamist political party is not "ready to work within the secular system" (Kinzer 1999, A7)—hinting that Kavakci's emergence was a deliberate provocation designed to disrupt orderly politics. The article concludes that Necmettin Erbakan, a banned Islamist politician, has "reportedly been running Virtue from behind the scenes, and placing Ms. Kavakci on its list of candidates was reportedly his idea" (Kinzer 1999, A7). Here, the *New York Times* foregrounds Kavakci as incapable of being anything more than a tool of scheming Islamist men. The article is dominated by a tone of suspicion, incredulity, and threat around Kavakci. Like the student dressed in uniform gray, she seems to be just following orders; her headscarf serves as the ultimate symbol of Islam's oppression of women, an equation that Lena Meari has demonstrated emerges in the *New York Times* during the 1990s (Meari, this volume, 90).

As the *New York Times*' mode of representation changes from a distanced observation of Muslim women to the personal profile, so too does its analysis of the <u>contradiction</u> seemingly embodied by Muslim woman. A later 1999 article on the same politician, Merve Kavakci, maintains a focus on the clothing of Muslim women as a clearly legible exterior sign of their beliefs and intentions. However, the headscarf here no longer signals an internal oppression or manipulation by men behind the scenes, as it did in the previous article on Kavakci. Now, it stands for her productive marriage of East and West. Although the article is by the same author and published only slightly later, its style of representation has changed dramatically, as the author apparently finds a new angle.

> Sitting demurely behind her desk dressed in immaculate white, Merve Kavakci does not look like someone who could send a nation of 65 million into turmoil. But because of what she wears, she has done exactly that.
>
> It is not Ms. Kavakci's chic white suit with gold buttons that caused the problem. It is the white scarf that covers her head, coupled with ideas of freedom she developed while living in Texas. (Kinzer 1999, A4)

In this new personal profile format, Kavakci is now directly quoted, rather than distanced by press appearances. Kavakci is presented to us as stylish, demure, immaculate—even wearing white, in a state of purity and calm—rather than angry, disruptive, and suspicious. Whereas the perspective of the first article is framed by a mediation and distance, which leads to an interest in uncovering motives and intentions, splits and suspicions beneath the frustratingly <u>covered</u> exterior appearance of Muslim women, the switch to a personal profile format brings with it a new interest in an understanding of the individual, humanized by her contact with the United States. The contradiction between Islam and the West is still central, but now it is portrayed not as a split but as a coupling of the "white scarf" with Western "ideas of freedom." East and West are still presented by means of a contrast, but this contrast is now presented as something integrated and particularly fulfilled by Muslim women.

Internal Orientalism: Obscured Images of Kurdish Women

As the *New York Times* increasingly positions Turkey as the home of an acceptable and individualized consumable Islam, the portrayal of distant and frightening backward Muslims does not go away. Rather, the distinction between good and bad Muslims identified by Mahmood Mamdani as crucial to Western representations (Mamdani 2004) becomes increasingly prominent in the *New York Times*. Not all Muslims are the potentially productive, potentially liberal subjects that the *New York Times* profiles. Good Muslims are flexible, like the businesswoman. Bad Muslims are inflexible and bound by tradition. In this case, this coding maps onto discourse with a long history in Turkish political discourse: the definition of the Southeast (Kurdistan) as backward, a code language used to target Turkey's Kurdish region for military intervention and top-down governance while avoiding mention of the Kurds' own political claims.

With the partial state recognition of Kurds and initiation of a short-lived peace process after decades of Kurdish armed and unarmed struggle, the AKP government positioned its maintenance of existing policies toward Kurds as an Islamically charitable development project—a language that the *New York Times* was able to comfortably work into its narrative of the Middle East. The *New York Times* adapts this established Turkish political theme to distinguish between good urban Muslim women, educated and choosing Islam as a modern identity (the good Turks), and bad rural Muslim women who are in need of intervention (often implicitly Kurdish, although they are not acknowledged as such).

This theme appears in the article on the pro-headscarf activist. While the *New York Times* characterizes her urban, educated Islamist politics as positive, they maintain that the headscarf is nevertheless oppressive for rural Muslim women:

> In many ways, Ms. Yilmaz's scarf freed her, but for many other women, it is the opposite. In poor, religiously conservative areas in rural Turkey, girls wear scarves from young ages, and many Turks feel strongly that without state regulation, young women would come under more pressure to cover up. (Tavernise 2008b, A1)

The rural Turkey referred to here is distant and undefined but clearly in need of some kind of intervention. Nevertheless, for the author, Turkey's cultural distinctiveness as Turkish still inclines it overall to good Islam, as against bad, traditional Islam. This echoes what Dicle Koğacıoğlu has referred to as "the tradition effect" (Koğacıoğlu 2004, 119–51), in which the invocation of "tradition" serves to create and legitimize the other of tradition—such as the "state regulation" mentioned in the article—while also categorizing these traditions as ultimately outside of time and unable to change on their own. In addition, these portrayals normalize other forms of violence against women (such as those perpetrated and supported by the state) by focusing only on supposedly traditional forms of violence—often distinguished from the more normalized forms of patriarchal violence by the use of terms like "honor killings."

In an article on so-called honor killings and honor suicides in Turkey, the author describes the plight of a "waiflike girl of 17" named Derya (Bilefsky 2006, 3) whose family tried to kill her for seeing a boy. The article ascribes honor killings to traditional culture in southeastern Anatolia (a toponym for the provinces making up Northern Kurdistan, which the Turkish government uses to describe the region without mentioning the Kurds). Such articles further solidify the narrative that, in the AKP's Turkey, the source of violence against women is the bad Muslims. Here, women are portrayed as "waiflike" and young, needing protection against tradition if they are to be saved from violence.

The article speaks approvingly of Turkey's changes to its penal code. Practices such as forcing women and girls to commit suicide are portrayed as the efforts of "tradition" to resist forward movement, represented by the state, as in this quote:

> Young women like Derya, who have previously led protected lives under the rigid moral strictures of their families and Islam, are suddenly finding themselves in the modern Turkey of Internet dating and MTV. The shift can create dangerous tensions, sometimes lethal ones, between their families and the secular values of the republic that the young women seek to embrace. (Bilefsky 2006, 3)

Here, the author portrays the Turkish state under the AKP as the source of good secular and Western values (represented by MTV and Internet dating), while the families of women like Derya (i.e., Kurdish families, which the Turkish state's narrative portrays as others and the source of backwardness) are the source of bad values. Regardless of the actual policies of the Turkish state (let alone the actual campaigns undertaken against patriarchal violence by Kurdish women themselves), the article aligns the state with modernity and good Islam, and the poor, rural Kurds with tradition and bad Islam.

The distinction between good Muslims and bad Muslims is also used to position Turkey as a whole as the good Muslim within the Muslim world. The article mentions, through a culturalist ethnographic argument, that Turks compare favorably with Arabs:

> In Turkey, traditional rules are often bent to accommodate modern life. Handshaking, for example, is a widespread Turkish custom, and most women follow it. Turkey is culturally very different from Arab societies, and for that reason interprets Islam differently. Islam here is heavily influenced by Sufism, an introspective strain that tends to be more flexible. (Tavernise 2008b, A1)

Urban Turkish Islam, restrained by the influence of the West, is continuously contrasted with a dangerously unalloyed traditional Islam that endangers liberal Islam (in this case through the puzzling pseudo-ethnographic fetishization of the handshake as the ultimate marker of Westernness). Another article contrasts Ramadan in Turkey approvingly with "the situations in Saudi Arabia and Jordan" (Frantz 2000, A15) because restaurants remain open. The appealingly flexible Islam of Turkey is always set off against a more pure and threatening form of Islam (whether Arab or rural).

Women and Islamic Capitalism

This more salutary Turkish Islam takes place in a temporality on the cusp that promises to join East and West in a productive way, with the Muslim woman as the key figure of resolution. One article particularly reflects this framing. This article takes the logic a step further by arguing that Islam itself, through the integration of the Turkish Muslim woman into the market, can be productive of value. The article, focused on booming business in the city of Kayseri and titled "Turks Knock on Europe's Door with Evidence That Islam and Capitalism Can Coexist" (Bilefsky 2006, 4), opens by addressing Western expectations about Turkey, framing the problem of Islam as a problem for capitalism:

> Many Europeans and secular Turks have dismissed this poor, largely agricultural region as the "other" Turkey, a non-European backwater where women in head scarves are more prevalent than businessmen in pinstripes. Islam, they argue, never went through its own Reformation and so is not receptive to capitalism and innovation. (Bilefsky 2006, 4)

Here, women (in headscarves) stand in for the East and backwardness, men (in pinstripes) for Europe and progress. Historical and economic positioning seems to be visibly legible through the exteriority of dress. The author dubs what is emerging in Turkey "Calvinist Islam" and embraces the secularization thesis presented—the idea that all societies must follow the same path of progress where the limitation of religion to its own sphere is connected to the growth of capitalism.

The assertion that Islam "never went through its own Reformation" echoes quotes from earlier articles that position Turkey as "not yet" having had its Renaissance. However, this author instead argues for the Weber-inspired thesis that Turkey is spearheading a "Reformation" of Islam, offering Turkey's economic success as its proof. The article finally culminates in an image of a Muslim woman as the epitome of this potential.

The article follows several businesspeople in the region of Kayseri. Most are men, but the article ends with a profile of a woman. This woman's profile leads into a hopeful assessment of this economic boom, which faces the best hope of continuing (the author tells us, citing a report on "Islamic Calvinists" (European Stability Initiative 2005)) if the woman problem—"the Achilles' heel of Central Anatolia's ambitions to catch up economically with the European Union" (Bilefsky 2006, 4)—can be solved. Women are presented as great economic resources, as well as the ultimate barometers of the degree to which Turkey has become sufficiently liberal and sufficiently capitalist. The portrayal of this figure of the successful Muslim businesswoman epitomizes the new Muslim woman of neoliberal capitalism in the *New York Times*:

> One person who is helping to overcome such clichés is Ikbal Cardaroglu, a successful chartered accountant in Kayseri. She is also active in the governing party, in which powerful women are scarce.
>
> Ms. Cardaroglu, who wears chic black suits and drapes her white silk designer scarf around her shoulders as a fashion accessory, said she had encountered few hurdles on the way to being a successful Muslim businesswoman,

though she said that when she began working in the 1980's, people pointed at her on the street, and women in her neighborhood expressed pity.

"When I first told my friends I wanted to go into business, they were surprised, since most women here are teachers or bank-tellers," she said. "I did not wear a head scarf at that time, and when I got married, my husband complained that his friends' wives wore head scarves and that I should do so, too." (Bilefsky 2006, 4)

For the *New York Times*, the headscarf is the center of interest in Çavdaroğlu's (her name was misspelled in publication) story. Her ambiguity toward the headscarf is read approvingly; she is undogmatic and independent. She is a flexible Muslim, like the Erdoğan supporter with the trousers and bare head. The reminder that the scarf is not on her head but "a fashion accessory" signals that she takes the proper attitude: she sees the headscarf as nothing more than an element of individualized, consumer self-expression, a commodity object that lets her couple East and West.

The headscarf is still an ominous sign of Islam's fanatical demands, which can, if left unchecked, unnecessarily restrict productive potential—but Turkey seems, for the *New York Times*, to be positioned to keep it in its proper place. One man is quoted as saying that "in the past people gave up trade to focus on making Islam the center of their lives," as proof that a fanatical submission to Islam is a danger to capitalism. But by ending the article with an example of a Muslim woman whose scarf obeys the demands of fashion instead of God, the *New York Times* gives us a hopeful image of what Islam should be. The woman is again the symbol of the future of the entire Muslim world, the figure who unites the contradictions of Islam and the West. She exists in a tense moment about to blossom into a more harmonious wedding of Islam with the West and with capitalist development.

In the above articles, the *New York Times*' representational and rhetorical tactics trace a distinct change in attitude toward Muslim women in Turkey, concomitant with the War on Terror's demand for an acceptable Muslim subject to mediate and domesticate the aggressive and masculine masses of the Muslim world. Additionally, ethnic or linguistic difference must be masked and subsumed under the single marker of identity relevant to the *New York Times*: Islam. The *New York Times* satisfies this demand with the representation of the Turkish Muslim woman, feminine and moderate, individualistic, and cheerfully appreciative of the virtues of hard work and the fruits of the global market. The genre for the representation is the individualized personal profile (such as those of Kavakçı, Yılmaz, and Çavdaroğlu); the temporality is that of a moment on the cusp of change. This temporality calls out for the intervention not necessarily of the old Kemalist state to drag the Turkish Muslim woman forward through history (as in earlier articles) but of the investor who can recognize her dynamic potential and productive value.

The literature on the representation of Muslims in the mainstream Western media tends to focus on rhetorical techniques that distance and exoticize Muslims in the figures of the fanatic and the oppressed woman. By tracing the revaluation of the Turkish Muslim woman in the *New York Times*, this chapter aims to incite critics to remember that the image of the Muslim woman as a familiar, commensurable individual in Converse sneakers is as much worthy of critical enquiry. This chapter provides an examination of how, given the *New York Times*' history of representing Muslim women as oppressed, backward, and without identity, a new figure of the Muslim woman came to be in representations of Turkey: full of potential and interiority, and suited for a role in neoliberal capitalism and the global economy.

References

Asad, Talal. 2003. *Formations of the Secular: Christianity, Islam, and Modernity*. Stanford, CA: Stanford University Press.

Bilefsky, Dan. 2006. "Turks Knock on Europe's Door with Evidence That Islam and Capitalism Can Coexist." *New York Times*, 27 August 2006. ProQuest Historical Newspapers: The *New York Times* (1851–2008): 14.

Cowell, Alan. 1994. "Career Women Finding Elbowroom in Turkey: Women Make Gains, but Don't Go Unchallenged." *New York Times*, 2 March 1994: A4.

Darnton, John. 1995. "Uneasy Crossroads: A Special Report. Discontent Seethes in Once-Stable Turkey." *New York Times*, 2 March 1995, late edition (East Coast): A22.

Doha, Tanzeen. This volume. "Specters of Islam: Anti-Islamist (Re)Presentations in Secular Media and Feminism in the *New York Times*, 1979–2011." In *Reporting Islam: Muslim Women in the New York Times*, edited by Suad Joseph.

El Shakry, Omnia. 2011. "Youth as Peril and Promise: The Emergence of Adolescent Psychology in Postwar Egypt." *International Journal of Middle East Studies* 43 (4): 591–610.

European Stability Initiative. 2005. *Islamic Calvinists: Change and Conservatism in Central Anatolia*. Berlin: European Stability Initiative.

Feldman, Noah. 2008. "Veiled Democracy?" *New York Times*, 8 February 2008: A19.

Fisher, Ian. 2002. "Party with Islamic Roots Likely to Win Turkish Vote." *New York Times*, 31 October 2002, late edition (East Coast): A3.

Frantz, Douglas. 2000. "Despite Turkey's Secularism, Ramadan Exerts a Strong Force." *New York Times*, 26 December 2000, late edition (East Coast): A15.

Haberman, Clyde. 1989. "As Islam Is Revived, Secular Turks Wince." *New York Times*, 26 March 1989. ProQuest Historical Newspapers: The *New York Times* (1851–2008): 14.

Howe, Marvine. 1982. "Turkey Planning Legal Abortions." *New York Times*, 7 February 1982, late edition (East Coast): A19.

Judge, Rajbir. This volume. "The Islamic World Is Flat(tened): Contesting Islam in South Asia, in the *New York Times*, 1980–2011." In *Reporting Islam: Muslim Women in the New York Times*, edited by Suad Joseph.

Kinzer, Stephen. 1997. "Secular Turks Alarmed by Resurgence of Religion." *New York Times*, 13 February 1997: A1.

Kinzer, Stephen. 1998. "A Woman, Her Scarf and a Storm over Secularism." *New York Times*, 17 March 1998: A4.

Kinzer, Stephen. 1999. "Islamic Woman in a Head Scarf Suddenly Galvanizes Turkey." *New York Times*, 4 May 1999: A7.

Koğacıoğlu, Dicle. 2004. "The Tradition Effect: Framing Honor Crimes in Turkey." *Differences: A Journal of Feminist Cultural Studies* 15 (2): 119–51.

Mamdani, Mahmood. 2004. *Good Muslim, Bad Muslim: America, the Cold War, and the Roots of Terror*. New York: Pantheon Books.

Meari, Lena. This volume. "The Material Life of Representation: 'Veiled Muslim Women' in the *New York Times*, 1980–2011." In *Reporting Islam: Muslim Women in the New York Times*, edited by Suad Joseph.

Naim, Hakeem. This volume. "Friends and Foes: The Pragmatic Liberal Biases in Representation of Saudi Women vs. Iranian Women in the *New York Times*, 1980–2011." In *Reporting Islam: Muslim Women in the New York Times*, edited by Suad Joseph.

Sengupta, Somini. 2001. "Campus Crowd Shrugs at Marital-Equality Law." *New York Times*, 28 November 2001, late edition (East Coast): A4.

Sengupta, Somini. 2002. "Some Progress for Turkish Women." *New York Times*, 19 June 2002, late edition (East Coast): A22.

Tavernise, Sabrina. 2008a. "Under a Scarf, a Turkish Lawyer Fighting to Wear It." *New York Times*, 9 February 2008: A4.

Tavernise, Sabrina. 2008b. "Youthful Voice Stirs Challenge to Secular Turks." *New York Times*, 14 October 2008, National edition: A1.
Toscano, Alberto. 2010. *Fanaticism: On the Uses of an Idea*. London: Verso.
Tuğal, Cihan. 2009. *Passive Revolution: Absorbing the Islamic Challenge to Capitalism*. Stanford, CA: Stanford University Press.

3

The Material Life of Representation: "Veiled Muslim Women" in the *New York Times*, 1980–2011

Lena Meari

Introduction

This chapter traces the representations of "veiled Muslim women" in the *New York Times* (NYT). It follows the discourses at work in NYT articles and locates the main thematic, continuities and shifts in the representations of "veiled Muslim women" over three decades (1980–2011). The term "veiled Muslim women" in this chapter refers to the constructed images and discourses on women who don the Islamic veil as represented in NYT articles. Media representations of "veiled Muslim women" in general are closely associated with representations of Islam, and the cultural racialization of "Islam" and "Muslims."

The American power elites' "material ideology,"[1] its political–economic interests, and its official foreign policies and practices in the countries in which the represented "veiled Muslim women" dwell precondition these representations. Thus, the examination of representations of "veiled Muslim women" in NYT and the racial formation of "Islamic culture" should be contextualized within the materiality and actuality of US foreign policies in order to understand associations between shifts in militarization and imperial practices and corresponding shifts in media representations.

Nadine Naber (2008) explicates "cultural racism" as a process through which culture, religion, and national origin become racialized. The gendering of the racial formation of "Islamic culture" emerges from the focused gaze on the "veiled Muslim women" as a site for the racialized disputation over

Islam and its "difference" from the West, in US print news media (and other media). One of the main ways Islam is gendered is through the "veiled Muslim woman." Gendered Islamic signs such as the veil have come to reoccupy the public's imagination. Discourses about the veil also attracted the attention of scholars interested in contemporary sexual and cultural politics in Europe and the United States as well as intellectual feminists. The Western liberal obsession with the veil has its colonial roots; the sexual interest in unveiling colonized Muslim women is associated with the colonial political interest of intervention in their countries. Frantz Fanon (1965) had referred to the Western-colonial unified stance regarding the veil by stating, "Taken as a whole, colonial society, with its values, its areas of strength, and its philosophy, reacts to the veil in a rather homogeneous way" (37). Joan Wallach Scott (2010) links the French colonial history with contemporary policies. Like Fanon, Scott points to the colonialist anxiety at the face of "veiled Muslim women" and discusses the place of the veil in the Algerian resistance against the French colonizers. Leila Ahmed (2011) maintains that in the colonial period, British and elite Egyptian arguments for unveiling conflated progress and modernity with the West. Lila Abu Lughod (2013) illustrates how discourses on the veil were deployed as political projects, and the ways in which "gendered orientalism has taken on a new life and new forms" (202) in the twenty-first century.

We can identify NYT's main shifting discursive pillars on the veil and veiled Muslim women within the racial, gendered discourses on Islam in the United States, especially since the 1980s and within various liberal feminist theories prevalent throughout the last three decades in US academia and its intellectual engagement with feminism, modernization, and developmental issues. As Tanzeen Doha illustrates in his chapter, corresponding intellectual liberal discourses to NYT transforming liberal discourses and their imperialist logic are reflected in the writings of Martha Nussbaum's ideas about internationalist liberal, humanist feminism prevalent in the 1990s and early 2000s, as well as in Syla Benhabib's work on the "discourse ethics" that includes some (e.g., moderate Muslims) as moral equals but excludes others (fundamentalists and indigenous people), ideas which became prevalent among liberals post-9/11.

This chapter argues that representations of "veiled Muslim women" in NYT reproduce colonialist, racist, and Orientalist discourses in various transforming ways. These discourses function alongside US foreign policy in

Arab and Muslim majority societies and work to legitimize and reinforce US domination and imperial expansion in the region. Like US foreign policy, the representations of "veiled Muslim women" in NYT are changing and take on different forms depending on the historical moments.

Although the complex "cultural discourses" on the veil established in NYT articles can take a life of their own, these cultural discourses operate primarily as a mystification to US political–economic interests. Mapping the representations of "veiled Muslim women" in NYT then assists in assessing the working of these discourses; their transformations, continuities, and ruptures; and their functions in the reign of US imperial interventions in Arab and Muslim countries. The questions considered in this chapter include: (1) Which images and thematic are associated with "veiled Muslim women" in the NYT and what forms of shifts have occurred over three decades? (2) What narratives do these images and thematic tell? (3) What political work does these images and thematic do? What do they conceal, what purpose do they serve, and how do they legitimize/justify US imperial domination?

The consideration of these questions exposes the processes of racial formation of Islam and its gendering. It renders contradictions, instabilities, tensions, and shifts that characterize the discourses displayed and constructed by the media on Arab and Muslim women and Islam in general. The workings of these religious–cultural–racial discourses and their intertwinement with US foreign economic and political interests allude to the complicated political role that the media plays in accordance and at the service of the US imperial desires, ambitions, occupations, and wars. US interests concern mainly the Arab and Islamic countries' oil resources and their geostrategic depth, as well as the protection of the interests of Israel, which was since its establishment an arm for Western interests in the region. These interests and the political economy beneath them are concealed from the media's "cultural discourses" provided to the public in order to secure the hegemony of the power elites in accordance with what Noam Chomsky and Edward Herman (2002) refer to as America's system of indoctrination, which includes a system of propaganda imposed by the media to serve the power elite who own and consequently control the media.

As the introduction to this book details regarding the relation of the United States toward the "Middle East," there are broad US foreign policy trends across the three decades (1980–2011) that all administrations followed for various degrees and with different priorities and nuances. These trends include: perceiving the region as an area to be controlled, a perception that reflects a combination of neocolonial and Orientalist views. Political-economic interests in the oil and gas resources of the region motivate the interest in the region and the desire to control it. Further, all administrations view the region through the lens of "terrorism" and the relation between "terrorism" and "Islam." Finally, all administrations determine their policies in the region in accordance with the interests of Israel, the United States' main ally in the region. Despite the diversity and at times contradictions in NYT representations of "veiled Muslim women," we can clearly notice the traces of the main foreign policy trends upon these representations over the three decades examined in this chapter. That is, these representations function by the "material ideology" of the American power elites.

American interests in the Arab and Islamic world are not recent. This region has been perceived as "immensely relevant and yet antipathetically troubled and problematic" (Said 1981, I) for Americans since the early 1970s. The West's relation to "Islam" and the troubled nature of this relation have a long colonial history. This history is beyond the scope of this chapter for it focuses on the recent and contemporary relation of the United States toward the Arab and Muslim world and specifically how the media, within the contemporary context, employs the veil. It is worth noting, however, that the contemporary relation is constituted by its history within the colonial encounter between the West and Islam that needs to be traced and studied deeply. The US political-economic interests in the region, particularly the interest in the region's oil resources, typify the contemporary relation to the Arab and Islamic world. The growing American interest in the Islamic world since the 1970s is motivated, as Said (1981, I) states, by the oil resources of the Arab and Persian Gulf, the Iranian Revolution, the rise of radical nationalism in the Islamic world, and the rivalry of the superpowers on the region including the Soviet influence in Afghanistan, and recently the Russian influence with its allies in Syria.

It is not surprising, then, to find that NYT articles on the issue of "veiled Muslim women" during the decade of the 1980s concern specific Muslim countries that are geopolitically relevant to US interests. Such countries include: Saudi Arabia that has one of the world's largest oil reserves and is one of the world's largest oil exporter; Iran that has a geopolitical significance and has one of the largest natural gas and petroleum reserves in the world and in which an Islamic Revolution took hold in 1979; and finally, Afghanistan sitting at a geostrategic location connecting the Middle East, Central Asia, and the Indian subcontinent, having crude oil and natural gas resources, rare minerals, and in 1979 witnessed a war between US-backed Mujahidin and Soviet-backed Afghan government.[2]

The NYT articles during the decade of the 1990s demonstrate a continuing interest in these countries and display old as well as new interests and forms of representations. Although "Islam" remains a troubling and problematic issue to the liberal American logic characteristic of the NYT, US political–economic interests and relations to each specific Islamic country shape the representational strategies of Islam and the Islamic veil. As Hakeem Naim illustrates in his chapter, NYT representational strategies of Saudi veiled women differ from the NYT representational strategies of Iranian veiled women in accordance with the US political relations with the Saudi and Iranian regimes that depend on the regimes' compliance with US political–economic interests and domination in the world order. The employment of different representational strategies illuminates the ways in which the media, and NYT in this example, constitute an instrument of propaganda in the service of the American power elite.[3]

In the beginning of the decade of the 2000s, the rise (and re-production) of Islamophobia in the United States and many parts of the world, stimulated by the events of 9/11, has reenergized formal and informal discourses on "the clash of civilizations" between Islamic and Western civilizations advanced during the 1990s by Bernard Lewis (1990) and Samuel P. Huntington (1993, 1996). The US regime's political, economic, and military practices that preconditioned the discourses have justified themselves on these discourses. Transported within these discourses is a modern racialization of culture and religion, now targeting "Islam" and relying on images of Muslim women similar to colonial discourse of previous century.

Meanings of race in the United States have changed across different historical and political circumstances.[4] In this sense, Omi and Winant (1994) define racial formation "as the social historical process by which racial categories are created, inhabited, transformed and destroyed." Since the 1990s, race has been reconceptualized civilizationally, with Islamic "culture" and "religion" as the ultimate other to Western "civilization." Samuel Huntington, for instance, who advocates the "clash of civilization" thesis, argues that the West should worry not about Islamic fundamentalism but about Islam itself.

Immigration historians have suggested that race plays a critical role in the adaptation of immigrant groups in the American society. American identity and American citizenship are associated with "Whiteness." Nevertheless, Sanchez (1999) contends that "Whiteness" is not simply a perspective on a white/black dynamic as most scholars of whiteness asserted. He calls for exploring how "nation and region play important roles in white identity formation" (Sanchez 1999, 69). This means that racial formations and their media representations are closely linked to the American administrations' foreign policy toward the original region and nation from which the represented group immigrated. The veil is central in these representations.

As the chapter shows in detailed examples, the NYT articles during the early 1980s provide multiple, unstable, and at times contradictory representations of the veil. The multiplicity, however, resides within an Orientalist and negative discursive frame (that has its roots in the colonial encounter between Western colonizers and Muslim countries). The references of this discursive frame are liberal assumptions concerning "what women are" and "what they desire." These assumptions contain the belief that women have an innate desire for freedom and autonomy and that they seek to challenge social norms imposed on them.[5] Within these assumptions, the veil is perceived as a main pillar of social norms imposed on Muslim women by Muslim men. Toward the end of the 1980s the equation of the veil with oppression was established in the NYT and the veil turns into the ultimate sign of Islam's oppressive practices toward women.

Hence, the main thematic on the veil in the NYT articles during the decade of the 1990s became the ethical role that the West should take in "protecting" and "saving" Muslim women from their oppressors. This "concern" serves the preexisting US material interventionist military plans and practices through justifying them on moral basis, eliciting Lila Abu-Lughod's explanation of how the global women's rights movement has developed into a "moral crusade" (2013, 81).

Following 9/11 the main theme in the NYT articles in the decade of the 2000s turns to the enemy from within, that is, the Muslim communities living in Western countries and their challenge to the "secular" regimes. As Nadine Naber (2008) argues, "September 11 was a turning point in that representations of 'terrorism' and 'Islamic fundamentalism' have increasingly replaced other representations ... and have become more fervently deployed in anti-Arab state policies and everyday patterns of engagement than ever before" (2008, 4). Correspondingly, representations of "veiled Muslim women" as subjugated victims during the 1990s were transformed post-9/11. As Sahar Aziz (2012) notices the veil's meaning was transformed post-9/11 from a symbol of female subjugation into a symbol of terror(ism). At the beginning of the decade of the 2000s, veiled/unveiled women corresponded in NYT articles to the schema of oppression/freedom. However, the representations of the "subjugated veiled women" had transformed as a result of the perceptions of veiled women as part of the Islamic "terrorism," not necessarily their victims. To deal with these two contradictory perceptions of veiled women as the victims of Islamic terrorism on the one hand and being sympathizers with it on the other, a new representational strategy (following a practical US political strategy) appears in NYT. After the establishment during the 1990s of the schema of veiled/unveiled women equating to oppression/freedom, the 2000s witnessed the new division of the modern and moderate veiled woman vs. the antimodern and militant veiled woman, a division that corresponds to the conceptual division of Good Muslims vs. Bad Muslims developed by Mahmood Mamdani (2005).

The abovementioned continuing and transforming representations have material life; they are embedded in the materiality of transforming US imperial practices in the countries in which the depicted "veiled Muslim women" reside. The NYT resort to "cultural discourses" to deal with "Muslim veiled women" and these discourses need to be scrutinized and analyzed. Nevertheless, the chapter does not wish to offer a "discourse analysis" that is devoid of US physical power employed in Arab and Muslim countries for the sake of capital profits and political domination. It wishes to contextualize the shifting representations within other forms of power relations, particularly those related to US foreign policies and its on-the-ground aggressive practices. This contextualization exposes how NYT "cultural discourses" operate as mystification of imperial economic–political interests and as moral justification for these interests.

Methodology

To examine the representations of "veiled Muslim women" in the NYT, the research team downloaded the articles that contain the key terms "Veil and Women" by manual searches through ProQuest of the NYT database for the 30-year period, 1980–2011. This method has its limitations for it is not comprehensive and does not provide all NYT articles on the issue. However, it does offer a sample of NYT articles on "veiled Muslim women." We employed a close reading for content analysis of the relevant 37 downloaded articles. The current chapter reflects only part of the thematic identified as reflected in 26 articles included in it.

For the sake of simplification and clarity, the following analysis is organized through the main thematic identified in NYT articles on "veiled Muslim women" throughout three decades. However, this analytical tactic, which presents separated and autonomous thematic, is artificial and misleading. In reality, the following identified thematic intersects in complex ways within NYT articles and their intersection conceals their intended impulse on the one hand, and complicates their message on the other hand. Therefore, we need to comprehend these thematic in their complex overlapping and cumulative effects.

The Decade of the 1980s

The representations of the veil and veiled Muslim women in the NYT during the decade of the 1980s were constructed mainly through articles on "veiled Muslim women" in specific countries such as Saudi Arabia, Iran, and Afghanistan. These countries were at the time the center of US interest for their oil resources and geostrategic positions. This seems to be the reason for the presence of NYT journalists and reporters in these countries, their encounter with its inhabitants, and the writing about them. NYT representations of "veiled Muslim women" during the 1980s are apparently multiple, unstable, and at times contradictory. However, inherent within the multiplicity of NYT representations of the veil were an Orientalist–colonialist tendency that constitutes "Islam" and the Muslim countries as the negative Other of the West in a way that serves the interests of the discourse producers. The Orientalist tendency is based on assumptions regarding the human nature and what is good and right for humans in general and women in particular. Within the apparent multiplicity of the representations of the veil, during the decade of the 1980s, we can identify a frame of reference that links the donning of the veil with oppressive and discriminatory practices against Muslim women. This frame of reference gradually equates the veil with oppression, discrimination, segregation, secondary position, and stupidity. During the 1980s, veiled Muslim women were more often than not depicted in NYT as Islam's oppressed victims. NYT articles employ a discursive frame that constitutes the veil as part and parcel of other repressive practices characterizing Muslim societies and demarcating their distinctiveness from Western societies.

The NYT articles in the early 1980s gradually construct the association between the veil and discriminatory practices against women. The accumulative effect of these associations turned the veil, toward the end of the 1980s, into a freestanding symbol that has the power to elicit negative and discriminatory associations. These discriminatory associations matched during the 1990s and the 2000s corresponding material practices reflected in Western military interventions to "save" veiled Muslim women, already constructed during the 1980s as the victims of Islam. Six main themes were identified in the 1980s.

The Veil as Multiplicity Governed by Negativity

The veil is represented in NYT articles as multiplicity that includes various dimensions such as faith, devotion, self-protection, and equalizing costume. However, this multiplicity is framed within a negative frame of reference. This representation corresponds to the Orientalist/colonialist fantasies of the East.

The following article from 19 June 1980 by A. G. Mojtabai, offers an example of the multiplicity of representations of the veil that reside within a negative frame of reference based on liberal fantasies and assumptions on what is universally "good" for women. The article is written in a question-and-answer form in which a Western woman is "investigating" another Western woman regarding her donning of the veil when she resided in Iran. The article begins with the following question:

> QUESTION: You are guilty, you know ... of compromise, conciliation, yes, I'd even say of collaboration with the oppressor ... When you lived in Iran ... you put on the veil.

After situating the donning of the veil as collaboration with the oppressor, the article provides multiple viewpoints about the veil and its meanings from the perspective of Western women. Part of the questions and answers that appear throughout the article read as follows:

> A: ... I thought of it as nothing more than one of those little concessions to circumstance that social life exacts from each of us now and then ... The chador was my passport to what otherwise I would not have been privileged to see ... Q: ... I'd like to suggest a certain amount of self-deception, bad faith, play-acting ... A: Well, let's at least look at the play-acting part. Sure, it's there. It's part of the reason that men in drag take to the chador. And prostitutes. Although, with prostitutes, it's also for self-protection. But coquettish women also use the chador to great effect. Beautiful eyes, but so-so nose? Banish the nose and expose the eyes; let the rest be inferred from the eyes ... For me, it was always something of a costume. For my mother-in-law, it was something very different, something closely bound up with her sense of self. It was more than the fact that she was a devout Muslim ... For poor women, who have few clothes, the chador is a great equalizer, a sort of uniform; it matters little what you are wearing underneath ... But when the covering held secure, and I gazed out, safe in my anonymity, that was something. I felt—somehow beyond reproach, invulnerable, snug, enclosed. I felt curiously free. Dead to the world, I was all alive. It was a little like that old dream of invisibility ... But, of course, I could put off the veil largely when I chose; I was not doomed to invisibility. (Mojtabai 1980)

The article ends and concludes with the following series of questions and answers:

> Q: Yet you put on the chador?
> A: Yes, but you see, the matter wasn't simple.
> Q: It never is.
> A: One small concession, as I said.
> Q: Which leads to yet another, and another. (Mojtabai 1980)

The above article exemplifies the representations of the veil, or should we say the Western women's fantasies on the veil and the assumptions on what is good for women as provided to the American readers in the early 1980s. It is written in a dialogic form, which in the liberal sense provides plurality of views. This form of dialogue, though, exposes the multiplicity of representations of the veil that reside within a negative discursive frame of reference. The multiple, unstable, and contradictory representations include depictions of the veil as: self-deception, playacting, self-protection, erotic, part of the sense of self for a devout Muslim woman, an equalizer for poor women, invisibility, and free feeling. Yet, these multiple and contradictory representations are depicted within a frame of reference that constitutes the veil as oppressive. The donning of the veil by women, as the article begins and concludes, represents a "concession" from the part of women that "leads to yet another, and another." That is, underneath the multiplicity of the representations of the veil there are assumptions regarding the human nature and its basic desires. One such assumption concerns the issue of the visibility of women. The veil is perceived as "covering" Muslim women, making them invisible while they should be visible and uncovered. The invisibility, it seems, disturbs the Western gaze and explains the obsession with the veil.

The Construction of the Veil as Discrimination against Women

Related to the Orientalist approach to veiled Muslim women and the negative frame of reference to the issue of the veil is the construction of the veil as discrimination against women. The framework of discrimination works through representing the veil as a discriminatory practice among other practices. Within this representation the veil becomes a symbol of oppression, segregation, and limited mental abilities.

The following quotations from an article about Saudi Arabia, published in the NYT on 22 January 1980 by Douglas Martin, is illustrative of the type of articles that construct an association between the veil and other discriminatory practices against women in Muslim societies. Although the article is concerned with the oil resources of Saudi Arabia, reflecting the interests of Westerners with this resource, as the first following quote shows, the article employs Saudi women's veil as a symbol of discrimination:

> Saudi Arabia has a deliberate policy of heavily subsidizing the price of gasoline through the state-owned Petromin oil company. The giveaway prices are embarrassing at a time when Sheik Ahmed Zaki Yamani, the kingdom's Minister of Petroleum, regularly tells Western consumers that high energy prices are good for them because they force energy conservation. Meanwhile, Saudi citizens regard cheap gasoline—about one-twentieth the price of bottled water—as almost a birthright ...
>
> On a social level, the automobile highlights one of the sharpest distinctions in Saudi society, that between men and women. Along with watching their fathers negotiate their marriages, having to wear black veils in public and being prohibited from working in professions with men, women may not drive cars. (Martin 1982)

The above article situates the veil within other discriminatory practices against women in Saudi society. The veil is constantly coupled with discriminative practices in NYT articles in a way that turns the veil into the visible symbol of the oppression and discrimination against Muslim women. That is, veiled Muslim women are being read as a text, which inevitably includes oppression. As the above quote illustrates, women who don the veil have no ability of marriage choice, are prohibited from working with men, and may not drive cars.

In addition to symbolizing oppression and discrimination, the veil is represented in many NYT articles as immediately linked to the segregation of Muslim women. Women are represented as segregated in their "black veils" and "secondary positions." The secondary position is directly associated with the veil as the following quote from NYT article from 3 September 1987 by Francis Clines shows:

> Officially, the Saudis brag that they are achieving their goal of taking their fortune into their own hands and displacing the American managers who arrived five decades ago with the first oil wells. But some sympathetic diplomats feel the Saudis are wasting the managerial resources of half the nation, the women, who remain firmly segregated in their black veils and secondary positions. (Clines 1987)

The above quote asserts that although Arabs-Muslims adopted the (Western) American modern managerial skills, unlike Americans they keep women segregated in second positions. The veil is central to the representation of the segregation of women and their distinctiveness from American women. Few articles in the NYT compare the segregation of women and the veil with the male/female segregation in Western public spaces. The following article from 15 December 1985 by Katha Pollitt provides an example:

> In the West we're horrified by such practices as the wearing of veils and chadors by Islamic women in public, a custom that seems to say that a woman who ventures abroad is so out of place she must symbolically deny she is there. But if you look around you in New York City, you'll see a lot of behavior that makes the same point more subtly. There's the constant low-level aggravation Kathy mentioned—"What are you reading? Want to have sex? Why aren't you smiling?" There's body language. On the subways, men sit with their knees apart, claiming space; women sit with their knees pressed together, ceding it. And there's the male sense of entitlement—on the street, men march boldly down the middle of the sidewalk, swinging their arms and looking ahead, swerving neither to left nor right for oncoming pedestrians. Women scurry along, clutching their shoulder bags, head down, weaving a zigzag path through the crowd while murmuring "Excuse me." (Pollitt 1985)

The above article reproduces the discourse that links the veil with oppressive and discriminatory practices against Muslim women. It constructs a homology between the function of the veil in Muslim societies and the function of gendered spatial discriminatory practices in the United States. The article aims to expose the subtle gendered discriminatory practices in the United States. Its frame of reference, though, is the construction of the veil as a horrifying practice.

The veil is represented in NYT articles not only as an oppressive practice imposed on Muslim women but also as a discriminatory practice that affects and limits women's mental abilities as the quotation from the following article from 27 March 1988 by Linda Bird Francke exemplifies: "Back in Long Island, I realize the veil has fallen over my mind as well. I resist having to make decisions, having to go out among strangers, having to be—a person. No wonder the women in Pakistan are finding their struggle so hard. They've been buried under the veil for a thousand years. I only felt its shadow for six weeks" (Francke 1988).

The above quote from an article written by a Western woman who spent time in Pakistan links the donning of the veil with the inability to make decisions, going out with strangers, and being a person. That is, the veil is associated with the objectification of Muslim women. Within such discursive frame the veil is represented as an ultimate constraint to women's mental capabilities.

The Veil as a Marker of Colonialist Binary

The veil is represented as a marker of the colonialist binary between us and them/Americans and Muslims. The theme of the colonialist binary works through representing American cities as tolerant compared to Muslim cities.

There are few articles in the 1980s that consider veiled Muslim women living in the United States. These articles depict US cities such as New York as a tolerant city in the eyes of Muslim women as the following article published in NYT on 24 September 1984 ends: "Despite objections to living in a city that clashes with their values, several women said New York gives them the freedom to live as they choose. 'Here everyone has his own cause, like saving the Indians, so nobody really pays attention to how I want to live,' said a young Iranian woman" ("The Moslem Veil in the City: A Matter of Tradition" 1984).

Following articles that depict the veil as discrimination against Muslim women, the above article illustrates that the American society is not discriminative even toward women who are veiled. In contrast to a Palestinian woman quoted in the above article as declaring, "I know I am right and everyone else is wrong," New York City is represented as a multicultural society that gives freedom of choice to all its residents in a way that ignores the institutional racism characteristic of American life experience.

The Veil as Anti-West Sentiment

Following the Iranian Revolution in 1979, the Iranian regime is represented in NYT articles as oppressive toward its citizens and anti-Western. The "repressive features" of the Iranian regime are objectified in NYT articles through the imposition of the veil on women. The veil is employed as the ultimate sign of repression toward women in the Iranian anti-Western regime. Thus, an association between the imposition of the veil and antagonism to the West is constructed in the case of Iran. The following articles from 9 July 1980 and 1 May 1985 provide examples regarding the representations of the Iranian regime and the veil:

> A drive to enforce Islamic rules in Iran was intensified by Ayatollah Khomeini. Seven men convicted of drug trafficking were executed by firing squad on a Teheran street, and 131 women were dismissed from the army and police force because they arrived for work without Islamic veils. ("News Summary" 1980)
>
> The Revolutionary Guards of Iran arrested about 500 people in Teheran in the past two days for violating the strict code of Islamic behavior, the semi-official Iranian newspaper Jamhuri Islami said today …
>
> Teheran residents reached by telephone from Athens said the announcement of the arrests "shows that the campaign to enforce the veil and discourage Western dress has continued." ("Guards Arrest 500 Iranians for Breaking Islamic Codes UPI" 1985)

The Representation of Veiled Muslim Women as Victims

As a result of the accumulated effect of NYT articles that depict the veil as an oppressive and discriminatory practice against women, the questions of whether veiled Muslim women are agents or victims and whether they fight the veil emerge. The following quote from an article from 13 April 1985 by Elaine Sciolino alludes to the centrality of this question in NYT: "One battle most Saudi women do not seem to be fighting is the battle of the veil. Many say they feel that veiling their heads and faces is preferable to the stares and insults of men" (Sciolino 1985).

While the article presents to the reader a Saudi veiled woman who works as a dean at a university in contrast to the stereotypical perception of veiled Muslim women, the article highlights the discrimination against women. The article is not interested in how women live social reality but in highlighting the repressive aspects of Muslim societies and women's readiness (or lack of) to fight against them. The article ends by stating that Saudi women do not seem to be fighting the battle of the veil. That is, Saudi women are represented as passive victims who don't rise up to the challenge of the fight they should wage. The frame of reference for the question of the agency of veiled Muslim women is the liberal discourse, which constitutes the human in general and women in particular as gearing toward freedom. In the liberal sense, freedom means the abolition of sociocultural norms, signified in the Islamic context by the veil.

Representation of the Veil as the Ultimate Sign of Muslim Women's Oppression

In the late 1980s we find several articles in NYT focused on Afghanistan. In these articles the veil/unveil is employed as a measure of women's oppression/freedom. The following quotes from two different articles from NYT, one published on 12 December 1988 by Henry Kamm, and the other published on 12 June 1988 by Donatella Lorch, provide few examples of how the veil was employed in articles about Afghanistan toward the end of the decade of the 1980s:

> Mrs. Wardak shares a concern felt by women of modern ways among the more than three million Afghan refugees in Pakistan. They fear that fundamentalist mullahs, or religious leaders, among the seven parties of the resistance alliance based in Peshawar want to turn back the clock on women's rights when they return to leading positions in this country. Mullahs have imposed strict confinement to the house or tent on the vast majority of refugee women and girls and severely limited their access to medical care and education provided by international agencies ...
>
> At the same time, she said, women have steadily gained in equality since 1959, when, as she said, "we were unveiled." (Kamm 1988)
>
> Mrs. Kakar leaned forward as she spoke of the past and the future in Afghanistan and her present exile, where a conservative Islamic current has swept many Afghan refugee women behind the veil, into seclusion. She unconsciously let her own veil fall as she spoke of her work as principal of the Lycee Malalai, a secondary school for Afghan refugee girls in Peshawar, and her anxieties about the role of women in a possibly Islamic state of Afghanistan after the war ends. (Lorch 1988)

The first of the above articles ends with an Afghani woman stating that Afghani women have steadily gained equality since 1959, when they "were unveiled." And the second article turns the veil into a fetish. Letting the veil fall becomes a symbol of freedom. These examples illustrate how NYT articles on the veil during the 1980s have gradually constructed the veil as the ultimate symbol of oppression against Muslim women. The veil became a freestanding symbol for oppression.

The sample of the NYT articles from the decade of the 1980s, presented above, shows an interest in the veil and veiled Muslim women, particularly in specific countries: those that are relevant to US political–economic interests. Apparently the representations of the veil are multiple, unstable, and contradictory. However, despite the multiplicity of representations the accumulative effect of reading articles about the veil is negative. The veil is represented within a discursive frame that constitutes the veil as part of repressive and discriminatory practices against Muslim women. Articles that include a consideration of the veil as a choice of women are read within this discursive frame.

With this frame of reference and the establishment of the veil as the symbol that condensates all that is negative and repressive in the Islamic societies, toward the end of the decade of the 1980s it was enough to provoke the veil in an article in order to elicit negative connotations toward the regime in Afghanistan. This formation of the veil played a critical role in legitimating and justifying US invasion and destruction of Afghanistan a decade after.

The Decade of the 1990s

One of the main thematic in the NYT articles on "veiled Muslim women" during the 1990s decade is the role of the West in "protecting" and "saving" Muslim women from their "oppressors." While NYT articles in the 1980s were concerned with the manifestations of the "oppression" of Muslim women in which the veil is constructed as a condensed sign of this oppression, NYT articles during the 1990s were concerned with "the growing strength of religious fundamentalism" and "Islamic militancy" in Arab and Muslim countries, which corresponds to the trend in American administrations' foreign policy that emphasizes the concern with "terrorism." The concern with Islamic movements is associated with an "ethical" discourse regarding the role that the West should take in assisting and saving Muslim women. The veil is represented as central to the rise of "religious fundamentalism," and Muslim women within these articles are represented as the victims of "religious fundamentalism." The representations of the Islamic movements and their "repression" of Muslim women in NYT articles within a culturalist discursive formation serve as a mystification for political–economic interests of the United States in the Arab and Muslim countries and the risk some Islamic movements would pose to it. Three main themes were identified during the 1990s.

Islamist Equals Fundamentalist

The NYT articles during the early 1990s were concerned with Islamic movements in the Arab and Muslim countries. In these articles Islamic movements are homogenized and demonized through their construction as fundamentalist repressive movements. In accordance with the growing discourses during the 1990s on the "clash of civilizations," NYT articles represent the condition in the region as a battle between secular and religious regimes. The following article published on 1 July 1990 by Youssef M. Ibrahim offers an example:

> ELEVEN years after Ayatollah Ruhollah Khomeini was swept to power in the Iranian revolution, Islamic forces in Algeria, Egypt and Jordan have peacefully secured footholds on power at the ballot box. Elsewhere, Islamic fundamentalists are seeking or consolidating power through the use of arms and intimidation.
>
> In the Sudan, a military dictatorship is implementing religious edicts by force. In Lebanon, Egypt, Tunisia and Morocco, armed fundamentalists are seeking to overturn secular regimes. Fundamentalists are challenging the Palestine Liberation Organization for leadership within the Arab uprising in the Israeli-occupied West Bank and Gaza Strip. Even in Saudi Arabia, where strict Islamic laws are already enforced, princes and technocrats privately complain that religious leaders are obstructing the ever-slow pace of modernization …
>
> Western diplomats have begun developing contacts with some groups that take part in elections. Among the many unanswered questions, however, are what the West can gain from such contacts, how effectively the fundamentalists would govern if they were elected to full national power, and whether they would preserve democracy, given that their basic demand is for a guarantee that the country be run by their religious rules.

"Islam, Not Revenge"

"The Algerian people have chosen Islam, not revenge," was the response given by Sheik Abassi Madani, the leader of the Islamic movement in Algeria, when asked in a recent interview whether his movement will seek to ban alcohol, end mixed bathing on beaches, and require women to wear veils. "These matters come through education and not otherwise," he said.

That remains to be seen. In Iran similar promises were made and broken. There are, in each Islamic movement, hard and moderate tendencies. What the fundamentalists share is a dream: to break with secularism and install Islamic regimes. (Ibrahim 1990)

The above article shows how the rise of Islamic movements in different Arab and Muslim countries is represented in NYT articles. The interest in Islamic movements is a political–economic one that concerns Western countries' political–economic interests in these countries and the fear that any change in the regional governments could affect these interests. However, the concern is represented in the article as a concern with the imposition of religious rules on the citizens of these countries, including the imposition of the veil on women. Further, the concern with the "liberties of the citizens of these countries" is justified in the article based on the Iranian example that was already demonized in many NYT articles throughout the 1980s. The article states that promises to protect the citizens' liberties in Iran "were made and broken."

Within the concern of the NYT articles during the 1990s with what they refer to as "Islamic fundamentalism" we notice an interest in different Islamic movements such as Hamas—the Palestinian Islamic resistance movement, which evolved in the late 1980s during the first Palestinian Intifada. In accordance with the United States' official position of unconditional support for the Israeli settler-colonial state, NYT articles focus on what is represented as the oppressive religious aspects of Hamas and not its anti-colonial struggle against Israeli colonialism. The whole Palestinian anti-colonial struggle is represented through the perception of Hamas as a religious movement, which "oppresses women and imposes the veil." This is an exemplary case of the function of NYT cultural–religious discourse in concealing the colonial-settler base of Israel and the Palestinian struggle against it. The following article from 22 August 1991 by Sabra Chartrand provides an example:

About 30 teen-age boys were spread up and down a busy street in small, distinct patrols, all nervously watching the women who passed. Some fingered little bags of black paint. Egging each other on, they began reprimanding girls, young women, mothers and daughters. Their mission was clear: warn, and if necessary punish, women and girls who dared appear in public without their veils.

Hana Surani came out of a dress shop and with one sweeping motion loosely wrapped a scarf around her head. She took five steps to the boutique next door and then yanked off the scarf as she crossed its threshold.

Before the door closed behind her an angry young man pointed at her head and commanded, "Put the veil on properly!" Startled and afraid, Miss Surani just looked away.

But a few minutes later two young women with dark hair curling under slack scarfs became angry at a similar challenge and in the middle of the street defiantly pulled off the scarfs. They were rewarded for their boldness with a squirt of black paint on their clothes …

"This will keep our morals and traditions intact," said one of the youths, a 19-year-old who said he was acting on orders from the Islamic Resistance Movement, also known as Hamas, a banned Islamic fundamentalist group active in the Palestinian uprising in the Israeli-occupied territories. "Only through Islam can we defeat Israeli intelligence agents who use loose women to lure Palestinians into spying for them."

To Islamic fundamentalists, loose women are any who do not cover their heads, as decreed by the Koran. Islamic fundamentalism has swept the Arab world in recent years, but in Gaza it has become a rallying point in the fight against Israel. It is only through devotion to Islam, adherents say, that the Palestinians will free themselves of Israeli occupation …

"The Islamic revival in Gaza is principally motivated by politics," said Ziad Abu Amer, a political science professor at Bir Zeit University who has written a book about Gaza fundamentalist movements. "This is a counterbalance to Judaism, Zionism and Israel.

I think it is done more to assert nationalist identity than for religion," he added …

Miss Hadidi, whose clothing is beyond reproach, approved of the scarf vigilantes. But women like Miss Surani, who are admonished or attacked by the youths, often have a different view.

"We put on the veil because we are afraid of these uneducated, ignorant boys," said Miss Surani, who defiantly drapes her scarf as loosely as possible over as little of her hair as she thinks will escape notice. "Their actions have nothing to do with religion. It's just their political mood." (Chartrand 1991)

The above article, written during the Palestinian first Intifada, focuses on Hamas young activists' practices against women and the ways in which they impose the veil on women. Palestinian women are represented as the victims of Hamas who are violently obliged to don the veil. The reiteration of such representations in NYT articles implies that any woman who dons the veil is a victim of the oppressive religious–fundamentalist movements.

Although the above article apparently brings different voices such as the voice of Hamas youth activists, the voice of a professor who analyzes the intertwinement of the religious and the nationalist aspects in the Palestinian anti-colonial struggle, and the voices of various women, there is a decontextualization of the Palestinian colonial context and a construction of Hamas and other Islamic movements as eliciting fear. Hamas is described in the article as "a banned Islamic fundamentalist group active in the Palestinian uprising in the Israeli-occupied territories." The article does not mention that all Palestinian political organizations, including self-claimed secular factions of the PLO, are banned by the occupation authorities, it also does not mention the colonial violence of Israel toward Palestinian men and women.

Although the article provides a voice of a woman who defends the donning of the veil and the niqab by Muslim women, the article depicts her voice within the many other voices of Palestinian women who refer to the veil as oppressive. Further, her voice is represented as a reflection of the voice of Hamas men. She is quoted as saying, "If a woman does not obey God, her father, husband and brothers must force her. If they fail to do so, others must intervene." As we will see, the depiction of Palestinian women in Gaza as victims of "Islamic fundamentalism" changes in the subsequent decade with the focus on the women of Hamas as "negative" agents and sympathizers with "terrorists."

The White Man's Burden

During the 1990s the "clash of civilizations" took a form through images that portray it as taking place within Muslim majority countries rather than between Western countries and the Muslim world. The "uncivilized enemy" of the West is represented as targeting modern Westernized communities in the region. Within this context, the issue of the "white man burden" arises.

The following article published on 7 February 1993 by Clyde Farnsworth illustrates the thematic of the link between "the growing Islamic fundamentalism" in the region and the role that the West should take for "protecting oppressed Muslim women":

> The Saudi woman just granted asylum in Canada because of her fears of persecution at home for her feminist beliefs predicts that there will be increasing repression of Saudi women because of the growing strength of religious fundamentalism in that country …
>
> Saudi restrictions on women are based both on the Koran and on conservative Arab traditions. Women are not allowed to mix with men in any public or work place. A woman must be veiled in public and is forbidden to travel alone or to drive a car …
>
> Islamic militancy has been on the rise throughout the Middle East, with proponents challenging practically every state …
>
> While still in that country, she tried to go outdoors without the veil, to travel alone and to pursue a university education in the field of her choice …
>
> She arrived in Canada in April 1991, seeking to further her education and to work eventually in women's counseling. She had to go into hiding, however, after an appeal for refugee status on grounds of sexual discrimination was denied, a decision that made her an illegal immigrant. She has lived on money from her family. That rejection was overturned Jan. 29 after Bernard Valcourt, the Minister of Employment and Immigration, intervened as part of a landmark change in Canada's immigration rules. Ottawa is drawing up guidelines, expected to be ready within the next month, under which it would grant refugee status to women who can show persecution as a result of their sex.
>
> The change potentially would open up Canada to abused women from many countries who are not protected by the laws of their homelands …
>
> Saudi Arabia's great wealth and the lack of any pressing need for women to work are among forces that keep women down in that country, she believes.
>
> "The way we are wealthy is different from the U.S.," she said. "I think in the U.S. and other countries the women's movement and the economy have grown at the same time, but for us there has been no change in the mentality

because there is no incentive for women to participate in public life. We let the men abuse us because we don't know any better." (Farnsworth 1993)

The above article includes thematic noticed earlier in the 1980s such as the association of the veil with other discriminatory practices against Muslim women, as well as the constitution of the West as the Other of the Islamic oppression of women. Added to these thematic is the question of the role Western countries should take for the protection of the oppressed Muslim women. This thematic is also illustrated in the following article that was published in NYT one month later on 10 March 1993 and that seems to refer to the same woman. In this article, however, the variety of discriminatory practices against women described in the earlier article was reduced to the donning of the veil:

> A woman from Saudi Arabia, identified only as "Nada," has helped Canada establish a new basis for political asylum: gender.
> Recently Canada's immigration minister, Bernard Valcourt, overruled a refugee tribunal to grant "Nada" the right to remain in Canada. She had argued that by refusing to wear a veil and otherwise opposing the subordination of women, she risked persecution if she returned home.
> Broadly this makes sense, and not just for Canada. But where does one draw the line? Suppose a Japanese woman claimed right of asylum on the same ground, since by tradition women are subordinate in Japan. No doubt this and other arguments will be heard now that Canada is due to issue new guidelines that expressly permit refugee applications by women who claim they may be persecuted strictly because of their sex ...
> The current definition of a refugee under United Nations rules and under most Western asylum laws is a person who has a well-founded fear of persecution for reasons of race, religion, nationality, membership in a particular social group or political opinion. It's hard to see why gender could not be added to the list, assuming that reasonable lines can be drawn. ("Asylum by Gender (Editorial)" 1993)

In the above article the veil turned to be the central aspect of Muslim women's subordination. We can notice that gradually the multiplicity in the representations of the veil was reduced to one meaning: oppression. While during the 1980s the veil was associated with the subordination of Muslim women and the frame of discourse about the veil held negative meanings, there were multiple, unstable, and contradictory representations of the veil. In the 1990s the representation of the veil was reduced to one sign—the oppression of Muslim women. Further, this sign turns to be the acclaimed concern of Western countries' policies and material intervention on behalf of Muslim women who reside in these Western countries and on behalf of Muslim women living in Arab and Muslim countries. This concern constitutes the West as a "liberating power."

The following article published in the NYT on 13 January 1995 by Marlise Simons provides one more example for the "Western ethical dilemma" of how to deal with the subordination of Muslim women by their own regimes, and to what extent these countries should take part in the activities of the "international community":

> The groups say sex discrimination is analogous to the racial discrimination that resulted in South Africa's being banned from the Olympic Games between 1964 and 1992. The Olympic charter states that any form of discrimination with regard to a country or a person on grounds of race, religion, politics, sex or otherwise is incompatible with belonging to the Olympic Movement ...
>
> Atlanta Plus members say that Iran is the only country they know of that has explicitly banned women from most sports but that others are doing so quietly, including Pakistan and Kuwait. Chahla Chafiq, an Iranian sociologist, said that in Iran women can participate only in those Olympic sports in which they can wear head-to-toe robes and veils ...
>
> Moroccan and Tunisian female athletes have said that social pressures against them are hard to bear. In Algeria, Hassiba Boulmerka was widely celebrated in her country after winning an Olympic gold medal in the 1,500-meter race in 1992. But she and her teammates have said that as they trained on the streets at home, people have also shouted obscenities at them. Boulmerka has also been denounced in several mosques for "scandalous" behavior "not worthy of a Muslim woman." (Simons 1995)

The Construction of the United States as a Liberating Force

Based on the thematic of the "white man's burden," the United States is constructed in NYT articles as a liberating force. The following article published in 1990 by LeMoyne James provides an example of the representation of the

United States as a liberating power that does not get even a "thank you" from those it saves:

> As the military deployment here lengthens and President Bush arrives to celebrate Thanksgiving, the cultural gap dividing American troops from their Saudi hosts appears to be widening, leaving each staring at the other across a chasm neither can easily bridge.
>
> The other day, I realized that none of us has gone into the desert and said thank you to the American soldiers for coming here to save us, a Saudi Government official said.
>
> "We haven't visited them. We haven't invited them into our homes. They must think we are terrible people."
>
> Asked why so few Saudis had made the effort to get in touch with American soldiers, the Government official said: "I don't really know. We're an insular people still, not very welcoming to foreigners. The whole experience is making me think a lot about being Saudi and about how we relate to others." ...
>
> "America's a democracy," said Lance Cpl. Tony Swofford of the Marine Corps. "But look at them here. There's no democracy. Women can't drive, they even have to wear veils. I don't think the Saudis really want us here."
>
> "We'll take all the casualties and then we'll go," Lance Cpl. Nelson Fountain said. "The reason we're here is because letting Saddam Hussein stay is worse. Otherwise, we wouldn't be in Saudi Arabia."
>
> Because the American military command is concerned not to offend Saudi sensibilities, American troops are charged with a long list of things they may not do here, including talking to women and wearing a crucifix or a Star of David in public ...
>
> "Why is it that the United States always has to be the one that goes and fights the bad guy?" Cpl. Kevin Krotzer asked. "The Arabs aren't coming here. Why do we have to be the ones who do it all here?" ...
>
> American troops have described the Saudis as arrogant, ignorant, prejudiced and basically hostile people who repress women, prohibit other religions and deny worldly pleasures while driving around in luxury cars blaring rock-and-roll ...
>
> Several American soldiers and officers said they were both bemused and offended by a speech last week by the Saudi Interior Minister, Prince Naif bin Abdul-Aziz, a leading member of the royal family, who declared a ban

on protests by Saudi women to expand their extremely limited rights in this male-dominated society. (LeMoyne 1990)

The above article represents the American troop as a liberating power, sacrificing their lives for Saudis who do not appreciate the American sacrifices. The frame of the discourse is a cultural one. It emphasizes cultural divides and conceals economic–political interests of the United States in the Gulf and the imperial aspects of their military bases in the region.

The sample of NYT articles from the decade of the 1990s illustrates the shift from the concern with the veil as an oppressive sign to the concern with the "ethical" role of the West in saving the oppressed veiled women. After the homogenization and demonization of the Islamic movements throughout the early 1990s, and the establishment of women as the oppressed helpless victims of these movements in NYT articles, the "ethical burden" of the United States and other Western regimes appears. The culturalist discourse presented in NYT articles and the ethical dilemmas mystify the political–economic interests of the United States and its imperialist presence and domination.

The Decade of the 2000s

The NYT articles in the decade of the 2000s witnessed continued interest with old concerns such as the Iranian regime and the employment of the veil to elicit negative sensibilities toward it. The main concern with the Iranian regime stems from its challenge to the American domination in the region and its position toward Israel; however, the concern is presented in the articles as a concern with women's freedom. The 9/11 events at the beginning of the decade, though, had energized the demonization of other regimes in Afghanistan and Iraq and strengthened the concerns of previous administrations with what is called "terrorism." "Veiled Muslim women" were more intensely employed in American print media and by American official politicians throughout these events. The success of this employment depended on the accumulated effect of the representations of the veil and "veiled Muslim women" during the previous decades. Fear of Islamic movements and Islamic signs was constantly produced through the media. The Muslim veil had been established as a main symbol of "the violence of Islam" imposed on women. At the beginning of the decade of the 2000s, veiled/unveiled women corresponded in NYT articles to the schema of oppression/freedom. However, the representations of the "subjugated veiled women" had transformed post-9/11 as a result of the perceptions of veiled women as part of the Islamic "terrorism" not necessarily their victims. Consequently, a new equation had been established regarding the veil. Veiled women had been divided into two groups: modern and moderate vs. antimodern and militant. This division parallels what Mahmood Mamdani (2005) refers to as Good Muslims and Bad Muslims. This strategy, it seems, was needed in NYT because the old schema of representing veiled Muslim women as the victims of patriarchal Muslim oppression became less convincing for the audience and mainly not effective in political terms.

The other main thematic that appeared intensely during this decade is "the enemy at home," reflected in the growing interest in Muslims and Muslim women who are living within Western countries. Muslim communities in the United States are represented as much more tolerated than in Europe despite revelations of the growing surveillance of Muslims in the United States. Three main themes were identified during the decade of the 2000s.

The Veil/Unveil as Corresponding to Liberation/Oppression

NYT articles post-9/11 focused on the "war on terror" including the one waged in Afghanistan. In some articles, the Muslim veil was used as a cause and measure for the justice and success of the war. The following article from 24 November 2001 by Ami Waldman provides an example:

> However, the merchants in back of the Jameh Mosque are not having such a good week. About 50 of them sell burkas, the face-covering, full-length shroud that the Taliban required women to wear. Many of the burka merchants opened their shops when the Taliban came to power. But now that the Taliban are gone, so, too, is a captive market. In the past two weeks, prices have dropped in half, and the average number of burkas sold each day has slipped to 5, from 20 …
>
> And they feel liberated from buying burkas, a trend that is prompting a lot of long faces on what can be called Burka Row. Practically every other store there features the garments, made from nylon that is crimped and stitched and attached to a head cap and mesh face covering. (Waldman 2001)

The above article employs the veil/unveil as a barometer for the liberation of Afghani women. Liberation of Afghani women is equated in the article to being liberated from buying burkas. Such superficial presentation of liberation, which ignores the material realities of women, is apparent in NYT articles. The other face of the veil/unveil as equal to liberation/oppression is apparent in the following article from 25 January 2002 by Elaine Sciolino, which refers to American women in Saudi Arabia:

> The United States military has quietly lifted an order from the gulf war era requiring servicewomen to wear long head scarves and black robes known as abbayas when off base. It also absolved servicemen of having to hide their uniforms under Western styled shirts while driving off-base, a practice adopted more recently for security reasons.
>
> Wear of the abbaya in the Kingdom of Saudi Arabia is not mandatory but is strongly encouraged, says the classified directive, released Saturday, adding that for men there is no longer "any requirement to wear civilian clothing to cover the uniform."
>
> The change in policy follows a lengthy review set off by complaints from Lt. Col. Martha McSally, the highest-ranking female fighter pilot in the Air Force.
>
> Colonel McSally, who is no longer in Saudi Arabia, filed a lawsuit last year that branded the dress code unconstitutional and charged that it improperly forced American women to conform to others' religious and social customs. She is also fighting regulations requiring military women to be accompanied by men and to ride in the back seats of cars when off base in Saudi Arabia.
>
> Colonel McNally's suit was regarded in some quarters in the Pentagon as frivolous, but as she pressed her case before the media after Sept. 11, the Pentagon reversed course. (Sciolino 2002)

The above article is concerned with what Col. McSally refers to in the article as forcing "American women to conform to others' religious and social customs." The article centers the dress code of US military servicewomen and completely ignores the implications of having these American women and men on this country's soil as part of an imperial policy of domination in the Gulf region through the constant establishment of American military bases to serve and protect economic interests.

A New Division: Good/Bad Muslim Women

The NYT articles are not only concerned with the imposition of the veil on women in Iran and Afghanistan, and consequently portraying these regimes as oppressive, they are also concerned with women who fight back. These women are regarded as part of the Good Muslims. The following article from 2 April 2003 by Elaine Sciolino offers an example. It is titled "Daughter of the Revolution Fights the Veil." This title alludes to the idea that some women within Islamic regimes are opposing the regime through opposing the veil. NYT articles portray those women as part of the modern, liberal group of Muslim women who are the potential allies for Westerners. This shows how the veil/unveil is employed now as the symbol for opposing/allying with the Western political regimes. An association is established between being a Muslim woman who do not oppose the veil and being anti-Western and sympathizing with terrorism:

> As a member of the ayatollah's family, Ms. (Zahra Eshraghi) is expected to embrace the trappings of the revolution and the Islamic Republic that followed. Nothing symbolizes the revolution more than the ankle-length black chador that covers all but a woman's face.
>
> Pale-eyed, with perfectly manicured eyebrows and slightly frosted hair, Ms. Eshraghi said she had always covered her hair in public—at least with a scarf—because of the dictates of Islam. She fought colleagues at the Interior Ministry, where she promotes women's issues, when they tried to force her to wear more modest dress and dark colors underneath her chador. Behind closed doors, she wears fitted pantsuits that do not conceal her full figure. (Sciolino 2003)

The above article focuses on veiled Muslim women who resist and fight back "Islamic repression" and the "imposition" of the veil. During the 2000s there were numerous articles concerned with this thematic that indirectly divides Muslim women into two groups: conservatives who are the allies of repressive regimes and movements, and moderns who are the allies of the West. This division is applied to Muslim women who live in Muslim countries and those who live in the United States as the following article from 5 April 2007 by Ruth La Ferla illustrates:

> FOR Aysha Hussain, getting dressed each day is a fraught negotiation. Ms. Hussain, a 24-year-old magazine writer in New York, is devoted to her

pipe-stem Levi's and determined to incorporate their brash modernity into her wardrobe while adhering to the tenets of her Muslim faith. "It's still a struggle," Ms. Hussain, a Pakistani-American, confided. "But I don't think it's impossible."

Ms. Hussain has worked out an artful compromise, concealing her curves under a mustard-tone cropped jacket and a tank top that is long enough to cover her hips.

Some of her Muslim sisters follow a more conservative path. Leena al-Arian, a graduate student at the University of Chicago, joined a women's worship group last Saturday night. Her companions, who sat cross-legged on prayer mats in a cramped apartment in the Hyde Park neighborhood, were variously garbed in beaded tunics, harem-style trousers, gauzy veils and colorful pashminas. Ms. Arian herself wore a loose-fitting turquoise tunic over fluid jeans. She covered her hair, neck and shoulders with a brightly patterned hijab, the head scarf that is emblematic of the Islamic call to modesty. (La Ferla 2007)

To deal with the question of how veiled Muslim women manage to live in the United States—a modern, liberal state that contradicts with the Muslim women's lifestyle—the article above divides the Muslim women into two groups. One group is modern and open and the other is traditional and conservative. More associations can be added to representatives of each group. To the first group we can add tolerance and pacification and to the second group we can add fundamentalist and militant. The following article from 26 August 2000 by Barry Bearak concerns a woman from the second group:

Asiyah Andrabi, conservative Muslim and radical feminist, believes that women should be heard and not seen, so she makes her demands for equal rights from behind the black cloth curtain of an all-enveloping burqa.

"The veil is for security as Allah wishes it," she said, pausing to refresh her hidden mouth with sips of Coca-Cola. "If gold is left uncovered along a roadside, anyone will grab it, because it is a precious thing. It is the same with an uncovered woman."

There are other reasons for Ms. Andrabi to conceal her face. She is a militant who opposes Indian rule here. For most of the last decade she has been living either in jail or on the lam, alternating her efforts between the liberation of women and that of Kashmir.

Indian intelligence agents say they suspect that she is a conduit for money to guerrilla groups.

But her notoriety is owed to flamboyant rather than clandestine activities. As head of Dukhtaran-e-Millat, or Daughters of the Community, she has led hundreds of women in street protests. At times they have carried brushes and paint cans beneath their burqas, blackening any advertisements that show scantily clad models.

With the same sense of righteousness, Ms. Andrabi has also tossed colored dye into the faces of Muslim women who shun the veil. Western dress is popular here in Srinagar, the summer capital of the state of Jammu and Kashmir. (Bearak 2000)

The above article provides an example of the representations of a "bad" militant veiled Muslim. She is not represented as a victim but as part of the oppressing group (which oppresses liberals and moderate Muslims). That is, a new representation arises, the veiled Muslim women sympathizers with Islam—"terrorism." Consequently, a new division is made between Muslim women who are victims of fundamentalist Islam and Muslim women who are agents of fundamentalist-terrorist Islam. In the same sentiment, the following article from 3 February 2006 by Ian Fisher and Steven Erlanger concerns the women of Hamas. While articles about Hamas during the 1990s focused on Hamas as repressive toward women, articles in the 2000s focus on women as part of the "oppressive system" of Hamas, not just its victims:

Hamas has been known and feared for its men, armed or strapped with suicide bombs. But in its parliamentary election triumph here last week, one secret weapon was its women.

To a degree specialists said was new in the conservative Muslim society of the Gaza Strip, Hamas used its women to win, sending them door to door with voter lists and to polling places for last-minute campaigning.

Now in surprise control of Palestinians politics, Hamas can boast that women hold 6 of the party's 74 seats in parliament—giving the women of the radical group, guided in all ways by their understanding of Islam, a new and unaccustomed public role.

"We are going to lead factories, we are going to lead farmers," said Jamila al-Shanty, 48, a professor at the Islamic University here who won a seat in parliament. "We are going to spread out through society. We are going to show the people of the world that the practice of Islam in regard to women is not well known."

If Ms. Shanty's prediction is true, the role of women will certainly not be along the secular Western lines followed largely, and with real strides for women, under decades of leadership by Yasir Arafat's now defeated Fatah faction. The model will be Islam: women in Hamas wear head scarves and follow strict rules for social segregation from men.

And one of their role models—one of the few women in Hamas well known before the election—has a pedigree particularly troubling to many in Israel and the outside world.

She is Mariam Farhat, the mother of three Hamas supporters killed by Israelis. She bade one son goodbye in a homemade videotape before he stormed an Israeli settlement, killing five people, then being shot dead. She said later, in a much publicized quotation, that she wished she had 100 sons to sacrifice that way. Known as the "mother of martyrs," she was seen in a campaign video toting a gun.

Now she is one of the six women who are Hamas legislators, elected on the party list. The election rules had quotas for women for all parties. She was swamped this week at a Hamas victory rally at the women's campus at the Islamic University by young, outspoken, educated women who see no contradiction between religious militancy and modernity. (Fisher and Erlanger 2006)

The above article deals with the uneasy question for the Western liberal logic: "how could women support a religious movement that oppresses them." The previous representation of women as the victims of Islamic religious movements cannot provide an answer for this question. Further, the focus on sociocultural aspects and ignoring political ones is not sufficient. The article itself contains inner contradictions. It starts with asserting that Hamas uses women but then it refers to Hamas women who send their sons for jihad against Israel. The solution for this contradiction, it seems, would be the abovementioned division of Muslims and Muslim women into two groups: the good (secular) and bad (Islamic). Good is good for the geopolitical interests of the West.

The Enemy Within

Following 9/11, the issue of Arab and Muslim communities in Western countries was considered widely in NYT articles. There is a focus on the possibilities of integrating Muslims in Western communities and the "risk" they pose to Western secularism. The issue of women's veil is central to these debates. The issue of the enemy within brings the colonized into the colonizer's backyard. This issue had been under focus as part of the effort to justify targeting Muslim immigrants post-9/11 and it illustrates how the US empire targets immigrants from the countries it invades.

The following quotes from NYT article published on 27 June 2002 by Dana Canedy, on the case of Sultaana Freeman, a veiled Muslim woman living in the United States, provide an example of the concern with the enemy within and specifically the connection of the veil with terrorism:

> The Florida Department of Highway Safety and Motor Vehicles revoked the license of the woman, Sultaana Freeman, in January after she refused to replace her photograph with one showing her face. Ms. Freeman, 34, a homemaker from Winter Park near Orlando says doing so would violate her religious beliefs, and she is suing the state in Orange County Circuit Court seeking reinstatement of her license. A hearing is set for Thursday to determine whether the state's demand is unconstitutional.
>
> In January 2001, Ms. Freeman moved to Winter Park from Illinois, where she had a driver's license with a veil for many years. She was issued a Florida driver's license that February. In December 2001, she received a letter from the Florida Department of Motor Vehicles instructing her to replace her photograph with one showing her entire face. After she refused, the state revoked her license in January. (Canedy 2002)

On 7 June 2003, NYT published another article on the case:

> A Florida judge ruled today that a Muslim woman could not wear a veil in her driver's license photo, agreeing with state authorities that the practice might help terrorists conceal their identities.
>
> The decision, by Judge Janet C. Thorpe of Orange County Circuit Court, held that the right to free exercise of religion would not be unconstitutionally infringed if the woman, Sultaana Freeman, 35, was required to show her face on her license.
>
> Judge Thorpe said that the state "has a compelling interest in protecting the public from criminal activities and security threats" and that "having access to photo image identification is essential to promote that interest."
>
> Ms. Freeman had argued that to show her face publicly would violate her Islamic beliefs. ("AP Florida Court Bars Veil in License Photo" 2003, A10)

In the article above an association between the veil and terrorism, criminal activities and security threats is established. NYT continued to follow the same case through the following years as the quotes from the following article from 8 September 2005 show:

> A Muslim woman who, for religious reasons, wanted to wear a veil in her driver's license photo must follow a state law that requires a picture of her full face, a state appeals court ruled. The Fifth District Court of Appeal upheld a 2003 ruling by an Orlando judge that the right to free exercise of religion would not be burdened by the photo requirement in the case of the woman, Sultaana Freeman. The Department of Highway Safety and Motor Vehicles issued Ms. Freeman, 38, of Winter Park, a license in 2001 showing her veiled with only her eyes visible, but later suspended it. Ms. Freeman sued, claiming her First Amendment rights had been violated. Her lawyer said he was considering an appeal. (the "AP National Briefing South Florida: No Veils on Driver ID, Court Rules" 2005, A20)

The interest in the case is exemplary to the fixed gaze on the veil and its constitution as the main sign of Islam's internal threat to Western countries. The sample from NYT articles from the decade of the 2000s shows the shift post-9/11 events toward focusing on the Muslims within the United States and the Islamic internal threat. The Islamic veil became the symbol of the "violence of Islam," and its threat within and outside the United States. Within this representational strategy the victimized veiled women had also become a threat.

Conclusion

In this chapter I followed the working of the representations of "veiled Muslim women" in the NYT articles during three decades (1980–2011). These representations are transformed and reconstructed along US political–economic interests and its imperial wars in the regions in which the represented women dwell. The transformations of the discourses that represent "veiled Muslim women" in the NYT can be read as traces to US imperialist interests in different historical moments. Each historical moment necessitated new and often contradictory representational strategies that work mainly through creating a cultural discourse that conceals political–economic material interests.

During the 1980s six representational strategies had been identified: (1) the veil as multiplicity governed by negativity; (2) the construction of the veil as discrimination against women; (3) the veil as a marker of colonialist binary (us/them); (4) the veil as anti-West sentiment; (5) the representation of veiled Muslim women as victims; and (6) representation of the veil as the ultimate sign of Muslim women's oppression. The cumulative effect of these representations in NYT articles led to the equation of the veil with oppression in a way that turned the veil into a freestanding sign of Islam's oppressive attitudes and practices toward women. This was employed as a political tool in the hands of the American interventionist imperial foreign policy in the countries relevant for US economic–political interests. Although the veil in itself had been constituted as a symbol of Muslim women's oppression and victimhood along an Orientalist approach, its employment depended on US political relations with each relevant regime. In this sense, the oppressiveness of the veil as constructed in NYT articles had been linked with anti-West in the case of Iran whose regime is not aligned with US imperial domination policies in the Gulf region.

During the decade of the 1990s new representational strategies appeared, they included: (1) Islamist equals fundamentalist; (2) the white man's burden; and (3) the construction of the United States as a liberating force. These representational strategies drew power from the previous representations of the veil as oppressive sign and added to them an ethical dimension that necessitates intervention under the auspice of "protecting" and "saving" the Muslim women from their oppressors. This had served the preexisting US material interventionist military plans and practices, mainly in Afghanistan through justifying them on moral basis.

During the 2000s, new representational strategies appeared and included: (1) the veil/unveil as corresponding to liberation/oppression; (2) a new division of good/bad Muslim women; and (3) the enemy within. These representational strategies concern US military interventionist policies and the homeland security anti-Islamist policies, in which the "veiled Muslim women" had transformed from a symbol of victimization into a symbol of terror.

Notes

1 I am employing the concept "material ideology" following Louis Althusser's thesis on the structure and functioning of ideology. Althusser (1971) argues that ideology has a material existence. That is, ideology does not have an ideal or spiritual existence but a material existence; an ideology always exists in an apparatus and its practice or practices.
2 For an alternative periodization for historical events, see the chapter by Tanzeen Doha in this book who argues for an "Islamist periodization" that troubles US vs. Soviet dichotomy in the analysis of Islamism. While Doha troubles the analysis that Islamists are either Soviet-backed proxies or US-backed proxies, in my chapter I focus on the geopolitical dimension at work in the region.
3 Likewise, Chomsky and Herman (2002) had showed that NYT covering of events in Cambodia and East Timor during the years 1975–79 differed in accordance with the interests of the American power elites, asserting the media, and NYT in this example, as an instrument of propaganda in the service of the power elite.
4 For a review of the system of racialization and its transformations in the United States see Nadine Naber (2008).
5 Saba Mahmood (2005) elaborates on the normative liberal–secular assumptions about human nature, the belief that all human beings have an innate desire for freedom and autonomy, and that human agency consists of acts that challenge social norms.

References

Abu Lughod, Lila. 2013. *Do Muslim Women Need Saving?* Cambridge, MA: Harvard University Press.
Ahmed, Leila. 2011. *A Quiet Revolution: The Veil's Resurgence, from the Middle East to America*. New Haven, CT: Yale University Press.
Althusser, Louis. 1971. "Ideology and Ideological State Apparatuses (Notes towards an Investigation)." In *Lenin and Philosophy and Other Essays*. Translated by Ben Brewster. New York: Monthly Reviews Press.
"AP Florida Court Bars Veil in License Photo." 2003. *New York Times*, 7 June: A10.
"AP National Briefing South: Florida: No Veils on Driver ID, Court Rules." 2005. *New York Times*, 8 September: A20.
"Asylum by Gender (Editorial)." 1993. *New York Times*, 10 March: A18.

Aziz, Sahar. 2012. "The Muslim 'Veil' Post-9/11: Rethinking Women's Rights and Leadership." *Policy Brief*. The Institute for Social Policy and Understanding and the British Council.

Bearak, Barry. 2000. "Behind the Veil, a Muslim Feminist." *New York Times*, 26 August: A4.

Canedy, Dana. 2002. "Lifting Veil for Photo ID Goes too Far, Driver Says." *New York Times*, 27 June: A16.

Chartrand, Sabra. 1991. "Gaza Journal; The Veiled Look: It's Enforced with a Vengeance." *New York Times*, 22 August: A4.

Chomsky, Noam, and Edward S. Herman. 2002. *Manufacturing Consent: The Political Economy of the Mass Media*. New York: Pantheon Books.

Clines, Francis. 1987. "A Reporter's Notebook: But under the Veils of Arabia, 'It's Another Story.'" *New York Times*, 3 September: A8.

Fanon, Frantz. 1965. *A Dying Colonialism*. New York: Grove Press.

Farnsworth, Clyde. 1993. "Saudi Woman Who Fled Predicts Crackdown." *New York Times*, 7 February: A19.

Fisher, Ian, and Steven Erlanger. 2006. "Women, Secret Hamas Strength, Win Votes at Polls and New Role." *New York Times*, 3 February: A1.

Francke, Linda Bird. 1988. "A Veiled Threat." *New York Times*, 27 March: A30.

"Guards Arrest 500 Iranians for Breaking Islamic Codes UPI." 1985. *New York Times*, 1 May: A10.

Huntington, Samuel. 1993. "The Clash of Civilizations?" *Foreign Affairs*. https://www.foreignaffairs.com.

Huntington, Samuel. 1996. *The Clash of Civilizations and the Remaking of World Order*. New York: Simon & Schuster.

Ibrahim, Youssef M. 1990. "The World; Islamic Fundamentalism Is Winning Votes." *New York Times*, 1 July: A5.

Kamm, Henry. 1988. "Afghan Peace Could Herald War of Sexes." *New York Times*, 12 December: A7.

La Ferla, Ruth. 2007. "We, Myself, and I." *New York Times*, 5 April: G1.

LeMoyne, James. 1990. "U.S. Troops and Saudis: A Silent Clash of Cultures." *New York Times*, 21 November: A10.

Lewis, Bernard. 1990. "The Roots of Muslim Rage." *Atlantic Magazine*, 30 January. https://www.theatlantic.com.

Lorch, Donatella. 1988. "An Afghan Exile, Her School and Hopes for Future." *New York Times*, 12 June: A14.

Mahmood, Saba. 2005. *Politics of Piety: The Islamic Revival and the Feminist Subject*. Princeton, NJ: Princeton University Press.

Mamdani, Mahmood. 2005. *Good Muslim, Bad Muslim: America, the Cold War and the Roots of Terror*. New York: Three Rivers Press.

Martin, Douglas. 1982. "Saudi Craze for Cars Is both a Blessing and a Blight." *New York Times*, 22 January: A2.

Mojtabai, A. G. 1980. "HERS." *New York Times*, 19 June: C2.

Naber, Nadine. 2008. "'Look, Mohammed the Terrorist Is Coming!' Cultural Racism, Nation-Based Racism, and Intersectionality of Oppressions after 9/11." In *Race and Arab Americans before and after 9/11: From Invisible Citizens to Visible Subjects*, edited by A. Jamal and N. Naber, 276–304. Syracuse, NY: Syracuse University Press.

"News Summary." 1980. *New York Times*, 9 July: B1.

Omi, Michael, and Howard Winant. 1994. *Racial Formation in the United States from the 1960s to the 1990s*. New York: Routledge.

Pollitt, Katha. 1985. "HERS." *New York Times*, 12 December: C2.

Said, Edward. 1981. *Covering Islam: How the Media and the Experts Determine How We See the Rest of the World*. New York: Pantheon Books.

Sanchez J., George. 1999. "Race, Nation and Culture in Recent Immigration Studies." *Journal of American Ethnic History* 18 (4): 66–84.

Sciolino, Elaine. 1985. "Saudi Women Start to Peek from Behind the Veil." *New York Times*, 13 April: 1.2.

Sciolino, Elaine. 2002. "Servicewomen Win, Doffing Veils in Saudi Arabia." *New York Times*, 25 January: A6.

Sciolino, Elaine. 2003. "Daughter of the Revolution Fights the Veil." *New York Times*, 2 April: A6.

Scott, Joan Wallach. 2010. *The Politics of the Veil*. Princeton, NJ: Princeton University Press.

Simons, Marlise. 1995. "Muslim Women's Exclusion Is Target of New Campaign." *New York Times*, 13 January: B15.

"The Moslem Veil in the City: A Matter of Tradition." 1984. *New York Times*, 24 September: B7.

Waldman, Amy. 2001. "In Herat, TV Man Is King, Veil Seller Is Lonely." *New York Times*, 24 November: B3.

4

Anti-Islamist (Re)Presentations in the *New York Times* and Academic Feminism, 1979–2011

Tanzeen Rashed Doha

Introduction

I trace historical developments in Islamist politics and mainstream feminism in relation to media representations of Muslim women.[1] By examining articles in the *New York Times* (NYT) published between 1979 and 2011, I suggest that secular representations of Islam, both in the media and feminist discourse, propagate what I call "anti-Islamism" (developed below). By constructing a periodization based on signature events within contemporary Islamist history, I identify tactical shifts within the larger, global strategy of anti-Islamism. As a conceptual frame, anti-Islamism moves beyond articulations that conceptualize Islamophobia as a behavioral–psychological disposition created through misinformation, or as a structural form of racial bigotry. Instead, anti-Islamism describes a consistent effort to counter and negate Islam's world-making aspirations. The Western discourse around gender, historically, has been a central site in this negation. Therefore, this chapter examines how feminism as a political and epistemic project (with three major exceptions) necessarily requires anti-Islamism—an incompatibility reinforced by media representations.

By examining articles published in the NYT between the years 1979 and 2011 and demonstrating their relation to feminist intellectual and political traditions, this chapter studies how patterns of representation within specific historical periodizations (re)articulate the structure of what I term anti-Islamism. As a conceptual term, anti-Islamism breaks with prominent theorizations that reframe Islamophobia as anti-Muslim racism.[2] Anti-Islamism as a framework allows us to understand not only how Islamophobia operates at the level of communal racial attitudes but also in relation to the historical, epistemic, and psychosocial effects of secularization and the War on Terror. Having said that, anti-Islamism both precedes and exceeds the War on Terror and earlier forms of war in the Islamicate world. It is both general and generative. Sociological case studies and ethnographic accounts provide us with empirical data but frequently fail to narrate a theory of how and why the anxiety and fear toward Islam has a generalizing consequence in modern secularity.

Conceptualizing anti-Islamism as secularization is generative, for secularization produces particular kinds of histories, social relations, psychologies, reasonings, and cultural formations. It promotes and mobilizes certain normative European values and political concepts. Meanwhile, conceptualizing secularism as anti-Islamism performs a negative function: the discursive and material evacuation of the world-making project of Islamism. Modern secularity aims to reduce Islam into culture by negating the centrality of the shari'a. Because the shari'a is not law in the modern sense, insofar as it does not separate the legal from the political and ethical, secular regimes try to delink the shari'a of Islam from its sociocultural expressions. It is precisely this disjuncture that demarcates the modern Muslim identity within the Western paradigm. But shari'a is not only law that is enforced from the outside, it is the mechanism that organizes the soul, trains the body, purifies the heart, refines the intellect, and disciplines the mind to produce proper Islamic subjects. By decentering the shari'a, modern secularity desubjectivates Muslims, and de-essentializes Islam.[3]

Methodology

In the documentary *Manufacturing Consent*—titled after a book by the same name—Noam Chomsky explains the central role of the NYT in not only organizing the social and political perceptions of its readers but also organizing historical knowledge. Chomsky explains that

The *New York Times* is certainly the most important newspaper in the United States and, one could argue, the most important newspaper in the world. The *New York Times* plays an enormous role in shaping the perception of the current world on the part of the politically-active educated classes. Also, the *New York Times* has a special role, and I believe its editors probably feel that they bear a heavy burden, in the sense that the *New York Times* creates history. That is, history is what appears in the *NYT* archives. The place where people will go to find out what happened is the *NYT*; therefore, it's extremely important, if history is going to be shaped in an appropriate way, that certain things appear, certain things do not appear, certain questions be asked, other questions be ignored, and that issues be framed in a particular fashion.

I focus on the NYT for my analysis of media representation in relation to gender and Islam examining its articles not only for an empirical analysis but also for its representations of Islamic discourse and subjects as part of a much larger social, political, and intellectual history.[4] They are not simply structural results of an ideological apparatus. Rather, they signify the workings of power, within sets of networked institutions that have specific geopolitical interests—and all of this emerges from a specific Eurocentric discourse in which anti-Islamism is a driving force. My focus on feminist intellectual history is not accidental. In my analysis, I describe how the NYT specifically focuses on the bodies of Muslim women and their use of the veil, which signifies political visibility in relation to the body. This representational focus on women's rights and its mobilization also comes with a specific understanding of the body, which has a particular genealogy in Eurocentric political–epistemic history. Because of this focus, then, I trace the relation between these representations in the media and more sophisticated intellectual discourse within the feminist tradition.

With that said, there are three kinds of texts sometimes considered part of the feminist tradition (yet existing in tremendous immanent tension with it) that are exceptions to the rule of hegemonic feminism, and/or the hegemony of feminism. By hegemony of feminism, I mean that within the ideological domain of mainstream and radical Western discourse, questions related to the condition of women are almost always readily addressed by the feminist systems of knowledge. I call into question efforts that try to make feminism paradigmatic for questions, concerns, problems related to women, sex, and gender in the Islamic world. However, I identify three specific texts that (alongside others like them) are crucial for understanding the uses and abuses of categories like gender, sex, and women in the contemporary discourse on Islam. While I emphasize the significance of the following texts for the mobilization of Islamism, I do not intend to make any evaluative gesture toward each author's oeuvre. Deauthorizing these texts also helps in thinking of each text as an exemplar of a particular genre of critique against Western hegemony, in which secular feminism is a constituent part.

First, consider "White Wars: Western Feminisms and the 'War on Terror.'" In this 2007 paper, Sunera Thobani identifies feminist texts published in the aftermath of 9/11 that articulate Western feminism's working relationship with whiteness and the global War on Terror. Thobani demonstrates how texts with very different political orientations "share surprising convergences in their treatments of violence and in their representations of white imperial subjects and Muslim Others" (2007, 174). While her dismantling of Phyllis Chesler and Zillah Eisenstein's writings is straightforward because one relies on civilizational arguments against Islam and Muslims and the other argues against patriarchy in a way that makes "American masculinity" and Taliban "misogyny" similar, Thobani's pointed critique of Judith Butler's psychoanalytic and philosophical approach to violence reveals the wide range of feminisms (liberal, Marxist, poststructuralist) entangled in anti-Islamist assumptions. Butler's secularity is obvious: she relies on "the primal vulnerability of the infant condition," which forms the basis for her notion of a collective "we." It is here that Thobani exposes Butler's uncritical comparison of the victims of 9/11 and the victims of US imperial aggression in Iraq and Afghanistan. Texts like Thobani's are outside of paradigmatic feminism because instead of offering prescriptions on gender and sex borrowed from a Western humanist tradition, they illustrate the relation between feminism (as a category) and the machinations of war.

Second, in the groundbreaking 1987 essay "Mama's Baby, Papa's Maybe: An American Grammar Book," Hortense Spillers explains how the conditions of slavery and its consequent history have inaugurated a process of ungendering for black subjects. The essay demonstrates the incompatibility of normative gender and blackness, not necessarily because of lack of interest in gendered relations but simply because civil society conceptions of gender—available only to the non-black, that is, the human—are articulated and organized through the subjugating structure of slavery or black social death.[5] Spillers writes, "Under [the conditions of slavery], we lose at least gender difference in the outcome, and the female body and the male body become a territory of cultural and political maneuver, not at all gender-related, gender-specific" (1987, 67). This theoretical observation troubles feminist conventions, and focuses the question of slavery onto the problem of flesh. She reads the "theft of the body" as "high crimes against the flesh" of the African female and male. In this sense, her analysis points to a generality of wounding, injury, and dishonor of bodies placed under slavery that become in their most immediate articulation "a primary narrative" of the flesh. When she speaks about the enslaved African female subject, she discusses the specificity of ungendering as well: "This materialized scene of unprotected female flesh—of female flesh 'ungendered'—offers a praxis and a theory, a text for living and for dying and a method for reading both through their diverse mediations" (Spillers 1987, 68). A text like Spillers'—which is in conversation with feminism—is foundational for any consideration of Islam in the contemporary world, not only because of the large and influential presence of African and black populations within the fold of Islam but also because modernity itself is grounded in the originary rupture of slavery. In fact, one should point out that Islamism is frequently described as a response to colonial history, but almost never as a response to slave plantations by the millions kidnapped from the shores of Africa. Spillers' essay provides the necessary historical, cultural, and material insights that help (re)position contemporary Islam, as a force in opposition to American (neo)plantations, as a retaliatory and guiding principle for the mobilization of slave revolts.

Third, in the 1983 essay "Can the Subaltern Speak?" Gayatri Spivak (1994) deconstructs the Western philosophical and theoretical interest in representation and "subjective essentialism" (74). She examines the text "Intellectuals and Power: A Conversation between Michel Foucault and Gilles Deleuze," critiques their reductive theorization of Marx, and demonstrates how they operationalize the speaking subject. Spivak is careful in not reducing Foucault and Deleuze to represent them as simply assuming that the oppressed subject can speak, but rather that what they consider "unnamed" and "nonrepresented" subjects are organized by power and desire. And, therefore, the intellectuals are self-represented as those who can, in fact, "analyze (without analyzing)" (Spivak 1994, 74). Spivak (1994) also points out how the philosophers miss the international division of labor, and how Foucault in particular due to his monist view of power is unable to see the relation between "localized resistance" and "macrological struggles" (85). She thinks that the two philosophers reinscribe the Third World as a legible Other, reliant upon "naturally articulate" subjects of oppression (Spivak 1994, 84). In the latter part of the essay, Spivak (1994) explains how the subaltern woman disappears in some ways between the British and Indian nativist narratives, the first being an example of "white men saving brown women from brown men" and the second a nostalgic assertion of indigenous authenticity. She then suggests, "The two sentences go a long way to legitimize each other" (93). In another passage, she makes clear the space of nonplace of the subaltern: "Between patriarchy and imperialism, subject-constitution and object formation, the figure of the woman disappears, not into a pristine nothingness, but into a violent shuttling which the displaced figuration of the 'third-world woman' caught between tradition and modernization" (Spivak 1994, 102). A text like Spivak's is an internal criticism of Europeanist thought as well as indigenous claims of tradition and authenticity within a discourse of gender. Overall, it does not promote any explicit feminist project, nor does it promote or valorize traditions. It is relevant for Islam-related conversations, partly because of the large subaltern population in the Islamicate postcolony—subjects who are not recognized by civil society—and partly because of contemporary Islam's calling into attention the line of conflict between programs of modernization and reforms of Islam.

It is important to note here that there are other very significant works of counter-hegemonic feminism—particularly in postcolonial and transnational feminist theory—that identify racial and colonial operations in traditional feminism. Works by Chandra Mohanty, Ranjana Khanna, and Rey Chow come to mind immediately.[6] Whether certain texts by these scholars are to be included in the three exceptional genres I outline above, I leave to the reader. What I do want to state explicitly, however, is that my preoccupation in this chapter is not to deconstruct "Western" (colonial) feminism but rather to think through how the epistemic, material, and historical grounding of feminism is secular. Just as identifying the Western orientation in particular forms of feminist discourse helps us determine their embeddedness in colonial power, investigating the secularity of feminism enables us to observe its embeddedness in what I term anti-Islamism.

It is impossible to generalize about an entire tradition. I do not use the feminist tradition in my argument to generalize it. I make a distinction between generalization and categorization. While the former requires a comprehensive study of patterns and systematic trends, the latter examines how as a theoretical form—something with historical unity and self-consistency—feminism requires anti-Islamism and, therefore, cannot enter the domain of Islamic orthodoxy.[7] This incompatibility gives rise to a structural relation of incommensurability and irresolvable conflict between modern feminism and orthodox Islam. In other words, feminism as a category is incompatible with Islamism, and at times it is explicitly engaged in the disarticulation of Islam. Often, this disarticulation of Islam takes the form of keeping the Quran—with reinterpretations of verses related to "wife-beating" and polygyny—but rejecting the basis of the hadith corpus and the shari'a. The necessary assumption is that the secondary texts emerged in the context of premodern forms of Islamic patriarchy and therefore must be rejected for their lack of concern about the social, historical, and political position of women. Again, my argument in this chapter is not moral but rather structural. Whether Islamic societies need feminism as a project requires a prescriptive discourse from which this chapter shies away.

Because my criticism of feminism is not comprehensive, I select specific texts in that tradition to discuss the relation between feminism and anti-Islamism within specific periodizations. I methodologically draw from Salman Sayyid (1997), who explains his own deconstructive reading of feminist writings:

> The reason for selecting these writers is not because they are necessarily representative of attempts to theorize fundamentalism (though the argument could be made that their conceptualization of fundamentalism shares many features with other such attempts), nor because I think their account is paradigmatic, but rather because their work makes clear the conditions of its discursive possibility. (27)

While my selection of specific texts is also due to their ability to make clear "the conditions of (their) discursive possibility," I want to stretch Sayyid's point further by suggesting that categorially, feminist interests counter

Islamism sometimes explicitly, and often implicitly. This incompatibility between modern feminism and Islamism arises from epistemic, conceptual, and material differences. Modern feminism's basis is the sovereignty of the radical subject, the subject of the Enlightenment. It assumes that (European) women as persons must have access to sovereignty, and therefore that any form of submission to authorities that violate this sovereignty must be addressed as an inhibition for the ultimate freedom and autonomy of women. While liberal feminism's preoccupation has been the enhancement of property relations, the politics of representation, and state-based "rights," Marxist feminism engages with the question of labor (reproductive and unproductive labor in particular), the wage relation, and value. But even within Marxist feminism, the economic critique of patriarchy (often through theories of value) relies quite heavily on the idea that the exploitative structure of capitalism targets women in a specific manner, and as a result denigrates their sovereignty. If one were to take these accounts of the subjugation of women under regimes of illiberalism and capitalism to their logical conclusion, and expand their vision to include the Islamic world, then one would obviously be confronted with the question of how in these societies the sovereignty of women is inhibited by—or their inhibition is justified by—the textual (and by extension material) tradition of Islamic orthodoxy. In an interview published in the *Journal of Politics and Culture* Silvia Federici is suspicious of sovereignty because of its close affinity to history of the nation-state, but retains the political use of the term, and promptly connects it to autonomy. Federici remarks,

> "Sovereignty," in this sense, has none of the monarchical or nationalistic connotations historically associated with the term. It is a call for autonomy, for self-determination, and it is a rejection of the capitalist model of agriculture, that expropriates people from their lands and their traditional knowledge, subjects them to deadly international regulations, and turns food into a poison. As Mariarosa Dalla Costa puts it, "sovereignty" is an affirmation "of the right of populations to decide what to eat and how to produce it," with a view of food as a "common good" rather than a commodity. (quote by Silvia Federici in Haiven 2009, 32)

It is important then to take note that sovereignty's meaning in liberal feminism and Marxist feminism goes through a significant shift, but the concept's fundamental association with autonomy remains constant. Whether one desires autonomy via a politics of the nation-state and reform in its laws, or through a political economic change, it is still a desire for the autonomy of the subject or, more precisely, a desire for the subject as autonomy. And, it is this subject—and autonomy—that is fundamentally contradictory to Islam's desire for subjects who are obedient to divine will, divine powers, and divine laws.

I begin each section with a contemporary periodization of Islamism. Without this periodization it becomes impossible to ground these articles within a system of contemporary history. I begin my periodization with 1979, the year of the Islamic Revolution in Iran, and end with 2011, the year that marks the death of Osama bin Laden and a specific articulation in the history of Islamist leadership.[8] Through this organization, I situate the discourses of media representation and feminism within a particular political terrain. After periodizing a decade in relation to Islamist history, I discuss the sets of reasonings and arguments that are dominant in the feminist intellectual tradition for that decade and then examine how the NYT's representations carry similar assumptions about Islam and its traditions. Despite the tremendous similarities in media representations and intellectual discourse between 1979 and 2011, there are also significant breaks, ruptures, and contradictions. However, I look at how anti-Islamism as a logic is operationalized in both cases, through a particular exercise of secular power and reasoning that produces an ensemble of knowledge about Islam, which is then rearticulated and reproduced within a particular economy.

In this chapter, I do not expand on these theoretical claims or provide a methodological paradigm. Rather, I focus on a shorter history, a manageable time frame between the years 1979 and 2011, to demonstrate how anti-Islamism is operationalized and mobilized within a particular genealogy of modernist crisis. But this shorter history contains within it a larger historical speculation about the spectral presence of Islam.

1979: Grounding Contemporary Islamism

This chapter interrogates contemporary history by demarcating periods between 1979 and 2011 that were influential in the rise of contemporary

Islamism as a threat to global colonial power. The year 1979 was a rupture in modern political history because it was the year Islamic clerics, under the leadership of Khomeini, were able to homogenize the rebellion against the Shah, seize state power, and create a constitutional basis for anti-Zionism. French philosopher Michel Foucault, working as a journalist at the time, wrote about the possible effect of the Islamic Revolution on Middle Eastern political geography: "Islam—which is not simply a religion, but an entire way of life, an adherence to a history and a civilization—has a good chance to become a gigantic powder keg, at the level of hundreds of millions of men. Since yesterday, any Muslim state can be revolutionized from the inside, based on its time-honored traditions" (Afary and Anderson 2005, 241). While such a fluent takeover of state power did not take place in other countries after all, one can easily recognize that Islam, in the 30 years since the Revolution, has become a stronger political force in non-Europe, and a concrete alternative to other forms of governance. The discursive political tradition of Islam with its tremendous corpus of knowledge provides for Islamists sets of laws, ethical structures, and political goals that are simultaneously stable and flexible. The stability originates from the structural fact that Islam, just like any other tradition, has its own discursive limit, and therefore has its internal texts, subtexts, and contexts. But the flexibility of Islam complements, stretches, and shakes this stability, by allowing for the possibility of various political–ethical maneuvers that can deal with the modern condition, and in the process expand its own availability.[9] In other words, even thinking simplistically within a nation-state frame, the solution that Islam brings to Iran is different from what it brings to Palestine, which again is different from what it brings to Afghanistan. In terms of political strategy, the Islamic solution can be about consolidating state power, destroying state power, nurturing political terror networks, decolonial praxis, or even illiberal systems of governance. The structure of the shari'a and the central domain of jihad not only give Islam its substantive content but also produce the condition for the applicability of each of the aforementioned strategies based on the historical demand of each situation.[10]

While the year 1979 inaugurated Islam's transition from a peripheral discourse to an authoritative discourse with concentrated state power, it also marked the possibility of an internal critique at the theological and geographical center of Islam—the Ka'ba. At the time, the revolution in Iran overshadowed the takeover of Mecca led by Saudi preacher Juhayman al Uteybi, but scholars now agree that this fanatic rebellion was in many ways the foundational event that created the possibility of al-Qaʻida. Yaroslav Trofimov observes,

> The significance of the Mecca uprising was missed at the time even by the most sharp-eyed observers. Too many other threats preoccupied the West. The seizure of the Grand Mosque—the first large-scale operation by an international jihadi movement in modern times—was shrugged off as a local incident ... But with the benefit of hindsight, it is painfully clear: the countdown to September 11, to the terrorist bombing in London and Madrid, and to the grisly Islamist violence ravaging Afghanistan and Iraq all began on that warm November morning, in the shade of the Kaaba. (2008, 7)

While this journalistic observation may reify the events at the Kaʻba, it reveals a particular kind of transition in the genealogy of Islamism within the larger structure of secular modernity. While the seizure of state power in Iran allowed for an anti-imperialist position with established military and defense apparatuses, the Mecca siege demonstrated Islamism's ability to reconfigure itself for the purposes of a critique that questioned not only the deviance of the House of Saud but the very category of the state itself. The simultaneity of these events destabilizes the linear assumption that Islamist politics merely changed its form from statism to antistatism due to economic history.[11]

The successful seizure of state power by religious clerics in Iran created the conditions for the possibility of Islamization at the level of political geography in the Middle East. The Islamic Republic's constitutional nonrecognition of Israel and its persistent interest in developing nuclear energy continue to demonstrate this political transformation. While the uprising in Mecca signaled a possible political critique of the established order among religious clerics, it failed to subvert the political power of the Saudi regime, which remains central to American geostrategic interests. This difference in foreign relations relates to the respective media representations of Iran and Saudi Arabia. Hakeem Naim demonstrates that while Saudi and Iranian women both are represented as repressed and disciplined, the causal structures of repression are conceptualized differently. Naim suggests that while in the case of Iran, the NYT identifies the Islamic Republic to be directly responsible for the repression of women's self-expression, women's immobility and docility in Saudi Arabia are understood to be rooted in a particular interpretation of Islamic law by conservative religious scholars. In the case of Saudi Arabia, the media representation seems to suggest that the state is interested in modernization that necessarily elevates women's social status, while the Islamic 'ulema (scholars) act as an obstacle in that process. Naim's comparative analysis demonstrates how the two major events of 1979—the successful revolution in Iran culminating in the seizure of state power, and the temporary siege of Mecca, which was stifled with the help of Western intervention—launched these two trends in media representation. In the first, the coalescing of religious and state power appears dangerous (for Western interests), while in the latter, the disjuncture between religious rebellion and state objectives serves as a useful site of difference, through which it becomes possible to maintain liberal sensibilities toward women's rights while simultaneously supporting the Saudi state.

When it became clear in the early 1980s that Ayatollah Khomeini would likely head an Islamic government, bourgeois feminists—both Iranian and Western—initiated a counterrevolutionary discourse deeply embedded in Islamophobia.[12] In 1978 Atoussa H. published a letter in *Le Nouvel Observateur* that denounced not only the specific interpretation of Islam by Iranian clerics but the foundational text of the religion itself. In her writings, the Iranian feminist cited decontextualized passages from the Quran, evoking feminist concerns in a manner that violates the Quranic text's own hermeneutic structure and promoted fear and suspicion among the French Left. She insists, "Clearly, the man is the lord, the wife the slave; she can be used at his whim; she can say nothing. She must wear the veil, born from the Prophet's jealousy toward Aisha!" At a press conference in Paris in 1979 philosopher and feminist Simone de Beauvoir delivered a speech targeting the Islamic Revolution, and in her articulation promoted a universal feminist solidarity: "(It) is important to have a demonstration—on the part of a very large number of Western women, French women, Italian women, and others—of solidarity with the struggle of Iranian women" (Afary and Anderson 2005, 114). The fact that de Beauvoir understood the "struggle of the Iranian women" to be outside of the immanent plane of the Islamic Revolution itself reveals not only her political presuppositions about gender, Islam, and history but also her particular alliance with Iranian women of a particular class position. In her uncritical conceptualization of "solidarity," she failed to elaborate on the relation between historical differences and how the experience of patriarchy relates to divisions between "first" and "third" world. Her parochial view on the condition of "Iranian women" not only promoted a notion of authenticity in an unproblematic way but also hinted at flaws in her feminist methodology. Instead of conceptualizing the Iranian Revolution—which has a genealogical structure with tensions, ruptures, divisions, and discontinuities—from within its own sets of reasons, arguments, knowledges, practices, and limits, both Atoussa H. and de Beauvoir assumed polemical positions against Islamism as a category, violating an entire corpus of knowledge for the sake of a politics that finds its originary impulse in a European crisis.

1980s: Consolidating Islamism(s)

In the 1980s, the Cold War split the world into two parts, generating an ongoing narrative of struggle in which dissociated political antagonisms are still represented as either products of a larger bipolar tension or simply as peripheral moments. Beneath this bipolar tension between states—frequently misrepresented as a struggle between capitalism and communism—there remained the real narrative of the crisis of capital. Indeed, the United States and the Soviet Union shared the same world system as its basis, and the differences between their respective societies had more to do with the manner in which the institutions of the state were instrumentalized in relation to economic history than their divergences at the level of political ideology. This structural economic reality disappeared in the larger framing of the Cold War, which representationally subsumes all political formations within its paradigm. In this context, various Islamist formations during this decade became mere products of the larger bipolar tension. Even after the revolution in Iran and the Mecca siege of 1979, there continued a full-fledged Islamic revival in the Middle East and South/Central Asia throughout the 1980s. Between 1979 and 1989 the mujāhidīn in Afghanistan engaged in defiant militant struggle against Soviet invasion; in 1982, Hizbullah formed in response to Israeli aggression in Lebanon; and in the aftermath of Palestine's First Intifada, Hamas emerged as a major political force. While these formations undoubtedly took place at the plane of world historical events, the idea that the almost decade-long fight by a heterogenous group of Islamic insurgents under the banner of the mujāhidīn in Afghanistan simply arose under US tutelage is not only a misreading of that struggle but also a direct attempt at distorting history through orientalist techniques consistent with the structure of anti-Islamism. Such representational strategies are based on the assumptions that Islamists fight without any self-direction and are politically gullible subjects without a moral history, easily bought off with imperialist funding. Similar assumptions are made by right- and left-wing experts about Hamas and Hizbullah. Hamas is described as a creation by Israeli intelligence for the purposes of undermining secular resistance by Palestinians, and Hizbullah is understood only as an extension of Iranian state interests in the region.

Lena Meari suggests that the NYT articles of the 1980s provide us with representations that are "apparently multiple, unstable, and at times contradictory." In my own research, I encountered empirical evidence that suggests a similar structure of representation. The 1980s comprise the decade during which media portrayals consistently emphasized fluidity, multiplicity, and complexity. During this time, so-called "cultural practices" rather than religion appeared in the media as the source of women's rights violations in Islamic countries. The "instability," "fluidity," and "multiplicity" of this period match the intellectual history of the time, during which Lyotard wrote *The Postmodern Condition* (published in French in 1979, in English in 1984) and defined "postmodern" as a form of "incredulity toward metanarratives" (1984, xxiv). While the text focuses on the philosophy of science and how knowledge is legitimized within a particular epistemic history, it renewed scholars' interest in marginal narratives across all areas of the humanities and social sciences. Lyotard's ((1979) 1984) emphasis on "local determinism" and "heterogeneity" contributed to the advent of Subaltern Studies and other forms of research on postcolonialism that questioned state-sanctioned historical archives and sought to mobilize history from the position of peasants, lower caste women, and Dalits.

In feminist theory, Kimberlé Crenshaw (2012), bell hooks (1984), Angela Davis (1981), and others emphasized the intersections of race, class, gender, and sexuality to think critically about the complex subordination of non-middle-class women—particularly black women. Indeed, the political heterogeneity of Islamism itself impacts and mirrors the complex character of its critique during the 1980s, during which the theoretical and political targeting of Islam largely took place indirectly—except by more directly Islamophobic thinkers located in Islamic countries themselves, including Nawal El Saadawi. Despite her Marxist focus on patriarchal class structure, El Saadawi explicitly cited Islamic fundamentalism as a major contributor to women's oppression. In her anti-Islamist polemic, she conflated all fundamentalisms to suggest that they perform the same ideological function for global capitalism. She wrote, "All fundamentalists—whether Christian, Jewish, Muslim or otherwise—are partners in the attempt to breed division, strife, racism, and sexism; they help international imperialism to maintain its control and to overcome popular resistance to policies that lead to war and increased exploitation" (El Saadawi 1997, 93). Her argumentation follows a pattern that is common in anti-Muslim writings. It begins with universal declarations against fundamentalism as a category but ends with the specific targeting of Islam, its legal structure, and its practices in relation to sex separation. El Saadawi criticizes Islamist success in organizing large numbers of men and women by suggesting that it merely provides a sense of return to an authentic past without addressing real contradictions.

However, El Saadawi herself constructs a utopian past in which—both prior to Islam and in very early Islamic history—women possessed rights that were subsequently overridden by Islamists, conceptualized as deeply patriarchal in the cultural sense, and antiquated in the political sense (El Saadawi 1997). There are two analytical errors in this supposition. First, the antimodernism of Islamists is framed within a particular notion of teleology, in which the progress of man is determined by how closely he is able to mimic European history. Because of this, Islamist critiques of liberalism, women's rights, secularism, and European modernity more broadly are not only represented as reactionary in a cultural sense, but Islamists themselves are identified as political reactionaries who work against the directional imperatives of modernist time. In this analytical frame, Islam itself must be transcended in order to reach the telos of progress. Second, El Saadawi fails to understand the actual directional structure of modernity in relation to history. The implicit teleology in her thinking is external to economic history and, consequently, lacks a proper conceptualization of the dialectical determinations of capitalist modernity. In this sense, her Eurocentrism relies upon a non-dialectical idealism, in which Islamism becomes an abstraction disconnected from material life, existing only as a category to be denounced by feminists. Given this theoretical catastrophe, and failure to grasp the most elemental dimensions of Islamism in terms of its actual material grounding in history—modernity included—it is not surprising that the initial utopia in El Saadawi's account serves as a strategic ploy to place Islam in an earlier history, a history that in her analysis is in need of exhaustion. This unidirectional view of history structurally debilitates Islam by evacuating its political content.

As mentioned earlier, the targeting of Islam during the 1980s—unlike El Saadawi's account—was largely indirect. Throughout this decade, media remained a central source of empirical information that validated a feminist project in which "cultural interpretations" of religion—rather than religion per se—are portrayed as the problem. This rewriting of religion as a cultural practice remains significant and relevant in anthropological debates. In *The Interpretation of Cultures*, Clifford Geertz describes religion as a "cultural system" to be understood at two levels—first, as an interpretive system of meanings and second, as a system immanent to social and psychological processes (Geertz 1973). Talal Asad critiques this two-level view by explaining how it essentializes religion, frames it within an interpretive hermeneutics, and places it outside of the field of power and social history. Asad writes, "The basic problem, however, is not with the idea of mirror images as such but with the assumption that there are two separate levels ... This resort to Parsonian theory creates a logical space for defining the essence of religion" (Asad 1993, 32).

In a NYT (1986a) article titled "Dispute over a Moslem Divorce Ensnarls Gandhi," a woman appears to defy an entire community by using the courts to reclaim her rights against oppressive, local, and male-dominated cultural practices. Muslim men are represented as particularly and peculiarly violent and domineering, while Muslim women are portrayed as being in opposition to the cultural logic of Islamic patriarchy. In the article a leading feminist writer and lawyer claims, "It is a dangerous trend when a minority community says it should be exempted from a Supreme Court judgment because of religion. A woman's right to claim redress before a court of law should not be compromised." Here, Islamic law is represented as the law of a minority culture that, in the end, should be subsumed within a universal (secular) law. In another article, "Islam: Feminists vs. Fundamentalists" (1985b), a feminist lawyer in Bangladesh insists on a separation between Islam proper and cultural practices. She argues, "Men play upon the religious sentiment of the people, and the people believe it is Islam when it's a custom or a tradition."

In the aforementioned articles, both feminist critics happen to be lawyers. Their reasoning demonstrates how secular law acts as a means of negating what is understood to be the cultural parochialism of Islam and/or Islamic law. While Lena Meari aptly illustrates how the NYT differentiates between Muslim societies and American society through discussions focused on veiled Muslim women, this chapter focuses on how the distinction made between the categories "culture" and "religion" is also consistently at work. For example, in the article "The Moslem Veil in the City: A Matter of Tradition" (1984) that aims to represent New York City as a tolerant place for veiled Muslim women, the author focuses on cultural values as the marker of religion:

> Of about 20 traditionally dressed women who were interviewed, most said they believe that Islam asks women to conceal all but their hands and feet. They said their outfits elicit little overt discrimination, but cause heads to turn ... Despite objections to living in a city that clashes with their values, several women said New York gives them the freedom to live as they choose. (1984, B7)

Other articles in the 1980s focus quite heavily on the instrumental role of secular law, and the negative cultural dimension of Islamic law. In the article "Saudi Arabia's Gospel Columnists" (1985a), Islamic law again appears as a set of parochial cultural codes:

> Moslems consider Islam a complete system that governs every aspect of life, and Saudi Arabia takes its role as guardian of the faith particularly seriously. It is the only country in the world whose Constitution and legal system are entirely based on the "sharia" or Islamic code of law. Details of social behavior, from what to wear to brushing one's teeth, are the subjects of continual debate. The most burning issues of the day concern women. (1985a, E9)

This appraisal of the shari'a continues in the article "Pakistan's Grim Islamic Law Is Not Just a Threat" (1981), in which middle-class women's organizations frame Islamic law as a mechanism that works against the advancement of women's rights. The author echoes the previous articles' analytical separation of culture and religion: "Islam preaches equality of men and women and this Government is committed to providing equality of opportunity for all. Such things as the favoring of the male children, these are not Islamic but rather they are cultural traditions of the subcontinent" (1981, A2).

This representation of the subcontinent as a region where cultural influence makes Islamization processes deviate from Islam proper is evident in other articles published in the NYT during the 1980s. In an article titled "The 'Islamization' of Pakistan: Still Moving Slowly and Still Stirring Debate" (1986b), the appearance of the word "Islamization" in quotes represents it as an inauthentic expression of Islam. The article itself elaborates on how women are specific victims of Islamic programs. In "Pakistani Women Take Lead in Drive Against Islamization" (1988), journalist Steven Weisman connects this notion of Islamization as a form of anti-feminism to the question of governance and religious authority's incompatibility with liberal institutions and rights. He quotes lawyer Amna Piracha, "But the issue is more than just women's rights. The issue is whether Pakistan is to be governed by elected representatives of the people or a group of clergymen answerable to no one" (1988, A1). The relation between governance and accountability in this articulation is curious. Here, if Islamization takes place—in which the clergymen do not derive their legitimacy through a secular notion of the law, due to their allegiance to a concept of divine order that is unverifiable—there is an absence of juridico-political legitimacy. This notion of juridico-political legitimacy, however, arises from a provincial history that is universalized through a logic of Eurocentrism that is itself unaccountable.

1991–2001: US Hegemony and Islamic Reconfiguration

With the end of the Cold War in 1991, the United States emerged as a global power inaugurating a unipolar world. With the demise of the Soviet Union, the focus of foreign policy largely shifted to the singular force of militant Islamist discourse in its various forms. By singular force, I refer to the concentration of Islamic discourse—regardless of its heterogeneity—conceptualized as a totality in opposition to the hegemonic and material expansion of the United States. While Islamic discourse is not without historical unity, it is not operationalized in the real social world by focusing on an essential enemy. Rather, militant Islamic discourse demonstrates tremendous flexibility in its ability to (re)ground itself within the domain of power. For instance, the assumption that Islamists were simply funded by the United States to fight the Soviets in Afghanistan demonstrates itself to be simplistic and false by the 1990s, a decade characterized by a new unipolar globality. During this period, Islamists took US hegemony as its fundamental opponent with tremendous moral and political seriousness. Between 1996 and 2001, the emergence of the Taliban as a governing force signified a transition from Islamic insurgency against foreign occupiers (in the 1980s) toward a retheorization of classical governance. The year 1996 is also the year of Osama bin Laden's relocation from Sudan to Afghanistan, inaugurating a new, tensed yet functional moral–political relationship between al-Qaʻida and the Taliban. In the 1990s, the overlapping and simultaneous development of Islamic governance on the one hand, and militarization on the other, created strategic pressure on US hegemony and Zionist ideology. This becomes evident in Hamas's creation of the al-Qassam Brigades in 1991, which works independently of Hamas's political wing. This period also marked Hizbullah's entry into the mainstream political sphere in Lebanon. These developments indicate how Islamism works through the distribution of tasks without isolating particular elements from the larger scope of its discursive tradition. In 1997, Hizbullah's leadership in forming multiconfessional Lebanese Brigades demonstrates Islamism's extra-discursive potential and political imagination beyond self-identity. Not only do we see the collaboration between various elements within the Islamic discourse itself, but also an interest to influence other forces of politics that are identified as functionally effective against Israeli political geography. Because of the concretization of Islam as the main enemy in foreign lands after the end of the Cold War, it is not surprising to see representations in media and feminist discourse to be more direct in their Islamophobia.

Contrary to the 1980s, the representation of Islam between 1991 and 2001 in the NYT is interventionist in a more pronounced way. The interventions—both political and intellectual—are rooted in a liberal, humanist internationalism. A collection of essays written between 1990 and 1997 by renowned feminist philosopher Martha Nussbaum under the title *Sex and Social Justice* is representative of this framework. Although her text is a broad, philosophically illuminating elaboration on liberal categories (e.g., justice, rights, universals, equity, reason, liberty), she is blunt about its purpose when she states in the introduction,

> The approach defended here refuses to take that step (of cultural relativism), arguing that an account of the central human capacities and functions, and of the basic human needs and rights, can be given in a fully universal manner, at least at a high level of generality, and that this universal account is what should guide feminist thought and planning. (Nussbaum 1999, 8)

Nussbaum uses Aristotle to conceptualize notions of "human functioning" and "capability" in order to make a philosophically grounded political case for liberalism. She thinks through the works of Kant and Rawls for the purposes of examining and justifying concepts like dignity, liberty, and justice. She also reinterprets John Stuart Mill via Aristotle to think of his work outside of utilitarianism. It is curious that while this philosophical–political project aims to reconstitute liberalism, by returning to Aristotle—an ancient philosopher—it grounds liberal categories in a discourse that is almost as old as philosophy itself. By doing this Nussbaum's philosophical project of "Kantian/Aristotelian liberalism" slips into a transhistorical imperative. Her text's emphasis on liberalism, which claims to ground itself in universally valid concepts of justice and rights, actually grounds itself uncritically within a naturalized vision of capitalist property relations.[13]

Nussbaum specifically addresses Islam with the following quoted conversation at the beginning of chapter 3, titled "Religion and Women's Human Rights." Here, a Bangladeshi woman involved with a literacy and skills program sponsored by the Bangladesh Rural Advancement Committee asserts, "The mullahs say: 'When they will die we shall not bury them.' Villagers say, 'Wherever they want, they go. They do not cover their heads. They talk with men. They will be sinners.' I said: 'If Allah does not see us when we stay hungry then Allah has sinned'" (1999).

This is not simply an articulation related to concerns about women's rights but rather an anti-theist questioning that foundationally and negatively interrogates Islam. The concept of Allah becomes reliant upon liberal categories. In fact, in this line of reasoning, it is only through liberalism that Islam can legitimize itself. Nussbaum's rhetoric against the Islamic Republic of Iran signals her political complicity in contemporary anti-Islamism. She defends her liberal universalist position by suggesting that Islamic tradition and history has many examples of toleration, and therefore, her critique of specific practices under the name of Islam is not a totalizing critique of Islam. While it is true that Islam has within itself a tremendous history that covers many spatiotemporal contingencies, it is misleading to think that Islam does not carry within itself its own systematicity that gives it a historical unity. One can think about this systematicity in a genealogical way, therefore not essentializing the internal history of Islam, which allows for both the maintenance of a certain kind of orthodoxy as well as reconstitution of its social dynamic within particular histories. There is much scholarly work on orthodoxy in relation to distribution of power and the immanent development of an authoritative discourse within the Islamic tradition. To reduce this corpus of knowledge to a matter of basic pluralism for the purposes of teasing out values commensurable to liberalism is anti-Islamist in the most elemental sense: it denies Islam its internal consistency, objectifies it as a simple whole with many parts, and breaks it up according to the rules of liberalism. Nussbaum, who in the introduction to her book openly rejects relativism in order to revive liberal universalism, paradoxically justifies plurality within Islam to select parts of it for the purposes of disciplining and domesticating Islam within a structure of liberal feminism.

Articles published in the NYT in the 1990s are less nuanced, and more directly anti-Islamist. They are consistent with Nussbaum's intellectual interest in women's human rights and her universalism. Here is an excerpt from an article titled "Turks March in Campaign to Preserve Secularism" published in 1997: "Thousands of Turks, most of them women, marched through the streets of Ankara today in the first major public protest against the policies of the Islamic-led Government ... Let Turkey shout 'Down with Sharia!' they chanted. One banner proclaimed, 'Women's Rights are Human Rights,' while another simply, 'Women Exist'" (1997, 4).

This article frames local women in an Islamic country as authentic yet subversive subjects who question Islamic law. The specific focus on the shari'a works as a technique to reduce Islamic governance into a particular orientalist imagination of religious jurisprudence. The NYT, of course, has no interest in the details of the massive history of jurisprudence and law in the Islamic tradition, and therefore, this kind of selective reporting does little more than supply the anti-Islamic historical unconscious of the Western reader with more raw data to help reproduce racial archetypes.

Barbara Crossette's article "Women's Rights Gaining Attention within Islam" (1996) focuses on women in various Muslim-majority countries who are organizing to develop specific sets of demands that are consistent with liberal values. Crossette writes,

> Throughout the Islamic world, from North Africa and the Middle East to Southeast Asia, a diverse assortment of individuals and women's rights groups, different in cultures but sharing a powerful faith, are creating a momentum for change that few would have predicted a few years ago.
>
> While the status of women can vary widely from country to country in the Islamic world, advocates of Muslim women's rights share a core group of demands. They want the right to education, both secular and religious, which is often denied to girls. They seek changes in economic practices to allow them to own and inherit property, enjoy the freedom to start businesses and share in decisions on the distribution of family income. They also want reform in Muslim family laws that often leave them at the mercy of men who can divorce them without warning, take away their children, deny them the right to travel and bequeath them as chattel to the next male relative. (1996, 3)

This article demonstrates direct, structural similarity with Nussbaum's arguments, insofar as it locates women in Muslim countries who, in efforts to "modernize" Islam, advocate for human rights. In this sense, Islam becomes a site for liberal interventions.

Another article by Barbara Crossette focuses on Afghanistan and vilifies Islamic militants. Here it becomes clear that the reasoning structure of anti-Islamism forcibly reduces and compares historically different regimes of power by essentializing women's autonomy:

> The circle of teachers, a doctor and several homemakers—sitting cross-legged on the carpeted floor of a mud-walled house—wanted to tell Ms. Bellamy, a woman to woman and without inhibitions, what life was like in Afghanistan after decades of political upheaval, a Soviet invasion, a holy war,

a civil war and now an era marked by enforces of Islamic militancy riding around in jeeps and pickups beating up sinners. (1998, 1)

In this article, "Soviet invasion," "holy war," and "civil war," three different regimes of power, are portrayed as commensurate and culminate in an "Islamic militancy" that restricts women's autonomy. Woman as a category becomes central in this discourse and is used as a way to promote internal tension within Afghan society. The following quote illustrates this logic: "In the midst of the session, when a man tried to deliver a message to Ms. Bellamy through an intermediary, she said firmly: 'No men here! This is a meeting for women.' Faces around the room broke into smiles" (1998).

This kind of framing strategically manipulates the discourse to not only compare different regimes but also highlight Islam as the higher point of domination. It also falsely identifies a cultural logic instead of an economic one for patriarchy, and fails to address the centrality of modern power within imperialist history. All of these errors contribute to the discursive rationale of anti-Islamism.

Islamic polygyny is frequently at the center of representational techniques that frame Islamic jurisprudence as a force of patriarchy. This particularly controversial subject helps to locate patriarchy within the instrumentalization of religion itself. The NYT published a "Letter to the Editor" in 1991 that critiques polygamy:

> The institution of polygamy is legal in Islam, but most Muslim countries, under the pressure of women's rights groups and others interested in strengthening social welfare, have since the 1960s placed legal restraints on its practice. These include requiring the prospective polygamist to obtain the written consent of his first wife before marrying a second. This consent is rarely given. The legitimacy of polygamy in Islam originated in the need to provide legal and social protection to widowed women and their children, as well as to unmarried women with little chance of finding a spouse, when Muslims were few in number and severely persecuted by the pagan Arabs among whom they dwelt ... The Koran is explicit, however, in making polygamy conditional on a man's being able to provide equally for all his wives, a theoretical possibility that is highly unlikely in fact. (1991, 169)

Another article published in 1990 reduces the heterogeneity internal to Islamism in a manner that allows for liberal interventions against a supposed coherent enemy: the category of the fundamentalist (Ibrahim 1990). The article begins by recognizing how Islamists in specific places (Algeria, Egypt, Jordan) have come to power through peaceful means, but "elsewhere, Islamic fundamentalists are seeking or consolidating power through the use of arms and intimidation." The article continues, "In the Sudan, a military dictatorship is implementing religious edicts by force. In Lebanon, Egypt, Tunisia, and Morocco, armed fundamentalists are seeking to overturn secular regimes." Not only does the representational technique dominant in this article essentialize the formation of Islamism, but it also involves an inversion in which it appears that "Islamic fundamentalists" have full agency to "break with secularism." This kind of inversion fails to grasp the genealogy of historical power that comes with secularism. To suggest that Islamists have political agency and can simply attempt to "overturn secular regimes" is to miss the force with which Eurocentrism establishes the secular—not only as a political doctrine but also as an epistemic field. To give Islamists full agency within secular modernity—a category with a particular genealogy in Enlightenment history—is to misconceptualize the materiality of the secular political episteme. The article suggests that "Islamic fundamentalists" share a common dream of disrupting secularism. Such journalistic attempts reveal a historical unconscious deeply anxious about the return of Islam—an unconscious beneath the spectacle of the modern West's self-perception.

2001–11: War on Terror and Discourse of Ethics

9/11 inaugurated a new global history. Two planes flew into the Twin Towers, a third plane managed to damage the western side of the Pentagon, and a fourth plane aiming to hit the White House fell short. The state immediately blamed al-Qaʿida and considered the attacks an act of war, and al-Qaʿida took responsibility through the release of a video. 9/11 is objectively the most comprehensive attack on the security, intelligence, and economy of the global superpower. Even though 9/11 clearly represented a global jihadist attack on the political and economic structure of Western domination, much of the commentary in the immediate aftermath of the attacks—leftist as well as rightist—involved civilizational, cultural, and identitarian explanations. In the immediate aftermath of 9/11, the Afghan Taliban government fell and refused to hand over Bin Laden to the United States, launching a full-fledged war. The war in Iraq, however, took a different form. Within the Sunni resistance, under the leadership of Abu Musab al-Zarqawi, al-Qaʻida in Iraq began a series of terrorist attacks and suicide operations. Zarqawi also released several beheading videos during this time. The central leadership of al-Qaʻida criticized Zarqawi, and considered his brutal sectarian tactics antithetical to the values of global jihad. Despite such internal critiques of political sectarianism, however, in this decade sectarianism became mainstream political culture—particularly given Iran's major role in reconfiguring the governing powers of the Iraqi state. The 2006 July War in Lebanon between Hizbullah and the Israeli Defense Forces, however, demonstrated an exception: the possibility of Islamic unity. Specifically, the collaboration between Shia Hizbullah and Sunni Hamas demonstrated the type of Islamist political action that, as Salman Sayyid claims, sustains Islam itself and keeps the tradition from dissolving into its constituent parts.

During this decade after the London bombings of 7/7, there was also a shift inward. Western and secular states not only focused on the external enemy combatant but also conducted sophisticated and detailed surveillance of potential homegrown terrorists. By 2009, with the beginning of the Obama presidency, US foreign policy moved toward contingency operations and precision warfare through the full-scale use of drones. The war expanded in depth and precision, and the state rhetorically and diplomatically shifted from emphasizing civilizational differences toward promoting a moderate "reformation" from within Islam. On 4 June 2009, Obama delivered a historic speech in Cairo in which he acknowledged the history of colonialism and tension between the West and Muslim world, but emphasized a dialogic ethical discourse:

> I have come here to seek a new beginning between the United States and Muslims around the world; one based upon mutual interest and mutual respect; and one based upon the truth that America and Islam are not exclusive, and need not be in competition. Instead, they overlap, and share common principles—principles of justice and progress, tolerance, and the dignity of all human beings. (Obama 2009)

This decade's state interest in promoting a (liberal) reformation within Islam parallels scholarly developments during the same period.

Seyla Benhabib's *The Claims of Culture: Equality and Diversity in the Global Era* (2002) provides a detailed theoretical grounding for this form of state intervention in a world shaped by a universalizing globalism. Her argument is a critique of naive cultural relativism in the post-9/11 era, and a call for a "discourse of ethics," a framework that allows for all morally autonomous individuals and social/cultural groups to arrive at a meeting point acknowledging each participant as a moral equal. "Discourse ethics" is informed by critical theorist Habermas's notion of "communicative ethics" (1990). For Habermas, unlike the first generation of Frankfurt School thinkers, modernity is an unfinished project. Habermas encourages the maintenance of Enlightenment-based values and believes that while history took a devastating turn with the Holocaust, revitalizing the modern project remains important. Benhabib's "discourse ethics" relies on this concept of modernity and remains open to all except indigenous people and "fundamentalists" (read: Islamists). She writes,

> It is the rejectionist fundamentalists who find it most difficult to live in a globalized world of uncertainty, hybridity, fluidity, and contestation. Unable to make the daily compromises that the practice of any firmly held religious belief in the contemporary world would require, these groups declare war on global civilization or consume themselves in acts of apocalyptic fervor … the "true Islam" dreams of the twenty-first century—are doomed to failure, but not before they cause a great deal of mischief and human suffering, instability, and fear. (Benhabib 2002, 186)

The specter of 9/11 looms behind the state policies, intellectual production, and popular media representations of this decade. Media representations during this decade reflect a realization that overtly interventionist approaches within the logic of imperialism have been ineffective, and that 9/11 may epitomize this failure of liberal-humanism. This decade involves a strategic shift from the militarist exportation of liberal values toward the encouragement of reformation within Islam itself (Mamdani 2004). In this decade the question of "women's rights" in Islam becomes a site of central contestation, and Islamic women interested in projects of liberal reform are represented as active actors working to challenge the threat of Islam from within.

While Benhabib's "Habermasian" notion of "discourse of ethics" gives us a quick preview of the epistemic environment during this period, it does not tell us much about Muslim scholars and their involvement in furthering the agenda of this decade. During this decade, not only secular feminists but some Muslim women scholars also participate in the discourse of internal reform. Through Quranic hermeneutics, these scholars attempt to overhaul the orthodox tradition of Islam from within, to free Islamic orthodoxy from patriarchal interpretations and other forms of exegetical distortion. Asma Barlas—a scholar critical of making hybrid Quranic and Western/feminist epistemologies—suggests that patriarchal readings of Islamic discourse result from historical patriarchy at particular periods, not from the Quran itself (Barlas 2002). Her aim is to return to a hermeneutic arrangement in which the Quran—as Divine ontology and Divine speech—is at the very center, and other secondary texts of the shari'a like the hadith corpus are read with a close eye on historical contingencies. Along with Barlas, Kecia Ali and Amina Wadud also publish texts dealing with similar themes during this decade. While the authors of these works have different political investments, during the 2001–11 period, Quranic hermeneutics as a genre was ideologically mobilized in conjunction with the reformist agenda of a "discourse of ethics."

A similar pattern is noticeable in NYT articles during 2001–11. For instance, in an article titled "Daughter of the Revolution Fights the Veil" (Sciolino, 2003) we see the representation of this reformist argument from within the authentic representation of the Islamic Revolution in Iran. The article suggests that there is internal tension within the Khomeini family about the status of the veil in revolutionary/reformist Islamic discourse. Elaine Sciolino writes,

> When it comes to credentials in Iran's Islamic Republic, Zahra Eshraghi's are cast in gold. Her grandfather was Ayatollah Ruhollah Khomeini, the cleric who overthrew a king and led a revolution in the name of Islam. Her husband's brother is the reformist president, Mohammad Khatami. And her husband, Mohammad Reza Khatami, is the head of the reformist wing of Parliament. In a society where women can derive enormous power from the men in their lives, those three pillars give Ms. Eshraghi enormous standing. Yet the 39-year-old government official and mother of two has a confession to make. She feels trapped by her family history. And she hates wearing the black veil known as the chador. (2003, A6)

The author is suggesting that Eshraghi is perfectly positioned within the discourse of Shi'i Islamic orthodoxy to question the Islamic Republic's normative legal focus. In another article titled "Half the Afghans, the Women,

Fight to Establish Their Rights" (2002), Barbara Crossette more openly highlights internal tensions within the discourse of Islam to promote women's rights. She discusses the significance of ideologically training women in Afghanistan so that they can question the Islamic legitimacy of the Taliban and establish "clandestine home schools for girls." She writes,

> Ms. Kabuli, 41, was among those who stayed and worked underground, and she is now a judge dealing with youthful offenders … During Taliban rule, from 1996 until last fall, she ran one of hundreds of clandestine home schools for girls. Ms. Kabuli said the problem with the Taliban was not that they were Muslims. "Islam brought a certain equality to men and women," she said. "The laws that the Taliban brought were from pre-Islamic times, based on traditional law." (Crossette 2002, A7)

The author, in this case, is using an argument similar to scholars of Quranic hermeneutics, namely deauthenticating one normative gender focus in traditional Islam on the basis of another, particular liberatory reading of Islam.

Sabrina Tavernise explores similar concerns in her article, "In Quest for Equal Rights, Muslim Women's Meeting Turns to Islam's Tenets" (2009). She discusses the patriarchy demonstrated by the National Fatwa Council in Malaysia in their call against the practice of yoga. The journalist uses local women's voices that argue for reform within Islam, instead of the 1990s tactic of dwelling on secular feminist critiques. Tavernise observes,

> (Muslim women's) mission was to come up with ways to demand equal rights for women. And their tools, however unlikely, were the tenets of Islam itself. "Secular feminism has fulfilled its historical role, but it has nothing more to give us," said Ziba Mir-Hosseini, an Iranian anthropologist who has been helping to formulate some of the arguments. "The challenge we face now is theological." (2009, A8)

This article fits neatly with the imperatives of Quranic hermeneutics and discourse of ethics, namely discourse within Islam via interpretive and reading strategies to dispel patriarchy. The article also provides an interesting periodization, demonstrating how secular feminism exhausts its utility, giving way to a reformist agenda concerned with theology. This is interesting, given the fact that the decade prior to 2001–11, as explained in the last section, was a decade of internationalist and interventionist secular feminism.

In an article titled "Turkish Terror Victim Espoused a Tolerant Islam" (2000), Stephen Kinzer represents Islamists as violent against Muslim feminists who fight for women's rights. The article suggests that male domination is not part of the essence of Islam and is the result of a perversion. Kinzer writes, "The woman, Konca Kuris, was often described as a Muslim feminist. In books, articles, lectures and television appearances, she had described Islam as a religion that guarantees women's rights, and asserted that male commentators over the centuries had twisted its essence in ways that led to the oppression of women" (2000, A3).

The message in this article resonates with the arguments in Barlas' monograph. The main point in this article is to historicize the orthodoxy of Islam as patriarchal. In other words, keep Islam but deconstruct and dispel its orthodox structure. In this sense, the "discourse of ethics" has a reductionist agenda. Islam's massive corpus, systematized over 1400 years, is reduced to a certain modernist interpretation of the Quran. Much of the hadith corpus and shari'a are questioned, and selective texts from different periods in Islamic history are kept so long as they adjust to modernist sensibilities. In NYT articles like the one by Kinzer above there is a tendency not only to show that interpretive textual manipulation and "perversion" create the basis of patriarchal societies but also to insist that Islamist men are also obsessively violent and perverted in their responses to feminism.

Interpretive openness is central for both Quranic hermeneutics and discourse of ethics. An article titled "In Jeans or Veils, Iraqi Women Are Split on New Political Power" (2005) illustrates this method well. The author expresses concerns about the future of Iraqi women, cites a scholar who argues for pluralism within Islamic thought, and suggests that this internal diversity may allow for women's rights and other forms of reform from within Islam's discursive tradition. The article states,

> Many secular women in the assembly agree that Western models cannot always apply in Iraq, and that Islam must play an important role. But, like Dr. Raja al-Khuzai, they argue that there are many schools of thought within Islam, and plenty of room for differing views, and they worry that Islamists will make inroads into Iraq's secular family law, which was established in 1959 and remains among the most liberal in the region. Today, for example, men can take more than one wife only under strict conditions. (Worth 2005, A1)

While it is certainly true that Islam's corpus of texts, reasoning structure, and scholars are full of contradictions and paradoxes, there is still a systematization of knowledge in which an orthodoxy is articulated. And to assume that the complex mechanism through which this articulation takes place over a period of 1400 years is simply a determination of history is to commit tremendous violence upon Islamic epistemology and methodology. The multiple contradictions and the existence of plurality of thought within the epistemic unity of Islam do not necessarily negate, undermine, or delegitimize orthodoxy. To assume such a delegitimization is to essentialize difference.

Concluding Remarks

The primary aim is to reveal a structural homology between two forms of secular representational strategies vis-à-vis Islam: media and feminism. My analysis covers the years 1979–2011, which I divide into three periods—1979–90; 1991–2001; and 2001–11—according to signature Islamist events. I examine how media and feminist discourse for each period overlap in their assumptions and disarticulation of Islamism. I also demonstrate that modern feminism (with three key exceptions) and Islamism are incompatible in their foundational assumptions—not only in terms of how they articulate subjectivity but also how they contradict (and antagonize) each other's visions of the world. Though I find three exceptions to this secular paradigm of feminism in Thobani, Spillers, and Spivak, I do not attempt to redeem feminism through them. Rather, I want to consider how their works generate, map, and deconstruct the categories of gender/sex outside the frame of anti-Islamism that modern feminism upholds. In this sense, there is a primary difference in their desires. At the risk of sounding too metaphysical, one may remark that at the most elemental level, there is a difference in each respective tradition's ethical dispositions.

The killing of Osama bin Laden in 2011 marks the end of a particular history of contemporary jihad. With the Arab uprisings in full effect, many Western and secular journalists and critics during this time begin to discuss the Arab Spring in relation to what they predict to be an "Islamist Winter" (Ghezali 2012; Totten 2012). In other words, there is a remobilization of a binary between Islam and the secular. Similarly, in 2012 controversial philosopher Slavoj Žižek suggests that the 1979 revolution in Iran was an authentic moment until the Islamists deauthenticated it by taking over its direction, and locates in Iranian reformist Mousavi (during the 2009 election scandal) the possibility of a political "return of the repressed (Leftists and secularists)." Elsewhere Žižek writes of Tahrir Square, "But then there are the Arab uprisings. Do they not offer an example of a collective act of resistance that avoids this false alternative between self-destructive violence and religious fundamentalism?" (2012, 61). For Žižek and others, the period between 1979 and 2011 is a history of political defeat and repression. And the period in the aftermath of the Arab Spring and death of Bin Laden is a time for the renewal of secularity. Of course, we know by now that the seductive dream of a new secularism ends very quickly—already we have witnessed Hamas militants firing rockets at Israeli forces in response to the Gaza massacre, a full-fledged and uncompromising jihad in Syria with hundreds of local rebel groups with more than 50,000 fighters, and a number of deadly attacks in the heart of Europe. Perhaps we have entered a new history of jihad with a new ensemble of problems and potentialities.

Notes

1 Another version of this chapter was published in the *American Journal of Islamic Social Sciences* in 2018.
2 See Mohammed Sidiq Seddon, Dilwar Hussain, and Nadeem Malik, *British Muslims Between Assimilation and Segregation: Historical, Legal and Social Realities* (Leicester: Islamic Foundation, 2004); Annelies Moors and Rubah Salih, "'Muslim women in Europe:' Secular Normativities, Bodily Performances, and Multiple Publics," *Social Anthropology* 17 (4) (November 2009): 375–78; Abdoolkarim Vakil and Salman Sayyid, *Thinking through Islamophobia: Global Perspectives* (New York: Columbia University, 2010); Sohail Daulatzai, *Black Star, Crescent Moon: The Muslim International and Black Freedom beyond America* (Minnesota: University of Minnesota Press, 2012); Tariq Modood, "Multiculturalism, Interculturalisms, and the Majority," *Journal of Moral Education* 43 (3) (2014): 302–15.
3 By de-essentializing, I mean Islam is forcibly conceptualized through a modernist discourse of state-based individual and group identity, instead of the Sharia. Islamic discourse is de-essentialized when the primary focus of the discourse

is to figure out how Muslims can live within the national and international imagination of the history of the state.

4 The majority of my analysis of NYT articles in this chapter emerged out of research conducted in the Suad Joseph Lab at the University of California, Davis, as part of a larger project on the representation of Muslim women in media. I accessed the articles by searching for key terms on ProQuest. The search was wide: it covered specific countries including Iran, Saudi Arabia, Iraq, Palestine, Lebanon, Pakistan, and Egypt; various terms related to the veil (e.g., veil, hijab, chador, niqab), terms related to women and Islam (e.g., women's rights, women in Islam, women and Islam, Muslim women), Islamic law and jurisprudence (e.g., various spellings of Sharia), and names of key figures and organizations (e.g., Khomeini, Hamas, Hizbullah, Taliban). Readers should note that the research required reading of more than 3000 articles. For example, if one searches for the words "Muslim veil," ProQuest releases 261 articles, or if one searches "Muslim woman" it gives 1928 articles within the time frame of three decades approximately. All articles published with these various key words and phrases were read.

5 See Orlando Patterson, *Slavery and Social Death* (Cambridge, MA: Harvard University Press, 1982) and Frank Wilderson, *Red, White & Black: Cinema and the Structure of U.S. Antagonisms and Slavery and Social Death* (Durham, NC: Duke University Press, 2010).

6 Chandra Mohanty, "Under Western Eyes: Feminist Scholarship and Colonial Discourses," *boundary 2* 12/13 (3/1) (1984): 333–58; Rey Chow, *Woman and Chinese Modernity: The Politics of Reading between West and East* (Minneapolis: University of Minnesota Press, 1991); Ranjana Khanna, *Dark Continents: Psychoanalysis and Colonialism* (Durham, NC: Duke University Press, 2003); Khanna, *Algeria Cuts: Women and Representation, 1830 to the Present* (Durham, NC: Duke University Press, 2007).

7 In Talal Asad's conceptualization of Islam as a "discursive tradition," the relation between Islam and Islamism is grounded in a specific description of orthodoxy, which he defines in his now classic 1986 essay: "Orthodoxy is crucial to all Islamic traditions … (O)rthodoxy is not a mere body of opinion but a distinctive relationship—a relationship of power. Wherever Muslims have the power to regulate, uphold, require, or adjust correct practices, and to condemn, exclude, undermine, or replace incorrect ones, there is the domain of orthodoxy." See Asad, "The Idea of an Anthropology of Islam" (Washington, DC: Center for Contemporary Arab Studies, Georgetown University, 1986). Islamism, then—as part of Islam's discursive tradition—is quite explicitly reliant upon the mobilization of orthodoxy. The contestations and disputations on whether orthodoxy is ontological or historical are irrelevant for a genealogical

understanding of Islamism. For genealogists, the important question is not whether orthodoxy is real or true, or if it is contestable, but rather the manner in which orthodoxy is mobilized, and what such a mobilization enacts. This chapter, then, should not be taken as a defense of orthodoxy but rather as an elaboration on how Islamism structurally legitimizes itself through a concrete engagement with orthodoxy, and therefore must have the appearance of a system of orthodoxy. In parts of the chapter where I use "Islamic orthodoxy" instead of simply "Islamism," I do so to ensure that readers understand that the antagonism secular feminism has with Islamism is due to its reliance upon the mobilization of orthodoxy. In other parts, where I do not explicitly mention orthodoxy, it should be assumed as inherent in my definition of Islamism. Moreover, it must be added that secular feminism's antagonism may also extend to forms of Islamic orthodoxy that do not necessarily fall within the explicit social, historical, and political projects of Islamism. For this reason, I cannot delimit my reading of feminist antagonism to the realm of Islamism alone. Feminism appears to have a broader antagonism with Islam itself—as long as it reflects orthodoxy—regardless of whether it organizes an Islamist programmatism.

8 There are significant works in religious studies that examine Islamism as one form of "religious violence" (e.g., Juergensmeyer's Terror in the Mind of God) or "fundamentalism" (e.g., Lawrence's *Defenders of God*) among many. In *Shattering the Myth: Islam Beyond Violence* (1998), however, Bruce Lawrence moves beyond essentialist accounts that represent Islam as violent, and suggest that the tradition is not a monolith. Bruce Lincoln on the other hand, in the text *Holy Terrors: Thinking About Religion After September 11* (2002), identifies religious reasoning behind the 9/11 attacks, and discursively investigates speeches and documents to suggest that figures like George W. Bush and Osama bin Laden are similar insofar as they both share a Manichean worldview. While this literature raises important points, it understates relations of power, and fails to specify Islam dynamic with global secularity. In other words, to conceptualize Islam through the category of "religion" is to already be entrapped in a secular logic. Moreover, the main point in my chapter is to show how the secular—both as media and feminism—is exceptionally oppositional and antagonistic to Islam in particular, not necessarily religion in general.

9 Sayyid writes about the relation between Islam and Islamism in terms of "availability." He writes,

> Islamism is not the mere reflection of Islam, but rather it is a political discourse that takes the availability of Islam as a means of undermining the Kemalist anciens régimes. Islamism makes use of the availability of Islam, but, at the same time, it increases the availability of Islam. In other

words Islamism is organized around Islam, but this is a two-way process since Islamism also organizes Islam. (*A Fundamental Fear Eurocentrism and the Emergence of Islamism*, 1994, 77)

10 See Wael Hallaq, *The Impossible State: Islam, Politics, and Modernity's Moral Predicament* (New York: Columbia University Press, 2012), for his use of Carl Schmitt's conception of central domain to discuss the significance of jihad in the Islamic tradition.
11 Another iteration of the same simplistic assertion is that Islamism changed its form from "culturalism" to "economism" due to capitalist crisis. Islamism's critique of colonialism in an earlier moment in history had cultural, economic, political, ethical dimensions, and therefore, other than pointing at the general directional structure of capitalism, such assertions fail to recognize even the most elemental grammar and syntax of Islam.
12 I use counterrevolutionary here specifically to mean any set of political articulations that deliberately attempted to subvert the massive clerical orientation of struggle in the late 1970s.
13 Nussbaum defines "control over one's environment" as the ability "to hold property … having the right to seek employment on an equal basis with others … In work, being able to work as a human being, exercising practical reason and entering into meaningful relationships of mutual recognition with other workers" (Martha Nussbaum 1999, 42).

References

Afary, Janet, and Kevin B. Anderson. 2005. *Foucault and the Iranian Revolution: Gender and the Seductions of Islamism*. Chicago: University of Chicago Press.

Akhtar, Sarah. 1991. "For Women, Polygamy's Just a Rotten Deal." *New York Times*, 2 June 1991.

Asad, Talal. 1993. *Genealogies of Religion: Discipline and Reasons of Power in Christianity and Islam*. Baltimore, MD: John Hopkins University Press.

Barlas, Asma. 2002. *"Believing Women" in Islam: Unreading Patriarchal Interpretations of the Qur'an*. Austin: University of Texas Press.

Benhabib, Seyla. 2002. *The Claims of Culture: Equality and Diversity in the Global Era*. Princeton, NJ: Princeton University Press.

Crenshaw, Kimberlé Williams. 2012. *On Intersectionality: Essential Writings of Kimberlé Crenshaw*. New York: Perseus Distribution Services.

Crossette, Barbara. 1996. "Women's Rights Gaining Attention within Islam." *New York Times*, 12 May 1996.

Crossette, Barbara. 1998. "Afghan Women Demanding End to Their Repression by Militants." *New York Times*, 6 April 1998.

Crossette, Barbara. 2002. "Half the Afghans, the Women, Fight to Establish Their Rights." *New York Times*, 7 June 2002: A7.

Davis, Angela Y. 1981. *Women, Race, & Class*. New York: Random House.

El Saadawi, Nawal. 1997. *The Nawal El Saadawi Reader*. London: Zed Books.

Geertz, Clifford. 1973. *The Interpretation of Cultures*. New York: Basic Books.

Ghezali, Rabah. 2012. "Arab Spring, Islamist Winter?" *HuffPost*, 17 July 2012. https://www.huffpost.com/entry/arab-spring-islamist-wint_b_1212794.

Habermas, Jürgen. 1990. *Moral Consciousnesses and Communicative Action*. Translated by Christian Lenhardt and Shierry Weber Nicholsen. Cambridge: Massachusetts Institute of Technology.

Haiven, Max. 2009. "Silvia Federici, On Capitalism, Colonialism, Women and Food Politics." *Politics and Culture* 2: 32.

hooks, bell. 1984. *Feminist Theory: From Margin to Center*. Cambridge: South End Press.

Ibrahim, Youssef M. 1990. "Islamic Fundamentalism Is Winning Votes." *New York Times*, 1 July 1990.

Kinzer, Stephen. 1997. "Turks March in Campaign to Preserve Secularism." *New York Times*, 16 February 1997.

Kinzer, Stephen. 2000. "Turkish Terror Victim Espoused a Tolerant Islam." *New York Times*, 26 January 2000: A3.

Lyotard, Jean-Francois. (1979) 1984. *The Postmodern Condition: A Report on Knowledge*. Translated by Geoff Bennington, and Brian Massumi. Minneapolis: University of Minnesota Press.

Mamdani, Mahmood. 2004. *Good Muslim, Bad Muslim: America, the Cold War, and the Roots of Terror*. New York: Three Leaves Press.

Meari, Lena. "The Material Life of Representation: 'Veiled Muslim Women' in the *New York Times*." In *Reporting Islam: Muslim Women in the New York Times*, edited by Suad Joseph.

Naim, Hakeem. "Friends and Foes: The Pragmatic Liberal Biases in Representation of Saudi Women vs. Iranian Women in the *New York Times*, 1980–2011." In *Reporting Islam: Muslim Women in the New York Times*, edited by Suad Joseph.

Nussbaum, Martha. 1999. *Sex and Social Justice*. New York: Oxford University Press.

Obama, Barack. 2009. "Remarks by the President on a New Beginning." Speech, Cairo University, Cairo, Egypt, 4 June 2009.

"Pakistan's Grim Islamic Law Is Not Just a Threat." 1981. *New York Times*, 17 September: A2.
Sayyid, Salman. 1997. *A Fundamental Fear: Eurocentrism and the Emergence of Islamism*. London: Zed Books.
Sciolino, Elaine. 1985a. "Saudi Arabia's Gospel Columnists." *New York Times*, 5 May 1985: E9.
Sciolino, Elaine. 1985b. "Islam: Feminists vs. Fundamentalists." *New York Times*, 25 July 1985.
Sciolino, Elaine. 2003. "Daughter of the Revolution Fights the Veil." *New York Times*, 2 April 2003: A6.
Spillers, Hortense. 1987. "Mama's Baby, Papa's Maybe: An American Grammar Book," *Diacritics* 17 (2): 64–81.
Spivak, Gayatri. 1994. "Can the Subaltern Speak?" In *Colonial Discourse and Post-Colonial Theory: A Reader*, edited by Patrick Williams, and Laura Chrisman, 66–111. New York: Columbia University Press.
Tavernise, Sabrina. 2009. "In Quest for Equal Rights, Muslim Women's Meeting Turns to Islam's Tenets." *New York Times*, 16 February 2009: A8.
"The Moslem Veil in the City: A Matter of Tradition." 1984. *New York Times*, 24 September: B7.
Thobani, Sunera. 2007. "White Wars: Western Feminisms and the 'War on Terror.'" *Feminist Theory* 8 (3): 174.
Totten, Michael J. 2012. "Arab Spring or Islamist Winter?" *World Affairs* 174 (5): 23–42.
Trofimov, Yaroslav. 2008. *The Siege of Mecca: The 1979 Uprising at Islam's Holy Shrine*. New York: First Anchor Books.
Weisman, Steven R. 1986a. "Dispute over a Moslem Divorce Ensnarls Gandhi." *New York Times*, 9 February 1986: A3.
Weisman, Steven R. 1986b. "The 'Islamization' of Pakistan: Still Moving Slowly and Still Stirring Debate." *New York Times*, 10 August 1986: A10.
Weisman, Steven R. 1988. "Pakistani Women Take Lead in Drive against Islamization." *New York Times*, 17 June 1988: A1.
Worth, Robert F. 2005. "In Jeans or Veils, Iraqi Women Are Split on New Political Power." *New York Times*, 13 April 2005: A1.
Žižek, Slavoj. 2012. *The Year of Dreaming Dangerously*. London: Verso Books.

5

Friends and Foes: The Pragmatic Liberal Biases in Representation of Saudi Women vs. Iranian Women in the *New York Times*, 1980–2011

Hakeem Naim

Introduction

The representation of Islam, Muslim women, and the Middle East in mainstream American media has been dominated by a simplistic nuance and with multifaceted dimensions. It is based on the conceptually established notion of two divided cultures: the "West" vs. the "East." It maintains the ideological claim of liberal righteousness and strategically emerging patterns that are associated with and/or echoes policies of the United States toward the Middle East. It constructs an ideological paradigm of power with an image of "objective representation" through different rhetoric.

A close study of the *New York Times*, the most important media outlet in the United States and the world, assists us to understand these multifaceted dimensions of a unified discourse about Islam and women in the Middle East. It also illustrates pragmatic shifts within the Orientalist dichotomy of the "East" vs. the "West." I present a comparative analysis of the *New York Times* representation of women in Saudi Arabia and Iran. The *New York Times* coverage of both countries falls under the broader paradigm of Orientalism and *liberal imperialism* within a hegemonic discourse that preserves US political and economic interests. By liberal imperialism, I mean that the economic and military domination of the United States over the Middle East has not only established a Eurocentric liberal discourse about the Middle East and Islam, but it also indicates network of institutions that benefits from and is influenced by the apparatuses of imperial power. The *New York Times* signifies this liberal imperialism through producing and reproducing an Orientalist discourse in which, in addition to Islam, the US interest is the driving force.[1]

It should be pointed out that it would be a grave misconception to suggest that the discourses on Muslim women and veil in the *New York Times* and/or the US media were produced to simply follow the interests of the US government and its associated agencies. These discourses do not have a single authoritative center. Michel Foucault makes the point that "Discourses are tactical elements or blocks operating in the field of force relation; there can exist different and even contradictory discourses within the same strategy" (Foucault 1980, 100). This ideological strategy serves to maintain the existing power structure, which provides the authority and means of production for representation and production of discourses within a complex relation of power and knowledge. As David Spurr argues, the US media depends on "institutional sources, their place in a market economy, and standardized discourses in terms of national policy and public opinion" (Spurr 1993, 8).

Even though US media strategies vary through time, space, and geography, the representation of Islam, Muslim women, and Islamic culture highly intertwined with US economic and political interests in a particular Muslim state.

In this chapter, I do not expand theoretical analysis of Islam, the Middle East, and Orientalism. Nor do I provide an historical and theoretical discussion of US foreign policy toward Saudi Arabia and Iran. Rather, I focus on the *New York Times* representation of Iran and Saudi Arabia, which followed different patterns and helped to preserve the structure of US strategies regarding these two countries. I would like to illustrate the discursive divergence in the *New York Times* representation of veiled Muslim women, which is based on US strategic interests in its relation to Saudi Arabia and Iran and presented within the discourse of Orientalism and liberalism. In Iran oppression of women was blamed on the state, whereas in Saudi Arabia religion, culture, and tradition were accused of the condition of women. Iran was the land of irrationality ruled by the Islamic tyranny, and Saudi Arabia was the land of contradiction ruled by Islamic tradition. For instance, the *New York Times* wrote about Iran:

> The one program the mullahs seem able to agree on is that women's hair must be covered. The only real program that the authorities seem to have

been for the total covering of women's heads. Violations of Islamic dress requirements for women are punishable by imprisonment and up to 70 lashes. (Kifner 1983, A2)

But, in another article about Saudi Arabia, the *New York Times* presents the women's veil as a dictate of ulema, religious scholars:

> Saudi women must be veiled in public. This edict of the ulemas is applied rigorously in Riyadh by the squads of the religious police, but it is more relaxed in Jidda and Dhahran, far more liberal cities. The Saudi royal family has been pushing strongly for the modernization of the country but has been doing so gradually and carefully so as not to alienate the powerful religious establishment. (Ibrahim 1990, A18)

In another article "repression" of Saudi women is acknowledged, but again it is said to be "reflection (of) their culture":

> Saudi Arabia is a bizarre place. It has McDonald's restaurants that look just like those at home except that there is one line for men and one for women. Al Riyadh newspaper has women journalists, but they're kept in their own room; when a male editor must edit a woman's copy, he does it by phone. Saudi women wear bikinis—but only in-home swimming pools or in all-women pools. They claim all this reflects not repression but a culture they cherish. (Kristof 2002, A35)

As a part of the Media Project Research team, I have searched and read 620 articles about Iranian women in contrast to 239 articles about Saudi women, published in the *New York Times* between 1 January 1980 and 29 June 2011. Twice the number of articles about Iran also tell us the need and interest of the United States in continuously spreading and regenerating the established wisdom about her "enemy." The key terms I used to conduct my research were "Iran and Women" and "Saudi Arabia and Women." I selected the articles after a carful thematic categorization. Therefore, each article that is referenced here is a quintessential example of many other articles that fall within the same category of analyses. For instance, I separated the articles that discussed about women previously banned from driving in Saudi Arabia. Then, I clustered the articles that pragmatically avoided the criticism of Saudi Arabian state ban on women driving and channeled the discussion to Islam and culture of driving in the Middle East.

The Ambivalent Power of Liberal Orientalism and the Continuous US Foreign Policy

Controlling a free flow of oil, protecting Israel's interests, cold conflicts with postrevolution governments of Iran, and neocolonial mechanisms, including "the war against terror," were the main foreign policy trends that US power structure has followed between 1980 and 2011. It is true that the Soviet invasion of Afghanistan, the Iranian Revolution, the Gulf wars, and the US "War on Terror" created strategic diversions for US foreign policy in the Middle East. For instance, the United States and its ally, Saudi Arabia, supported anti-Soviet Afghan groups with a discourse of Islamic liberation and religious freedom while the Islamic Revolution in Iran was demonized by associating Islam with punishment, autocracy, and cruelty.[2] This paradoxical ambivalence, however, is constructed to recognize the US interest around a strategic continuity, based on the US preservation of economic and political interests. This continuity is the established guiding principle of the different US administrations in their relations with Saudi Arabia and Iran in the last three decades. Protecting the Saudi Arabia regime as the most important economic and strategic ally has been one of these continuous "pillars" of US foreign policy in the region. The Iranian Revolution of 1979 made Saudi Arabia the only "reliable" source of energy for the United States. On the other hand, Iran was seen as a model of "instability" for US interests. Moreover, Israelization of US policies toward the Middle East has constituted the main aspects of US involvement in Saudi Arabia and Iran.[3] Since one of the main elements of the Iranian Revolution was its ideological hostility to Israel, Israelization of US policy of the Middle East is also strengthened in a continuous ground of conflict with Iran. Thus, representation of Saudi Arabia and Iran in the *New York Times*, which has preserved a degree of continuity, ensues an amalgamation of US foreign policy toward these two countries, and an Orientalist liberal discourse. American Orientalism, similar to the traditional sort that has existed in Europe, developed as a direct relation of military and political power of a new emerging empire with the Oriental world.[4] The common and strategically unchangeable concept of the representation of both Iranian and Saudi women in the *New York Times* falls within this politically and socially established liberal Orientalist paradigm. The distinction between the "civilized" "us" and the unpleasant "them" was reconstructed, maintained, and stated. This facile division, although presented with contrived complexity by the *New York Times*, can be understood within consistently claimed "objective truth" of transcended knowledge of liberal modernity. The backwardness of Iranians and hypocrisy of Arabs was the received knowledge that was reproduced and recycled. In one article veil was compared with the airplane, a symbol of civilization. "Air Iran flight attendants have been issued a sort of hooded cowl to top off their smocks, giving them a strangely medieval appearance as they stand at the door of a Boeing 747" (Kifner 1982, A1). In another article "Arab hypocrisy" was explained to the readers: "The Saudi women went into the bathroom on the jetliner and emerged swathed in black veils, their expensive high-fashion clothes from the West—and more strikingly their dark eyes—totally muted for the landing in Arabia. 'Hypocrites, see?' said the Saudi airline crewman quite appreciatively. He was a Briton working for the Saudis" (the *New York Times* 1987, A8). Orientalism as a conceptualized and pragmatic "knowledge" recycles itself so as to follow the path of power. The exercise and image of power enables the process of formation, production, and distribution of this particular knowledge. It makes it the established "knowledge" so as to set the stage, to reconstruct itself, and to be imitated by others. The *New York Times* mostly flavors this established consensus with the liberal democratic values and creates a "normal" and "professional" image.

Since Islam has been the most important means of production in representation of the Middle East, the critiques of Saudi Arabia and Iran by the *New York Times* reveal an ambivalence between US foreign policy on the one hand and the Orientalist binary of the West vs. Islam on the other hand. As the articles of this book detail, the story of veiled Muslim women on the *New York Times* is a story of Islam, power, and representation. Branded with extremism, irrationality, anti-Westernism, despotism, punishment, and conflict, the subjective interpretation of "Islam" not only redivides the "East" and the "West" but also creates a situational environment, which allows representation of the "other" by the power without any self-questioning. The American press, particularly the *New York Times*, can write about "Islam" within the strong assertion of power because they can maintain the discourse about Islam. It relates to the manifestation of their power over the "other." It helps them to contribute to the political and economic interests of the US power structure in the Islamic world. In the following article Islam is presented as a set of strange and bizarre law codes in contrast to Western secular and rational law:

> Moslems consider Islam a complete system that governs every aspect of life, and Saudi Arabia takes its role as guardian of the faith particularly seriously. It is the only country in the world whose Constitution and legal system are entirely based on the "sharia" or Islamic code of law. Details of social behavior, from what to wear to brushing one's teeth, are the subjects of continual debate.
>
> On smoking, for example, a multipart series in the daily newspaper Sharq al-Awsat concluded that 'Complete abolition is the only way to get rid of this disease. It is a sin, the same way as alcohol is a sin.'
>
> As for the young man who forced his pregnant sister to drink poison, he was told that under Islam, he should have tried to get her to marry her child's father in order to legitimize the child. If that failed, he should have waited until the baby was born; then the couple could have been officially punished with a public lashing. The brother was wrong, said the scholar, because "the great scholars of Islam forbade individuals from taking the law of God into their own hands, fearing aggression, conflict and civil strife."
>
> Dr. Ibrahim al-Awaji, Deputy Minister of the Interior, who holds a Ph.D. from the University of Virginia, said, "One can always use two guiding questions: Is it in the public interest? And will it help prevent un-Islamic activities from occurring."
>
> The most burning issues of the day concern women. In the case of elderly women, "is all right for them to be a little less conservative," says one advisor. "They can wear jewelry and wear makeup to a certain extent and can associate with men. The only debatable issue is how old she should be—some say after menopause, some say until the lady's face looks ugly." According to other recent discussions, birth control is acceptable as long as there are good financial or medical reasons, but only if the wife consents to it.
>
> As for wife-beating, a recent column in the daily newspaper Sharq al-Awsat, counseled, "Women can be beaten, but not too severely." The reason? The Prophet Mohammed said that a man would be ashamed if he "beat his wife like an animal" and then made love to her.
>
> In practice, Islamic norms of behavior often depend on the problems of the moment. A few weeks ago, for example, women were banned from video cassette stores, which were becoming meeting places. Particularly delicate

subjects, such as the role of women in the workplace, tend to be avoided. (Sciolino 1985b, A9)

Moreover, withing the established analytical tradition, the liberal Orientalist notion, as Edward Said argues, creates epistemological and ontological differences between the East and the West, which takes superiority of the West for granted (Said 1979, 2–5). The "knowledge" produced by the institutions of Orientalism can claim self-awareness, authenticity, and authority about Islam, Islamic culture, and Islamic lifestyle. This "self-awareness" comes from the political and economic power that made available Islam and the Middle East for subjective interpretation and representation (Said 1997, 140–44). Thus, interpretation and representation of Muslim women and Islamic veil is projected in the *New York Times*, by power-centric discourses. Therefore, Orientalism frees the constructed "West" from any skeptical self-questioning about the "East." Its discourse is humanistic, liberal, and pragmatically "convincing" in contrast to the dehumanizing practices in the East. The following excerpt from an editorial article of the *New York Times* is a good example:

> The dress restrictions are dehumanizing, submerging the individual identity of women in a colorless sea. Not a single woman in Teheran, a dusty metropolis of 12 million people, dares wear anything other than a dark, bulky raincoat or black chador, the traditional Islamic cloak, and no woman leaves home without a scarf or other head covering, even on scorching summer days. But many women I met, while resentful of the dress standards, are troubled more by inequities in the law. Men can divorce their wives without cause at any time and are automatically awarded custody of children. Wives who outlive their husbands are generally permitted a much smaller inheritance than men who outlive their wives, regardless of variations in income. A woman who kills a child is subject to capital punishment; a man who commits the same crime is not. (Taubman 1997, A38)

Another article makes even shopping malls, the symbols of global capitalism, a symbol of dichotomy between the "West" and the "East":

> The American shopping mall is often considered a metaphor for the sterility of suburban life. The Saudi mall is the opposite, a self-contained live experiment where a conservative religious culture confronts the

restless energy of one of the fastest growing populations in the world. Here many Saudi young people come to shock as much as to shop, to nudge the boundaries of what is considered socially proper and to transform a Western icon into something that fits their own traditions. (Sachs 2000, A4)

Saudi Arabia and Women in the *New York Times*

Liberal imperialism focuses on the cultural interpretation of the "other," in this case the veiled Muslim women, to determine the forceful penetration of power into a specific society. The racially established and focused gaze on the veiled Muslim women that Lena Meari mentions can be different from one place to another.[5] The veil is a symbolic object not only of fecundity but also sexual exoticism, irrationality, and revenge. It promises opportunity, desire, and at the same time deadly threat. It needs to be conquered, studied, dominated, and penetrated. As Lena Meari states the symbolic representation of a strategic "other" in terms of female body and feature is a colonial practice. It symbolizes the difference between the colonized and colonizers. The existing power differences between the colonizer and the colonized and domination of a society is seen and presented through the symbolic feature of gender. Political and economic access of the West to a society rationalizes the colonial gaze. Thus, the gaze on the veil takes different purposes of penetration. The deeper the US political and economic interests conquer, the further the gaze penetrates. For instance, the close relations of the United States with the Saudi regime correspond to the conquest of Saudi women beyond the veil. It is a deep penetration into interior economic and political space of the Saudi society. Thus, the stories that go behind the veil are more important. The *New York Times* constantly mentions a progressive image of Saudi women under the veil. Reports such as "Saudi Women Start to Peek from Behind the Veil," "Under the Veil of Arabia, 'It Is Another Story,'" "Saudis in Bikinis," and "they wore black abayas or long gowns but the abayas were open, showing their jeans and T-shirts (under the abayas and gowns)" are often published in the *New York Times* to illustrate the female body under the veil. It is important to mention that these articles are largely published in the last decade, between

2000 and 2011, when political and economic penetration of the Saudi State by the United States reached its summit. The following article symbolizes the deep relations of the United States with the Saudis that go beyond the veil, that is, the surface:

> On my first evening in Riyadh, I spotted a surreal scene: three giggly black ghosts, possibly young women enveloped in black cloaks called abayas, clustered around a display in a shopping mall, enthusiastically fingering a blouse so sheer and low-cut that my wife would never be caught dead in it. Afterward, I delicately asked a Saudi woman to explicate the scene.
>
> "What do you think the 'black ghosts' wear underneath their abayas?" she replied archly.
>
> Saudi women may be regarded in the West as antique doormats covered in black veils, but the women themselves vigorously reject that stereotype. "It hurts when you hear what people say about us, that we're repressed," Monira Abdulaziz, an assistant professor, said reproachfully.
>
> "I cover up my body and my face, and I'm happy that I'm a religious girl obeying God's rules," a dietician named Lana scolded me after I wrote a typically snide reference to repressed Saudi women. "I can swim and do sports and go to restaurants and wear what I want, but not in front of men. Why should I show my legs and breasts to men? Is that really freedom?" (Kristof 2002, A35)

On the other hand, women's veil as a source of oppression and backwardness is blamed on societal irrationality and absurd traditions of Islam. A strong but implicit narrative to separate the Saudi regime from the "plight" of women was developed and publicized. However, it should be pointed out that the *New York Times* strategic discourse about the Saudi regime, more than a simplistic pro-Saudi propaganda, maintains some complex but ambiguous patterns, which enforces and reinforces the liberal ideology within the West-centric authority. It is incoherent, it does not contain a single center, but it is authoritative, self-righteous, and in the service of the dominated power. Here, focusing and blaming on "Islamic tradition" provides pragmatic and ideological means. The conceptualization of Islam and targeting its related culture as an oppositional dichotomy to the liberal and humanist West not only reinforces the West vs. East binary but also pragmatically provides an important means to produce strategic divergence within that established discourse.[6] Thus, the Arab culture, ulema, Islamic culture, and religious fundamentalists are declared responsible for the repression of women rather than the Saudi royal regime:

> Restrictions on Saudi women are more a reflection of Arab tradition than of religious directive. Saudi society's Government and its restrictions on women are not based on written laws, but on Sharia, the edicts of the 14-century-old Koran. The restrictions spring from interpretations of this Islamic code as offered by senior religious figures, known as the ulemas. Saudi ulemas are the most conservative of all Islamic scholars in the world and have been adamant in their interpretations of the Koran that impose severe strictures on women. (Ibrahim 1990, A18)

The following article provides another example:

> Saudi restrictions on women are based both on the Koran and on conservative Arab traditions. Women are not allowed to mix with men in any public or work place. A woman must be veiled in public and is forbidden to travel alone or to drive a car.
>
> Islamic militancy has been on the rise throughout the Middle East, with proponents challenging practically every state.
>
> While still in that country, she tried to go outdoors without the veil, to travel alone and to pursue a university education in the field of her choice.
>
> Bernard Valcourt, the Minister of Employment and Immigration, intervened as part of a landmark change in Canada's immigration rules. Ottawa is drawing up guidelines, expected to be ready within the next month, under which it would grant refugee status to women who can show persecution as a result of their sex. The change potentially would open up Canada to abused women from many countries who are not protected by the laws of their homelands.
>
> Saudi Arabia's great wealth and the lack of any pressing need for women to work are among forces that keep women down in that country, she believes.
>
> "The way we are wealthy is different from the U.S.," she said. "I think in the U.S. and other countries the women's movement and the economy have grown at the same time, but for us there has been no change in the mentality because there is no incentive for women to participate in public life. We let the men abuse us because we don't know any better." (Farnsworth 1993)

Moreover, since the Saudi state structure is responsible for the rights of its citizens, an ambivalent rhetoric to redefine the concept of individual "rights," different than the established liberal image, is promoted by the *New York Times* within a political context and without some serious opposition. Unlike Iran, the idea of modernization, economic freedom, and progress of the Saudi women is generally attached to the accepted narrative of "women plight in the Middle East" in order to produce a complicated image of reality about veil and what is called "restricted social rights" of women in Saudi Arabia. The argument was made that if Saudi women cannot walk freely without having a male relative in the public, she has a lot of money to spend freely. In an article titled, "Saudi Banks for Women Thriving," the *New York Times* reported that

> Despite their inferior social status, however, Saudi women have plenty of money-an estimated 30 to 40 percent of the hundreds of billions of dollars of private wealth in this country-and the Koran guarantees them personal control over it. As a result, banks run by women and catering solely to women have begun to spring up in the major cities of Saudi Arabia. This is an unusual development in a country governed by strict interpretations of Islamic fundamentalism. (Martin 1982a, A2)

The concept of "gradual change" was one of the main points that was repeated multiple times:

> Fawzan wears the traditional head-to-toe veil, but in her furniture, store she appears in fashionable European clothing. "If a woman in Saudi Arabia wants to work, she can," Mrs. Fawzan said. "The veil won't stop you. In running a business, I am contributing to the economic growth of Saudi Arabia, and I am doing so by observing all our Islamic traditions and practices."
>
> As the Saudis race to invest their oil riches in ambitious economic-development programs, the roles played by Mrs. Fawzan and many other urban women indicate that the traditionally conservative Islamic social structure is gradually yielding to change. The changes taking place are manifest in increasing educational and employment opportunities for women—opportunities that, in effect, are being provided within a wholly separate and self-contained sector where there is little contact with men.
>
> Like Mrs. Fawzan, scores of women are becoming entrepreneurs, scores more are entering educational careers and increasing numbers are physicians, administrators in governmental agencies and members of bank staffs.
>
> "It is true that change has been tremendous, and its impact on women is far-reaching," said Dr. Fatma Mandily, vice dean of the University Studies

Center for Girls at Riyadh University. "We are fortunate that this change has taken place within the framework of our Islamic traditions and the old code of ethics. Their modernization, so to speak, has made Saudi women more sociable, more open-minded, and more open-hearted. Yet we are still adhering to our Islamic way of life."

A number of women say that the key to change is more education. "Education is the basis of the change that is taking place in Saudi society for women," Mrs. Rouchdy said. "But for the most part Saudi women do not want to change their social norms. They don't want to run away from Islamic values and from religion. They are saying, we don't want the superficial aspects of Westernization but only the scientific part of it." (Gupta 1981, C1)

In other article the same topic of "gradual change" and progress was publicized and linked to the Saudi regime:

There is a popular perception that all Saudi women stay at home, unseen by the outside world. But Dr. Khuthaila is part of the growing number of Saudi women who are getting educations and going to work. And despite occasional declarations by conservative "ulema" or religious leaders, who rein them in, the trend seems irreversible. The King Saud University Women's Center, for example, with 500 students and a staff of all women, seems very much like a private convent school. Elderly, bearded guards stand at the gates. Once inside, the students throw off their veils. Dr. Mahmoud M. Safar, Deputy Minister for Higher Education and one of the Government's most articulate spokesmen, said: "We have already passed the stage of such questions as to whether we should let our women work or not. We have no illusions about the contributions Saudi women can make to the development of our country. But our great challenge is to allow her to work and at the same time to maintain the characteristics of the Moslem woman." (Sciolino 1985a, 1.2)

As reflection of US continuous policy toward Saudi Arabia, discussed above, the *New York Times* coverage of veil in Saudi Arabia has not followed a drastic change between 1980 and 2011. US relationship with the Saudi state increasingly strengthened and the coverage of Saudi Arabia drastically dropped or favorably compared with other Muslim countries such as Afghanistan and Iran. For instance, the one issue that the *New York Times* was critical of and firmly covered was the previous ban on driving by women in Saudi Arabia.[7] However, the coverage of this issue was mostly presented with some apologetic reasons in order to maintain the liberal balance of criticism when it came to the United States' main ally and one of the biggest oil suppliers. Since the coverage of Islam, Middle East, and Islamic culture is an assertion of power, the knowledge and its mechanism of interpretation enables and justifies the established cultural humanism. The axiomatic concept of cultural humanism, construed by the enlightened *human*, serves to claim a dogmatic and uncontested concept of objectivity. The power that defines and maintains this asserted objectivity is ignored, not contested, and taken for granted. Thus, an ambivalent but pragmatic diversion, paradoxically, employed to preserve the authority of the discourse since pragmatism is seen as a natural and rational feature of enlightened *human*.[8] The primary affirmation of this discourse is to maintain the power of producing and controlling it. Thus, associating with any party that contributes to maintain this existing power structure is a strategic imperative. The *New York Times* coverage of ban on women driving in Saudi Arabia also should be studied within this ambivalent liberal humanism. Even though the ban has generally been criticized as an Oriental irrationality, it has been unsubstantialized by connecting it to cultural, economic, and religious apparatus of an Islamic society. It is represented as an irrational counterpart of the represented subject. In the 1980s, the Saudi people's driving habit and Saudi Highways were given as an excuse for the driving ban on women:

> From a safety standpoint, the women might be better off not driving. Driving on Saudi highways is reminiscent of "dodge-em" cars in an amusement park. Cars drift from lane to lane without signaling. Left-hand turns from right-hand lanes are commonplace, and Saudi men approaching one another from opposite directions appear inclined to prove their masculinity by aiming directly at one another until one of them swerves away at the last moment. "It's the worst driving I've ever seen in my life," said an exasperated American living in Riyadh. "Cops? You see them, but they don't do a thing." (Martin 1982a, A2)

Nevertheless, it is worth mentioning that after 9/11, particularly in the first couple of years when the narrative of liberating Afghan women and bringing freedom to the Middle East was the common liberal fashion, the *New York Times* coverage of Saudi's ban on driving was extensive. However, after 2008, when the Iranian nuclear issue started dominating the news of the Middle

East, the repressive conditions of Saudi women were linked to the Islamic Republic as the following quote shows:

> The driving ban stems from universal anxiety over women's unrestrained mobility. In Saudi Arabia that anxiety is acute: the belong to men. Should women need to get around? she can do so in a taxi, with a chauffeur (there are 750,000 of them) or with a man related to her by marriage or blood behind the wheel. Although the Islamic Republic of Iran could not implement similarly draconian driving laws after the 1979 revolution, the theocratic regime did denounce women riding bikes or motorcycles as un-Islamic and sexually provocative. Iran's supreme leader, Ayatollah Ali Khamenei, proclaimed in 1999 that women must avoid anything that attracts strangers, so riding bicycles or motorcycles by women in public places involves corruption and is forbidden. (Milani 2011, A22)

Here, we can see the continuous Iran-centric criticism of the Middle East. The second Gulf War, the rise of Islamophobia after 911, and the restructuring of the Middle East, which brought a sectarian dichotomy of the Sunni and Shi'a, further strategically put the Middle East, the veil, and women in the center of an inimical liberal discourse for the *New York Times*, focusing on Iran and Iranian regime.

Iran and Women in the *New York Times*

In sharp contrast to Saudi Arabia, the *New York Times* representation of Iranian women and the veil, on the one hand, was an important image of oppression, brutality, and cruelty and, on the other hand, was the symbol of resistance, division, and criticism of the Iranian regime. Here, the enemy was clearly defined. Iran was an "Islamic Republic" ruled by the "anti-American" clerics. The institutionalized Orientalism, which is an important theoretical, cultural, economic, and political structure, divides the subjected societies into binaries of those who are oppressed and those who are oppressive. More than a cultural and theoretical representation of the Orient, it forms, maintains, and reinforces the foundation of Occidental power. It establishes consensuses to define the enemy within the economic and strategic vital interests of the Occident. Therefore, pressure must be maintained on the "enemy." This pressure is a natural ramification of construed *humanism* and "compassion" that institutionalized Orientalism produces within that established and dichotomous rationale. The *New York Times* liberal Orientalism is an important example. It manufactures conventional consensus, borrowing Noam Chomsky's terms, which is based on constructed liberal Orientalism and its well-institutionalized apparatuses. It constantly draws lines between the "good" and the "bad" within the conceptualized paradigm of "national security" and "Clash of Civilizations."

The Iranian women's veil, hijab or chador, was used as a weapon to criticize the Iranian regime. Hijab was called to be an oppressive tool at the hands of a tyrannical regime. Most of the reports in the first decade after the Islamic Revolution were about the harsh punishments of women who did not wear the veil. In a report, titled "Amid Hardship, Islamic Zeal Still Grips Iran," the *New York Times* wrote,

> Indeed, the covering of women has become almost a national obsession. Stores and restaurants in Teheran carry placards saying Islamic dress, meaning the hijab, or scarf-like head covering, must be worn. A kind of religious police, called the Anticorruption Organization, can fine shopkeepers for waiting on women without proper covering, and many stores keep a basket of spare scarves near the door. A few women can be seen on the sidewalks defiantly carrying a scarf in hand, shaking out their hair, between shopping stops.
>
> Women working in Government offices or private businesses are required to wear a kind of uniform of a long, dark smock-like garment that reaches below the knees; trousers or thick black stockings, and, needless to say, a thick, dark scarf that must be pulled forward so that no hair shows. Even this outfit is considered a little too racy for any place outside Teheran, where only the traditional black chador is seen.
>
> Government agencies are going through their personnel files and plucking out old identification photographs and replacing them with new pictures that show only a little bit of face. The scarf on the woman who reads the news on television has gotten noticeably longer. Air Iran flight attendants have been issued a sort of hooded cowl to top off their smocks, giving them a strangely medieval appearance as they stand at the door of a Boeing 747.
>
> The religious checker by the door of the Intercontinental Hotel refused to let a young woman into the lobby one recent morning, telling her that her scarf was "too thin."

The rules, and the behavior of self-appointed enforcers who challenge women for smoking or speaking to men, are not universally popular. "A living hell," said one well-educated Iranian woman on a Swissair flight from Teheran, one of the few flights by foreign carriers. Every woman on the plane pulled off her scarf as soon as the doors were closed and the air was thick with the smell of banana oil as they applied bright red nail polish. Multiple-Choice Tests on Islam. (Kifner 1982, A1)

This rhetoric increasingly continued and reiterated as a dominant theme throughout the aforementioned three decades:

This is a time of vehement intolerance in Iran, a backlash against the incremental loosening of clerical control over the last few years in the arenas of politics, education, the arts and social activities. Today, castigation comes not only through official channels but also in the form of free-lance attacks by the Partisans of the Party of God, shock troops devoted to the most puritanical Government factions. The atmosphere is inescapable. A new television program singles out specific writers and professors as Israeli spies or social misfits; the university system is being purged of "un-Islamic" elements whose loyalty to the revolution is deemed insufficient; professors who are considered dissenters have been beaten; publications are being shuttered, and the outdoor social season provoked a frenzy of raids on private celebrations.

Militants overrun areas where people tend to mingle with members of the opposite sex or engage in other suspect activities. Last year Chitgar, a sprawling 3,500-acre municipal park on Teheran's outskirts, brimmed with laughter. Women in baggy T-shirts and loose scarves, flaunting Islamic dress codes, often waited in the bicycle rental line for two hours.

Today the park's loudspeakers boom out repeatedly: "We ask our dear women to respect the Islamic code and we ask men and women to ride on their own paths."

In an unusual address broadcast nationwide, Ayatollah Khameini said that in the parks and cultural centers of a model Islamic capital, "the corrupt should find no refuge for degeneration."

Women are not the only targets. Two male students were recently detained in the park—one because his T-shirt contained too many Western images and the other because his long shorts left eight inches of calf exposed. "The police told me that if they saw me in the park again, they would send me someplace where neither I nor my bicycle would be found for 50 years," one said. (MacFarquhar 1996, A1)

And in another example in 2007, the same theme of "Islamic dress" as a symbol of oppression of Iranian regime is published:

> Violations of Islamic dress requirements for women are punishable by imprisonment. More than 800 women were arrested for dress code violations in Teheran, with many detained for wearing sunglasses. Women have been required by law since the 1979 Islamic revolution to cover their hair and wear long, loose clothing. Women were flogged, jailed and fined for what was considered immodest dress. (Fathi 2007, A6)

On the other hand, the pragmatic obsession with women's headscarf in Iran provided an important cultural, racial, and religious discourse for the *New York Times* to criticize the Iranian regime. As previously mentioned, I wish to concentrate on the use of discourses on reproduction of malignant Others. Representation is an important part of "Otherization" process. The power to represent a defined "Other" requires ideological and rhetorical strategies. By continuing its received antiregime notion, the main theme of the *New York Times*' coverage of Iran in the second and third decades after the revolution was to reconstruct a generalized, broad, and extensive discourse that illustrates division and revolt in Iran. Aligned with US liberal consensus, regarding Iran, there are many articles that present the dichotomy of women vs. Mullahs, ethnic and religious minorities vs. the ruling clerics, and, in general, Iranian people vs. Iranian regime. Although the oppression of the Iranian regime against its people cannot and should not be denied, the *New York Times*' overemphasis of division between people and regime was an important strategic method of dividing the enemy with a highly established narrative. Since the veil was declared an oppressive tool in the hands of the Iranian regime, it was useful to be portrayed as the source of resistance for the Iranian women against the regime:

> Several clashes between the vice squads and the public were reported, and a Western European diplomat was said to have been beaten on Sunday for refusing to allow the authorities to search his car. The crackdown, which began on Saturday, three days before the start of Muharram, the newspaper Salaam reported today. The hard-line daily, which called for "an unfailing

combat against social decadence," said 300 people had been arrested. In the 13-year revolution, perhaps no other issue has been debated with such fury as the rules for what constitutes "good hijab," or head covering. (Sciolino 1991, A8)

Another article provides more example of this rhetoric:

Hundreds of demonstrators in the city of Isfahan who were trying to prevent the arrest of women charged with wearing improper dress clashed with the Islamic security force known as the Komiteh on Friday, the newspaper Salaam reported today. The hard-line daily, which called for "an unfailing combat against social decadence," said 300 people had been arrested. Violations of Islamic dress requirements for women are punishable by imprisonment. and up to 70 lashes of the whip. They consist of showing one's hair or wearing sheer stockings or makeup. (Sciolino 1991, A8)

In another article, "Daughter of Revolution Fights the Veil," resisting the veil is individualized and presented as an opposition to the regime:

As a member of the ayatollah's family, Ms. Eshraghi is expected to embrace the trappings of the revolution and the Islamic Republic that followed. Nothing symbolizes the revolution more than the ankle-length black chador that covers all but a woman's face.

"I'm sorry to say that the chador was forced on women," she said over tea and cakes in her upscale apartment decorated in ornate furniture in northern Tehran. "Forced—in government buildings, in the school my daughter attends. This garment that was traditional Iranian dress was turned into a symbol of revolution. People have lost their respect for it. I only wear it because of my family status." Those are the words of a rebel. Ayatollah Khomeini called the chador the "the flag of the revolution," and early in the revolution of 1979 encouraged all women to wear it. Eventually, all women were forced to wear garments that cover their heads and hide the shape of their bodies.

Pale-eyed, with perfectly manicured eyebrows and slightly frosted hair, Ms. Eshraghi said she had always covered her hair in public—at least with a scarf—because of the dictates of Islam. She fought colleagues at the Interior Ministry, where she promotes women's issues, when they tried to force her to wear more modest dress and dark colors underneath her chador. Behind closed doors, she wears fitted pantsuits that do not conceal her full figure. (Sciolino 2003, A6)

Paradoxically, the "Other" is not only an established antithesis of the "civilized" and liberal West but also the concept that completes the ideological power of the West. It reinforces its "values," enables its authority to implement its strategies, reestablishes its binary structure, and divides the subject into friendly and inimical groups according to their stand to the dominated power's interests. The struggle of women with the regime in Iran is portrayed as a revolt of women against the Iranian government. Faiza Hashemi, daughter of the former Iranian president, Hashemi Rafsanjani, and Shrin Ebadi, the Nobel Peace laureate, were depicted as two liberal faces of the Iranian society. Not surprisingly, the *New York Times*' coverage of Shrin Ebadi depended on her stand in relation to US policies. While she is one of the important symbols of struggle for the Iranian people, in an editorial article, on 11 October 2003, she was called "A Champion of Iranian freedom" and praised for winning the Nobel Peace Prize:

> Shirin Ebadi, who won the Nobel Peace Prize yesterday, is not particularly well known outside Iran, where she is one of the country's most persistent champions of human rights. Yet the selection of this courageous Muslim woman by the Nobel committee will probably have worldwide impact. Ms. Ebadi was one of the first women to serve as a judge in Iran, before Ayatollah Ruhollah Khomeini banned women from the bench. Throughout her distinguished career she has upheld the principle that Islamic faith is compatible with the rule of law, and in particular with the rights of women, children and outspoken intellectuals. Honoring her will encourage millions in the Islamic world who share that belief.
>
> Iran's disheartened reformers are encouraged by her selection, while conservatives complain about what they call a nefarious European plot to promote human rights in Iran. Although the Nobel committee's choice came as a surprise to most outside observers, the choice of Ms. Ebadi upholds the finest traditions of previous prize winners who peacefully struggled against repressive regimes, like Lech Walesa, Aung San Suu Kyi and Archbishop Desmond Tutu. If honoring her efforts advances the human rights of all Iranians, so much the better. ("A Champion of Iranian Freedom" 2003, A14)

However, after Ebadi criticized the United States in her Nobel Peace Prize acceptance speech, she was linked to "political Islam" and Iranian regime in another article by the *New York Times*:

In her acceptance speech, Ms. Ebadi reserved her strongest reproach for the United States, declaring that "some states have violated the universal principles and laws of human rights by using the events of Sept. 11 and the war on international terrorism as a pretext." Ms. Ebadi offered only oblique criticism of Iran's conservative Islamic government. Many Iranian exiles have complained that by awarding the prize to a woman working within the legal system in Iran, the Nobel Foundation is supporting political Islam over a secular alternative in the country. Indeed, the Iranian government has taken Ms. Ebadi's prize as an opportunity to showcase recent reforms and put the best possible light on the position held by women there. (Smith 2003, A20)

The above article shows that the propaganda of power, as aforementioned Foucauldian concept of "tactical elements of force" illustrates, creates different discourses within the same strategy. It is a circular "relation" of discourses and in the path of this relation, contradicted discourses are constructed, and then destroyed, and reconstructed again. Good, bad, moderate, and extremist are defined by their acts and stands in relation to the policies and interests of the power or particular ideological discourse that is produced and reproduced within the structure of power.

Conclusion

The existing representation of Islam and Muslim women in the *New York Times* is an ideological discourse, which was constructed and reinforced through dichotomy of the West vs. the East. Important divergences within this unified discourse illustrate some certain strategic patterns that constructed differences in relation to the matrix of power for a particular place and in a particular time period. It is based on uncertainty that illustrates disavowal of certain liberal "standards" for one place and strict inquiry of the same "standards" in another place. This ambiguity is a product of the *New York Times* reliance on ideological and strategic institutions that provide discursive power for it. It should be pointed out that the reporters and writers might claim "objectivity and independence," which is comprehensible within that standardized discourse of "objectivity" and its relations to US power structure. However, the *New York Times*' discourse of Islam and Middle East produces and reproduces an ideology that should be studied and explained in terms of national security, the US interests in the region, public opinion, and American values. The American journalism's subliminal understanding of its connection with US power structure might be explained within the notion of patriotic Americanism. As Roger Cohen said in a conversation with the author, the *New York Times* is an American outlet and of course has an "American bias."[9] But the point that Cohen failed to mention is that this is an ideological bias. A conditional bias within the established garb of objectivity. The bias is originated and reproduced by a self-claimed righteous ideology that is culminated in a fixed set of American-centric values. Thus, the multiple discourses that are employed by the *New York Times* in representation of women in Saudi Arabia and Iran can be easily explained within this ideological American centrism, which echoes changes in political and economic interests of the United States in differentt countries and at different periods of time.

Notes

1. See Tanzeen Doha's chapter in this volume for an analysis of an anti-Islamic discourse that is produced by the *New York Times*.
2. See Paul Fitzgerald and Elizabeth Gould's (2009) book, *The Invisible History: Afghanistan's Untold Story* and Steve Coll's (2004) book, *Ghost Wars: The Secret History of the CIA, Afghanistan, and Bin Laden, from the Soviet Invasion to September 10, 2001*, for further information on US support of Afghan Mujahidin against the Soviets in the 1980s.
3. See Beinin (2003), "The Israelization of American Middle East Policy Discourse," for Israelization of US policies of the Middle East.
4. See Said's (1979) *Orientalism*.
5. See Lena Meari's chapter in this volume.
6. See Tanzeen Doha's chapter in this volume.
7. In September 2017, the Saudi King, Salman, issued a decree lifting the ban on women driving in Saudi Arabia.
8. See Edward Said's (1997) *Covering Islam: How the Media and the Experts Determine How We See the Rest of the World*.
9. I discussed the different patterns that the *New York Times* followed covering Saudi Arabia vs. Iran at a semiofficial meeting with Roger Cohen, foreign affairs columnist of the *New York Times* on 23 April 2013 in Davis, California.

References

"A Champion of Iranian Freedom." 2003. *New York Times*, 11 October: A14.

Beinin, Joel. 2003. "The Israelization of American Middle East Policy Discourse." *Social Text* 21 (2): 125–39.

Coll, Steve. 2004. *Ghost Wars: The Secret History of the CIA, Afghanistan, and Bin Laden, from the Soviet Invasion to September 10, 2001*. New York: Penguin Press.

Doha, Tanzeen. Forthcoming. "Specters of Islam: Anti-Islamist (Re)Presentations in Secular Media and Feminism, 1979–2011." In *Reporting Islam: Muslim Women in the New York Times*, edited by Suad Joseph.

Fathi, Nazila. 2007. "Enforcing a Single Hue for Islamic Fashion in Iran: Black." *New York Times*, 4 May: A6.

Fitzgerald, Paul, and Elizabeth Gould. 2009. *Invisible History: Afghanistan's Untold Story*. San Francisco, CA: City Lights Books.

Foucault, Michel. 1980. *The History of Sexuality*, vol. 1. Translated by Robert Hurley. New York: Vintage.

Gupte, Pranay B. 1981. "Saudi Men Still Hold Firm Rein, But Women Have Easier Time." *New York Times*, 13 May: C1.

Ibrahim, Youssef M. 1990. "Mideast Tensions; Saudi Tradition: Edicts from Koran Produce Curbs on Women." *New York Times*, 7 November: A18.

"Iran's Police Begin a Dress-Code Drive as Complaints Rise." 1993. *New York Times*, 23 June: A4.

Kifner, John. 1982. "Amid Hardship, Islamic Zeal Still Grips Iran." *New York Times*, 21 April: A1.

Kifner, John. 1983. "Cracks in the Wall of Khomeini's Power." *New York Times*, 25 April: A2.

Kristof, Nicholas D. 2002. "Saudis in Bikinis." *New York Times*, 25 October: A35.

MacFarquhar, Neil. 1996. "Backlash of Intolerance Stirring Fear in Iran." *New York Times*, 20 September: A1–12.

Martin, Douglas. 1982a. "Saudi Craze for Cars Is both a Blessing and a Blight." *New York Times*, 22 January: A2.

Martin, Douglas. 1982b. "Saudi Banks for Women Thriving." *New York Times*, 27 January: D1.

Meari, Lena. Forthcoming. "The Material Life of Representation: 'Veiled Muslim Women' in the *New York Times*, 1980–2011." In *Reporting Islam: Muslim Women in the New York Times*, edited by Suad Joseph.

Milani, Farzaneh. 2011. "Saudi Arabia's Freedom Riders." *New York Times*, 13 June: A23.

Sachs, Susan. 2000. "Saudi Mall-Crawlers Shop Till Their Veils Drop." *New York Times*, 5 December: A4.

Said, Edward. 1979. *Orientalism*. New York: Vintage Books.

Said, Edward. 1997. *Covering Islam: How the Media and the Experts Determine How We See the Rest of the World*. New York: Pantheon Books.

Sciolino, Elaine. 1985a. "Saudi Women Start to Peek from Behind the Veil." *New York Times*, 13 April: 1.2.

Sciolino, Elaine. 1985b. "Ideas & Trends; Saudi Arabia's Gospel Columnists." *New York Times*, 5 May: A9.

Sciolino, Elaine. 1991. "300 Arrests Reported in Iran in a Clash over Dress Code." *New York Times*, 30 July: A8.

Sciolino, Elaine. 2003. "Daughters of Revolution Fight the Veil." *New York Times*, 2 April: A6.

Smith, Craig S. 2003. "In Speech, Nobel Winner Rebukes the U.S." *New York Times*, 11 December: A20.

Spurr, David. 1993. *The Rhetoric of Empire: Colonial Discourse in Journalism, Travel Writing, and Imperial Administration*. Durham, NC: Duke University Press.

Taubman, Philip. 1997. "The Courageous Women of Iran." *New York Times*, 26 December: A38.

6

The Islamic World Is Flat(tened): Contesting Islam in South Asia in the *New York Times*, 1980–2011

Rajbir Singh Judge

Introduction

The *New York Times* generates a particular reality about the South Asian subcontinent that evokes colonial tropes about the plight of women that have been continually produced and reproduced in the public sphere since the nineteenth century. In this essay, I argue that just as the media, including the *New York Times*, played an essential role in the contestation over Hindu tradition that legitimated colonial ideology in the late nineteenth century, the *New York Times* from 1980 to 2011 functioned as a key site in the contestation over and clash with the Islamic tradition that was, and continues to be, central to American interests within Pakistan and Bangladesh.[1] Rather than centering how "traditions, when vital, embody continuities of conflict," the *New York Times* privileges a certain reading of Islam in order to provide a "correct" and "objective" narrative of that tradition—a moderate and liberal Islam that follows a unilinear temporality associated with a liberal secular logic that legitimates a capitalist order of things (MacIntyre 1981, 222).[2] Those who are believed to follow this reading of Islam, rendered as a stage associated with the end of history, become the custodians and legitimate voices of the entire tradition in contrast to the "other" Muslims who are deemed ideological, fundamentalist, and barbaric.

Central to the contestation of both the Islamic tradition from 1980 to 2011 and Hindu tradition in the nineteenth century was the suffering of women in which the veil and sati became signifiers of the oppressive constraints of tradition contra liberal freedom and tolerance. However, women within this discourse, as Lata Mani argues, were "neither subjects nor even the primary objects of concern" but rather were "the ground for a complex and competing set of struggles" over what constituted the tradition (1998, 2). Through this process, various features and practices located within specific traditions, such as the veil, became, as Mani writes, "potent signifiers" for the oppression of all women within the society (2)—a point scholars have ably traced (Ahmad 2009; Abu Lughod 2013; Scott 2007). The *New York Times* plays a central role in cementing these signifiers or, as Amira Jarmakani writes, "cultural mythologies" about the plight of women because newspapers, alongside other forms of media, do not simply reflect the certainty of the discourse but actively produce an "objective" reality through representations of history, culture, and religion (Abu Lughod 2013; Jarmakani 2008; Mani 1998; McLarney 2015; Mitchell 1988 Said 1979).

This essay explores these contestations over tradition by examining the bifurcation between liberal and fundamentalist Islam (good Muslims and bad Muslims) that the *New York Times* perpetuates. I argue that this Good Muslim/Bad Muslim discursive frame of the *New York Times* echoes centuries earlier discursive constructions that hinged on the veil and sati. Indeed, women function as the lynchpin of this discourse: they are neither subjects nor objects but the grounds of this debate. Within South Asia, this binary between liberal and fundamentalist Islam is mirrored in the binary posed between Pakistan and Bangladesh—a binary that is rooted in a racialized construction of a Middle Eastern Islam against an Indic cosmopolitan religious milieu. Such renderings by the *New York Times*, I argue, are premised on a temporalized historicity in which a secular becoming displaces a Muslim backwardness; and the success of such a displacement hinges on the outcome of the civilizational war between liberal good Muslims against fundamentalist "bad" Muslims. However, the success of "liberal" Muslims and the danger of "fundamentalist" Muslims continually shift according to particular historical circumstances. My essay historicizes key nodal points and ruptures, such as the rise of the Islamic Republic of Iran, the end of the Cold War, and 9/11 that altered the marking of this civilizational war within the discourse of the *New York Times* from 1980 to 2011.

My argument, it should be noted, explores the liberal impulses and those nettlesome silent referents within the discursive frame of the *New York Times* that legitimated changing state discourses and material interests from 1980 to 2011 (Abu Lughod 2013, 86). Even though the media, as Ellen McLarney contends, "sees itself as 'both autonomous and sovereign with respect to the state,' the verbatim reiterations of state discourse on Islamic totalitarianism and American freedoms betray a 'structural blindness to the material conditions of the discourses it produces and circulates'" (2011, 11). In this respect, the media, including the *New York Times*, works as a "hall of mirrors" that produces and reproduces justifications for the material interests of the state that impede the enunciation of a political subjectivity outside the framework of liberal secular democracy (McLarney 2011). Of course, the *New York Times* often presents multiple narratives, and at times contradictory, of the role of women within Pakistan and Bangladesh. Yet a certain conception of the human subject that privileges freedom and autonomy within singular progressive notions of historical time is the silent referent for these contradictions. The only political possibilities then are either to be liberated from the shackles of fundamentalism through an engagement with neoliberal secular politics that are presumed to grant women agency or to remain outside the purview of history and bound within patriarchy and tradition.

Temporal Shifts

Such employment onto the geographies of South Asia has differed depending on the geopolitical situation within a specific historical moment. Following Hakeem Naim's work in this volume, I trace these shifting representations for two nation-states: Bangladesh and Pakistan. A key rupture within this representational framework occurred in 1979 after the formation of the Islamic Republic of Iran.[3] After 1979 and into the early 1990s, the *New York Times* began to link Pakistan closely both geographically and temporally with Iran. The *New York Times* represented this assumed move "backward" to a fundamentalist Islamic politics through the prism of gender relations that signaled oppression and the inability for democracy to flower. In contrast, throughout the 1980s and into the 1990s, Bangladesh was considered more likely to experience the blossoming of a liberal secular democracy due to its nascent neoliberal economic policies and its ethnic Bengali heritage understood as marked by secular nationalism. This grounding of Bangladesh within a secular milieu gestured toward the possibility of gender equality. The complex political positions and negotiations of the two political figures that emerged within this discourse, Khaleda Zia, the prime minister of Bangladesh from 1991 to 1996 and 2001 to 2006, and Benazir Bhutto, the prime minister of Pakistan from 1988 to 1990 and 1993 to 1996, within their politics and the dynamism of Islam within the political landscape of the two nations were ignored in favor of a singular focus on their gender and the constitution of a liberal "good" Islam.

In the early 1990s the presumed inability of Bhutto and Zia to fully "liberalize" their traditions led to a backlash highlighted by the controversy over the publication of Taslima Nasreen's novel Lajja [Shame] in Bangladesh. These disappointments and other perceived failures of Zia and Bhutto led to the representations of Islam within Bangladesh and Pakistan as fundamentally irrational because of the failure of their respective secular nationalist projects that were manifested most clearly in the bodies of Zia and Bhutto. This failure of liberal political projects in Bangladesh and Pakistan supposedly exposed the fundamental divide between civilizations—Muslim and the liberal West—that was also reproduced within the work of Bernard Lewis (1990) and Samuel Huntington (1993). The *New York Times*, following these analyses and drawing upon earlier colonial Orientalist discourses, posited that the populations of Pakistan and Bangladesh were engaged within a micro-civilizational warfare that had become constitutive of politics in the post-Cold War period.

However, at the end of the 1990s and through the millennial years, the "success" of neoliberal economic policies within Bangladesh coupled later with a shift in global interests of the United States after 9/11 that emphasized macro-level civilizational warfare in order to impede the supposed specter of Islamic terrorism led to a reassertion of the gentler Islam of Bangladesh contra the harshness of Pakistan's. This image of Bangladesh was measured through its proximity to India's image as a flawed, but leading example of women's autonomy within South Asia. Bangladesh emerged once again as home to "good Muslims" since they became grounded in a colonized Indian Bengali milieu who had possibilities of gender freedom contra the "bad Muslims" of Pakistan who remained mired in the haze of Islam and patriarchy (Mamdani 2004).

Pakistan in the 1980s to Early 1990s

Islamization of Pakistan

At the beginning of the decade, the *New York Times* rendered General Mohammad Zia-ul-Haq, the head of state of Pakistan from 1978 until his untimely death in 1988, as the prototypical Oriental despot who "tells hard truths with mischievous eyes, practical wisdom and a smile beneath his mustache" who ushered in the age of Islamic politics into Pakistan ("Pakistan After Zia" 1988, A1). In an article entitled "Backward March in Pakistan" published on 19 October 1979, the *New York Times* decried General Zia's decrees that suggested "the intensely Islamic president is in some ways emulating the 'Islamic Republic' that is being constructed in neighboring Iran" (A34). The article continued,

> Americans should be saddened by these blows to freedom in a friendly nation. The evolution toward democracy was far from complete during the [Zulfikar Ali] Bhutto interlude of civilian government. But it is now clear that General Zia has put the process into full reverse. ("Backward March in Pakistan" 1979, A34)

The Islamic politics of General Zia, according to the *New York Times*, derailed the evolution of Pakistan within the historical timeline enunciated by West and actively inverted the nation into a noncontemporaneous mode, which violated its liberal inheritance and temporal uplifting from British colonial rule. However, though the *New York Times* throughout the 1980s raised the specter of the Islamization and Islamic policies that would be forced upon women, the threat of Islamization was coupled with the hope of liberal Islam—Pakistan could never become fundamentalist within the discursive framing of the *New York Times*. Pakistan had the civilizational capacity to challenge or slow down the process of Islamization, which meshed with its strategic importance during the Cold War as an ally of the United States in which the United States looked to Pakistan as a bulwark against the Soviets.

Yet the threat of Islam remained. For example, one article examined how Islamic politics rendered Pakistan "backward" through a focus on women's autonomy, a focus that is evident in Frank Prial's article "As Pakistan 'Islamizes,' Feminists Rise Up in Anger" published on 8 November 1980. The article, which begins with an anecdote about women forcefully being segregated to eat in different quarters than the men, reads,

> The unexpected segregation was yet another step toward what has been called the Islamization of Pakistan, a process that many feminists here predict will set back, if not destroy the cause of women's rights in this traditionally male-dominated Moslem county. (Prial 1980, 2)

The theme of being "set back" through the process of Islamization continues with the next section of the same article entitled "Rumors of a Backward Step" that argues,

> Of concern at present is the persistent rumor that the Government plans to repeal what amounts to a bill of rights for Pakistani women, the Family Laws Ordinance of 1961. The Islamic Ideology Council, which has no lawmaking power, has endorsed repeal with but one dissenting vote, that of its lone women member. Both the Law Ministry and Religious Affairs Ministry have reportedly recommended repeal. Both ministers have denied this and so has the President." One can't be sure," said a woman who attended the Lahore dinner. "It's not difficult to see what direction the conservatives want to take." (Prial 1980, 2)

The course of history that Pakistan takes, plotted through the coordinates of gender and freedom, is marked by regression into a previous mode of being that is correlated with an "Islamic society," in which progress is only possible through state-sanctioned rights.

> Yet the possibility for equality within Islam remains possible—though what is calculated as a "good" Islam. This liberal Islam appears in the article in the voice of Rashida Patel, who argues:

> "There is a strong ongoing effort to take away what we've won in the last 20 years, which isn't much," said Rashida Patel, a feminist and Karachi lawyer. "But educated women here will not brook any pushing back of any kind." Mrs. Patel, who has written a book, "Women and Law in Pakistan," insists that Mohammed, the founder of Islam, demanded equal rights for both sexes and that the severe repression of women that characterized latter-day Islam was and is a distortion of the Prophet's teaching and the Koran. (Prial 1980, 2)

In Patel's interview, Islam emerges with two distinct possibilities—a continuation and, thus, a temporal stagnation, of latter-day repressive Islam or the possibility of moving forward toward an ideal Islam marked by "rights." Islam, embedded within a historical timeline that finds its telos within liberal rights, then emerges within this narrative as needing to strive toward its teleological end, a stage that would end repression that marked "Islamic society," eliminating contestations on what constitutes both ethical and virtuous behavior.

However, in Steven R. Weisman's article "The 'Islamization' of Pakistan: Still Moving Slowly and Still Stirring Debate" that emerged six years later, there was a recognition that though "Pakistan started to make its laws conform with the teachings of Islam, religious and political leaders agree that the changes in the country have been largely marginal or cosmetic" (Weisman 1986a, 10). Moreover, these changes did not significantly alter the lives of women either as Weisman noted:

> Fears among some that all women would be forced to wear veils have also not come true … The practice of purdah, or covering the face, is common among women in most towns and urban neighborhoods. But women in the upper classes and in rural areas, where most people live, appear to have been unaffected … "The day-to-day life of most women is no different than it was," said Abida Hussain, a Member of Parliament. "As a woman who moves around in public, I am probably stared at more today than I was 10 years ago." (Weisman 1986a, 10)

Though Prial and Weisman note that many of the problems identified by the *New York Times* did not resonate within the Pakistani landscape, Pakistan still remained framed as moving toward a dangerous Islamization. This dual image of Pakistan, as a country near Iran, yet also against the Soviet Union, played out through multiple contradictions within the discourse of the *New York Times*. For example, as we learn in Weisman's article, the practice of purdah is common within towns and urban areas, and upper-class women and women in rural areas have remained unaffected. Nevertheless, the fear of Islamization, intimately interwoven with the veil, though acknowledged to have little material foundation throughout the 1980s, remained central for the *New York Times*. The trope of Islamization, of which the veil became a key image, was a potent marker of the possible threat that "fundamentalist" Islam posed to the becoming of the liberal subject in Pakistan.

Yet, though articulating the relative nonexistence of the intense Islamization marked by the veil, the article remained centered upon how the rights women attained could be encroached within the assumed patriarchal tradition of Islam. Weisman continued,

> "Women have always been the greatest sufferers in the enforcement of their rights in this country," said Hina Jilani, a lawyer and activist in the 450-member Women's Action Forum in Lahore. "Now we are about to take another step backward." ... Among the laws Miss Jilani said would be rescinded are curbs on a man's power to decree a divorce by himself or take a second wife. She assailed the advocates of such changes as "fanatics and obscurantists who don't think about what is beneficial for society." (Weisman 1986a, 10)

Even though General Zia's policies did not result in the fervent Islamization that the *New York Times* imagined, Pakistan is still construed as taking another step backward into its traditional Islamic heritage in which women, then, are continuously oppressed. Because Jilani occupies a temporal space of the liberal subject as a lawyer and rights activist, her analysis of Pakistan—in which Islamization is imminent and women will be oppressed—takes on an objectivity and concrete reality not granted to the Islamic scholars who are also interviewed within Weisman's article. She becomes, to follow Lila Abu-Lughod, a protagonist who does not "want to remain trapped in their strange and sordid worlds" (2013, 88). Whereas she provides an analysis that examines what is beneficial for society as a whole, others within the article are engaging only in blind ritual or fundamentalism. By constructing alternatives to Jilani's feminism in this manner, the specific practices of the 450-member Women's Action Forum become the legitimate agentival political expression of women within Pakistan.[4]

Benazir Bhutto

At the end of the 1980s, Benazir Bhutto emerged as a political challenger to Zia's alleged Islamizing government and within the frame of the *New York Times* came to represent the liberal custodian of the "correct" Islam. Gender remained the key site within which Pakistan's politics were staged. Bhutto emerged within this staging of the *New York Times* as a politician who, in order to be elected, would have to overcome and challenge the patriarchal presuppositions of fundamentalist Islam in order to propel Pakistan forward into democracy. Unlike General Zia who was associated with Iran, Bhutto is associated with South Asia:

> Here in South Asia, women have long been subordinate to men, with lower health and literacy rates. But there is also ample precedent of female heirs to political dynasties ... The most powerful was Prime Minister Indira Gandhi of India, who was assassinated in 1984. She was the daughter of Prime Minister Jawaharlal Nehru and mother of the current Prime Minister, Rajiv Gandhi. Women have also picked up the standards of their husbands or fathers in Sri Lanka and Bangladesh. (Weisman 1986b, A2)

Though within the *New York Times* there remains a distance between India and the West because of a long history of "subordination," Bhutto's placement within a genealogy of South Asian women politics that have women heirs to their political familial dynasties provides optimism for progress in Pakistan.

Yet, as another Weisman article from 25 August 1986, entitled "For Bhutto, a Big Issue Is Her Sex," relays, Bhutto is located within Pakistan, which is tied to patriarchy. Paradoxically, as Weisman notes, "in a country where men still tend to consider most women weak and ineffective, the most popular and charismatic opposition leader is a 33-year-old woman whose fiery oratory has brought cheers from millions of men" (Weisman 1986b, A2). Another Weisman article, "The Return of Benazir Bhutto: Struggle in Pakistan," published on 21 September 1986, states,

> In an Islamic state in which women are generally expected to be subservient, the 33-year-old unmarried woman, educated at Radcliffe and Oxford universities, has established herself as Pakistan's most popular opposition leader—indeed its most popular politician. (Weisman 1986c, A40)

These contradictions within the *New York Times*—though men considered women "weak and ineffective" and women are expected to be "subservient" while simultaneously "millions of men" supported her and she was the most popular opposition leader—existed because the *New York Times* reduced Bhutto and Pakistani politics to the logic of gender relations. Rather than presenting the complexity of Bhutto's relations with the public through the various political negotiations that Bhutto engaged in, the *New York Times* remained focused on her gender.

The key site for debates of Bhutto's gender emerged in the *New York Times* through the *New York Times* representation of the aforementioned Islamic scholars. The *New York Times* reported in 1986, "Islamic religious leaders have been debating the suitability of a woman as a leader of Pakistan" (Weisman 1986b, A2). The focus on the Islamic clergy is a theme that occurs throughout the *New York Times*, for example, in an article cited earlier, "The 'Islamization' of Pakistan: Still Moving Slowly and Still Stirring Debate," where a Karachi politician in an interview with the *New York Times* argued that "Pakistan is simply not a conservative or orthodox country ... The clergy has pushed this agenda to advance its own power" (Weisman 1986a, 10). Yet, the examples that the *New York Times* utilizes show that Islamic clergy had complex understandings of gender that defied the *New York Time*'s notions of simple discussions about the suitability of Bhutto as a prime minister or a power grab through an Islamic fundamentalist discourse. Weisman's article, "For Bhutto, a Big Issue Is Her Sex," goes on to note that

> One scholar in Lahore cited an old teaching that a state led by a woman would court misfortune. But another scholar countered that this did not matter because Miss Bhutto sought to become head of the government as Prime Minister, not head of state as President. (Weisman 1986b, A2)

Islamic scholars were debating within the parameters of the Islamic discursive tradition the complexities of gender relations that were also continually negotiated impinged by relations of power cultivated within secular modernity—there was no set policy that could be implemented by an "Islamic fundamentalist" nor would Benazir Bhutto by the virtue of her election "liberalize" and "reform" gender relations within Islam; instead, the issue was contested within the Islamic tradition itself.

Yet, within the *New York Times*, there emerged a priori assumptions about Islamic orthodoxy as fundamentalism, in which there is a refusal to recognize the dynamic nature of orthodoxy. The Islamic clergy did not act upon its audience and impose "fundamentalism" upon the Pakistanis, but rather the attempt to obtain orthodoxy, as Talal Asad (1993) shows quite forcefully, is a "collaborative achievement between narrator and audience," therefore, "the former cannot speak in total freedom"—a challenge to the depictions of manipulation that are employed when discussing Islamic reform/change (210). The discursive framing within the *New York Times*, however, disregarded new political formations and struggles over orthodoxy that have their own rational coherence, and instead produced narratives that foregrounded the presumed static and fixed irrationality and patriarchy of Islam within the geographic space of Pakistan that Bhutto had to contend against.

Bangladesh in the 1980s to Early 1990s

Neoliberalization of Bangladesh

In contrast to Pakistan, Bangladesh's specific historical moment in the 1980s was marked not by closeness to the Islamic Republic of Iran but rather by increasing neoliberal economic policies. These policies centered around autonomous choices that women could harness in order to break the constraints of Islamic tradition and poverty. For example, Seth Mydans' article "In Bangladesh, Women Can't Go Home Again," relays,

> Shafia Khatun has made a pioneering journey from rural poverty to a low-paying job in a crowded garment factory, and she may never be able to go home again ... Part of a small new industry fueled by American imports, she and 200,000 other women have defied Islamic tradition and planted the seeds of a slow social transformation in this nation. (Mydans 1988, A8)

Mydans celebrates the increasing neoliberal policies of Bangladesh that opened the economy to investments and made the market an ethos because even though Khatun's labor was exploited in a garment factory, she was free to sell her labor on her terms, thus breaking the hold of Islamic tradition and instituting a social revolution. Mydans continues with this point and cites

> Roushan Jahan, a scholar who has researched the new phenomenon of women workers, said factory owners sometimes lock their doors to keep women at their places for overtime work. She said the women often have too little schooling to compute the wages due them and are frequently shortchanged. Deepening poverty and landlessness throughout the country

has forced a compromise with cultural norms, said Mrs. Jahan. In traditional Bangladesh, women are in effect the property of their fathers or husbands. They receive less education, less food and poorer health care than their brothers. (Mydans 1988, A8)

The image that emerges in the article posits that the inability of women to sell their labor more effectively, which led to poverty, stemmed from tradition (less schooling) rather than the exploitative practices of the garment industry and deregulation. Even though poverty deepened because of the neoliberalization of the Bangladeshi economy, the article frames neoliberal policies as a form of progress because of their undoing of a traditional Bangladesh that beckoned in a new hopeful stage of history. The key to this rupturing of Bangladeshi history is the place of property in the collectivity. Whereas in traditional Bangladesh, women are conceptualized as property and bound within a family unit, within the marketplace, women become self-governing subjects (individuals) that are able to sell their property, their labor (Asad 2009, 28). Neoliberal policies and the opening of new markets, therefore, according to the discourse of the *New York Times*, annihilated traditional values for the better and opened the possibility for the emergence of an autonomous liberal subject in Bangladesh and, thus, progress—even though the reification observed might itself be a mirror (McLarney 2015, 247).

Though these neoliberal policies in Bangladesh were also accompanied by the declaration of Islam as the official religion in Bangladesh, Islamization was not framed as a threat as it was in Pakistan because Bangladesh was located spatially and temporally within a colonized Bengali heritage rather than a frontier Middle Eastern one. For example, Barbara Crossette's article "Official Islam Proving Gentler in Bangladesh" puts forth that

Bangladeshis say, a continuing religious harmony can be credited to the mitigating influences of Bengali culture, a Bengali political sagacity and the gentler tropical atmosphere that distinguishes Muslim Bangladesh from the harsher, colder desert and mountain nations of West Asia and the Middle East. Among Muslim-majority nations, Bangladesh has more in common with Indonesia, the southern Philippines or Malaysia than with Pakistan, the country of which it was once part. Here the warm evening air is often filled with music; the songs of the Indian poet Rabindranath Tagore are favorites. (1990, A17)

Crossette's article, "Bangladeshis Keep the Hard Edge off Islam," posits similar points:

> Though part of Pakistan from 1947 until 1971, Bangladesh, where 85 percent of the people are Muslim, feels little kinship for the harsher, more uncompromising, frontier brand of Islam found there, in Afghanistan and Iran. The cultural links that are most important to many Bangladeshis are those with the Indian state of West Bengal, where music and poetry flourish. Rabindranath Tagore, an Indian writer and educator known throughout the world, is a cultural hero. (1991a, A11)

The key to this Islam rendered gentler and private is the uncovered women's body made visible through unveiling within an open marketplace. Crossette continues and relays that "women in brilliantly colored saris, walk with their heads uncovered in public. Unlike in Pakistan, alcohol is sold and served openly" (Crossette 1991a, A11). The tolerance and gentleness that becomes constitutive of modern Bangladeshi culture and climate renders it vastly different than the harsher and closed Middle East and Pakistan. Instead its climate creates an acceptable liberal Islam that values openness and autonomy in which Islam is rendered a cultural heritage rather than a political challenge.[5]

This shift of religion into cultural specificity occurred in Bangladesh as it enters the historical timeline of the West through the sublation of religion into nationalism. According to an article in the *New York Times*, this occurred with the break from Pakistan in 1971:

> When Bengal was split along Hindu-Muslim lines in 1947, what is now Bangladesh became a distant part of Islamic Pakistan. In 1971, putting Bengali nationalism ahead of religion, Bangladeshis opted for a precarious independence instead, and slid rapidly into hopeless underdevelopment. (Crossette 1993, E9)

Bangladesh emerges as marked by a "temporal competence" it garnered through the alleged successes of the colonial project in Bengal and its radical break in 1971 with the desolate and unchanging image of the Middle East that within this narrative also railroaded Pakistan's foray into modernity (Bannerjee 2006, 4).[6]

Moreover, Bangladesh's "hopeless underdevelopment," that the *New York Times* alluded to, was negated because of the neoliberal "successes" and the perceived openness of Islam within Bangladesh, which then led the *New York Times* to note that

> Officials at the World Bank, in the Bush Administration and in private organizations no longer call Bangladesh a "basket case." Over the last five or six years ... Bangladesh has shown that progress can be made in critical areas of economic and social development with very slender resources ... In South Asia, Bangladesh is gaining a reputation as the most innovative and receptive nation in making use of grass-roots organizations, like the rural Grameen Bank movement, which gives support to village entrepreneurs. (Crossette 1992, A8)

Employing the rhetoric of progress, the *New York Times* placed Bangladesh within a narrative in which, as Scott notes in a different context, "the future overcomes the past, and in which the present is a state of expectation and waiting for the fulfillment of the promise of social and political improvement" (Scott 2014, 5). In order to overcome, Bangladesh required a break with the past, which necessitated the reconstitution of tradition, through a process, labeled innovation, that ruptured older forms of subjectivity and created forms that functioned with ease within the new economic paradigm of neoliberalism that proliferated within the 1980s and early 1990s, for example, "the grassroots women" (Grewal and Bernal 2014, 17).

Khaleda Zia

This new woman is celebrated within this discourse because of the break with tradition in which NGOs and neoliberalism play crucial roles. One article on the Grameen Bank highlights this role:

> The salute reflects steps taken by the Grameen Bank to improve the outlook and habits of its mostly female borrowers and to achieve what it maintains is an extraordinary 98 percent rate of loan repayments ... Despite their subordinate role in this Moslem society, 74 percent of Grameen borrowers are women. "Women are better clients in terms of repayment, and in terms of the objectives of the bank, the alleviation of poverty," Mr. Huq said. "We have found that poverty, hunger and disease are primarily women's issues." (Mydans 1987, E3)

Even the key to Khaleda Zia's politics became intimately intertwined with the success of neoliberal NGO policies as the success of NGOs and the "renown of the Grameen bank" functioned as "a form of governmentality" (Karim 2011, 188). An article states,

> Prime Minister Zia has benefitted from the help of strong Bangladeshi nongovernmental development organizations, which even in the Ershad years managed to steer clear of the pervasive official corruption that weakened or paralyzed government aid projects. (Crossette 1993, E9)

Whereas governmental aid projects are petrified and frozen by corruption mimicking the representation of Islam within Orientalist discourse, freedom and gender equality become constitutive of neoliberal NGOs and stable governance.

Khaleda Zia emerged within this framing, much like Bhutto, as a liberal custodian for the tradition. However, unlike Bhutto, Zia's role as the custodian of Islamic tradition did not require her to reconstitute the tradition but rather continue to uphold a gentler liberal Islam in the face of the constant threat posed by Islamic fundamentalism to women's rights. For example, in Crossette's article, "Conversations: Khaleda Zia: A Woman Leader for a Land That Defies Islamic Stereotypes," the interviewer relays that

> Although a militant Islamic fringe tries to curb the public role of women, Prime Minister Zia, the daughter of a provincial businessman and a prominent social worker, is confident that Bangladeshis will reject the fundamentalist message. (1993, E9)

Within this narrative, Zia embodied the position of the Bangladeshi nation of itself—a liberal Islam trying to fend off a militant Islamic fringe.[7] For example, the interviewer represents Zia as "born in an Asian Islamic milieu, not a Middle Eastern one," and that she ruled over a country that was "a Muslim-majority country largely without the chador or the system of purdah that keeps women secluded" and where "both the Prime Minister and the leader of the opposition, Sheik Hasina Wazed, are women, as are at least 10 percent of the members of Parliament" (Crossette 1993, E9). The lack of the veil, which leads to the emergence of women in the public sphere, is, once again, directly correlated to the culture of Bengal contra a Middle Eastern one.[8]

Bangladeshi women within this framing became differentiated from Pakistan's because of their presumed ability to engage freely within a rational public sphere that is absent of religion, which, thanks to Bengali culture, is imprisoned within the private realm. The interviewer relays,

> Mrs. Zia was more eager to make the point that while Bangladeshi women still suffer great privations, as do most South Asian women, there is no longer anything unusual about women in Bangladesh taking part in public life. (Crossette 1993, E9)

Moreover, the article continues:

> "We allow and encourage women to participate in all fields of national life," said Prime Minister Zia, 48, clad in a cream silk sari. "In the villages, women work in the fields. And in the towns also, women work outside their homes. Women are taking part in cultural activities and politics; they are working in the offices and in government departments, and as doctors and teachers." (Crossette 1993, E9)

Within the article, a shift emerges from the cloistered Muslim woman of Pakistan to an unfettered Bangladeshi woman taking part in public life. This division of the Muslim woman into a private realm who needs to be brought out into the public perpetuates the Western phantasm of the harem that found its most forceful signifier in the veil and its supposed imprisonment of Muslim women by making the woman inaccessible to sight and, thus, modernity (Alloula 1987). The women on display, visually able to be catalogued and surveilled, are celebrated within the discourse of the *New York Times*. For women on display and visible—whether in the fields or offices—are considered autonomous, endowed with rights, and able to sell their labor freely—further limiting patriarchy, as Tanzeen Doha writes, to "a cultural logic instead of an economic one" (Doha xxxx, 27).

Rather than conceptualize the public sphere as historically constituted and central to organizing a particular economic arrangement, the understanding of the public sphere that appears in the *New York Times* is an empty space (Asad 2003, 185). This empty space, decreed secular, is thought of as "the space in which real human life gradually emancipates itself from the controlling power of 'religion' and thus achieves the latter's relocation" (Asad 2003, 191). Belief and religion within this space can "either have no direct connection to the way one lives or be held so light they can easily be changed" (Asad 2003, 115). This type of religiosity is critical to the *New York Times*. The article continues,

"We are religious people, certainly," Mrs. Zia said. "But we are not extremists or fanatics, and therefore we are more liberal, and we consider that our women are more free. We have women who are very famous singers, and women who take part in drama on the stage and in the cinema." (Crossette 1993, E9)

The body of the woman, on display for public consumption in theater and film, became central in demonstrating Bangladeshi society's openness and freedom, its temporal advancement. Though Islam remains, it became strictly a marker of cultural difference that has no bearing on the autonomous liberal subject and his/her action within the public sphere. Temporally, once again, Bangladesh moves toward competence and the desired liberal end of history that sees Islam exist but stripped from any lifeworld or even heterogeneity.

Bangladesh's entry into the temporal competence wrought by modernity rested upon gender, for just as gender was central in anticolonial nationalist discourse on becoming modern, in the postcolonial state, gender functioned to legitimate a nation's progress—a nation's entry into the horizon of Western expectations (Chatterjee 1994; El Shakry 1998; McClintock 1995; McLarney 2015; Mitchell 1988). For example, within the article in the *New York Times*, family planning, just as motherhood did within the colonial period, became the signifier for this movement into modernity. The article reads,

> Population experts are stunned at this Muslim society's acceptance of family planning, including some abortion and sterilization. "It is a wrong conception that Islam is against family planning," Mrs. Zia said. "That may be true of the Catholics, but not Muslims. There is nothing in Islam that accepts that convention. Certainly in Bangladesh we do not have that constraint. Family planning is widespread and has been accepted in every corner of the country. Women and men are aware of its importance, and they are practicing it. That is why our birth rate has come down." (Crossette 1993, E9)

In contrast, in Pakistan, the article "Pakistan's Gamble with Quick Reform" notes,

> "For 27 years, the Government of Pakistan has had a population control program on which we've spent $1.4 billion," said Abida Hussain, who in May was appointed adviser to the Prime Minister on population. "All we've managed to achieve is a one percentage point increase. At 3.2 percent we

have about the highest population growth rate in the world. Our 2,700 family planning centers are obviously hopelessly inadequate." (Crossette 1991b, 9)

Whereas the average Pakistani woman, according to the *New York Times* article, "bears six children and is restricted to the role of wife and mother," within Bangladesh, women did not bear the same restrictions freeing them from the burden of the family (Purdum 1995, A1). Family planning, therefore, facilitates a woman's entry into the public sphere, removing the burden of children that restrict labor to the home—even though it is within liberalism that these paradox most manifest.

The Mid-1990s and the Clash of Civilizations

Bhutto and Failure

During the early to late 1990s, a new discursive strand was woven into the tapestry of representation employed by the *New York Times* as the cautious optimism for Bhutto gave way to the despair of Bhutto's failures in Pakistan evidenced by her exclusion from power and constant reelections/removals through the decade. With this discursive strand, the representation of Pakistani politics shifted from one marked by the constitution of a noncontemporaneous civilization to one that emphasized the contemporaneity of Islamic civilization and its attempt to establish civilizational hegemony within Pakistan. This narrative hearkened to the "Clash of Civilizations" thesis propagated by Sam Huntington (1993) in which there existed no established universal teleology that would lead to the eventual becoming of a liberal Islam—an Islam as a nonpolitical private identity. The narrative, within the *New York Times*, shifts from emphasizing Islamic civilization moving Pakistan backward temporally to the notion that two civilizational forces, one tolerant and the other barbaric, were battling within Pakistan with an undetermined, though required, victor. Reform or reconstitution of the tradition through the espousal of tolerance and liberal values became a tenuous position and confrontation became the key within the discourse of the *New York Times*.

This framing within the *New York Times* followed Huntington's assertion that the civilizational clash occurred at two levels: the macro and "at the micro-level, adjacent groups along the fault lines between civilizations struggle, often violently, over the control of territory and each other" (Huntington 1993, 29). For example, this micro-level clash between the two within Pakistan is reported in an article that states,

> Little more than three years since a return to democratic government, Pakistan is caught in a spiral of increasing lawlessness in many parts of the country. It is at war in all but name with neighboring India. A conflict between a resurgent Islamic clergy and an urban, Western-educated elite undermines efforts to forge a consensus on how Pakistan will approach the 21st century. (Gargan 1991, A17)

The inability to forge a consensus highlights how Islamic civilization, though synchronous with the West and the assumed unilinear time of history, still created chaos, representing a backward being. And a battle existed to see which civilizational values would emerge victorious heading into the twenty-first century.

Within this constant clash of two opposing forces within a singular nation-state, at the micro-level, there existed no redemptive telos for Pakistan, but it was instead characterized by an open war that took place in the terrain of gender. In this narrative, the *New York Times* framed Bhutto as a failure. One article reported that

> Ms. Bhutto accomplished little in her 20 months in office and introduced almost no legislation. Under her administration Pakistan's economy deteriorated, its people remained among the world's poorest and the oppression and mistreatment of the country's women, widely deplored by human rights organizations, continued. (Gargan 1993, A12)

Bhutto's political project became no longer tenable within Pakistani politics as "Islamization" continued to make strides and endangered women's rights. For example, the article, "A Pakistani Plan for Islamic Code," stated,

> The Government introduced legislation today that would make the Koran the supreme law of Pakistan and subject all aspects of life, from social behavior to civil liberties, to Islamic tenets … Opponents contend that the legislative package would promote sectarianism, pave the way for a militant and repressive Muslim theocracy, confine women to their homes and bring the press and the educational system under control of Islamic clerics. Women

expressed concerns that the bill could force them to wear veils in public and give Muslim clerics power to dilute or scrap family laws that protect Pakistani women in matters like child custody and divorce. (1991, A5)

Confinement and the veil remained significant tropes of the civilizational values of Islam and these values were measured through the politics of the family.

Yet though the discourse shifts slightly where it is now a battle between civilizations in determining what constitutes the best space for women, women still remain neither subjects nor objects but merely the ground for contestation. Although the *New York Times* promotes the liberal values of the West, these values are no longer conceptualized as developmental within Islam; rather Islam constitutes an antithesis to a distinct nonuniversal cultural formation of the liberal West. An appropriate Islamic tradition, within this narrative, is still constituted into the image of the West, but rather than emerging from within the Islamic tradition itself, it is framed as part and parcel of a Western tradition. Within this discourse, as the articles show, the choice between which tradition is best remains contested through gender.

The Taslima Nasrin Case in Bangladesh

Similarly, the crisis inaugurated by the publication of the controversial novel Lajja (Shame) by the Bangladeshi writer Taslima Nasrin heightened the framing of civilizational difference between the liberal secular West and fundamentalist Islam within Bangladeshi politics. Published in 1993, Nasrin's novel, which examined the protests in Bangladesh against the destruction of Babri Masjid through the eyes of a Hindu family in Dhaka, caused an outcry and large protests. But the publication of the novel alongside its accompanying protests was a complicated affair. Indeed, Habiba Zaman (1999) notes, "to comprehend the Nasrin affair in the context of religion, politics and feminist issues in the sub-continent, one needs to go beyond her case and look at both the local context and the postcolonial socio-political processes crosscutting national boundaries" (49). The international media outcry, however, ignored such complexities and instead created an image where Nasrin was, Zaman (1999) writes, "a lone fighter against the religious fundamentalist onslaught avoided questioning or examining colonial legacies, inter-communal politics and violence, the role of the state, and the transnational socio-economic, political processes" (52).

The *New York Times* was similar in its representations. Indeed, this controversy was framed as a political struggle between Islamic civilization and the liberal West. One editorial states,

> As often as not, this ultimate form of censorship springs from a political struggle. Ayatollah Khomeini exploited "The Satanic Verses" to reassert his flagging leadership of Iran's Islamic revolution. And Karim Alrawi, a human rights advocate in Cairo, says it is not only militant Islamicists who assail writers and artists in Egypt: "Members of Parliament are also having a go. They know a good headline grabber when they see it." ("Censorship by Death" 1994, A18)

This "exploitation" of the Nasrin controversy by the Islamists was then posed as a direct challenge to the secular Bangladesh that manifested itself most clearly within the body of the woman and the politics of the family. Another article continued,

> Bangladesh has a secular civil law code, but it is perennially challenged by Islamic fundamentalists and the Government often bows to the pressure. The Islamic crusade, Ms. Nasrin says, has fallen hardest on women. (Crossette 1994, E7)

Islam, framed as a fundamentalist crusade, became a constant challenge to Bangladeshi secular society that continually falters. These failures of Bangladeshi secular society are then experienced as an encroachment on the liberal secular woman. Nasrin, therefore, emerges as a subject that needs to be defended since she upholds liberal secular values.

Criticism of Nasrin's work, on the other hand, is deemed as an attack upon foreign institutions and NGOs that are aiding women:

> Ms. Nasreen is a former gynecologist and has attracted attention for a number of her views: She has said women should have the right to marry four times in Islamic societies, just as men do. She also said that she was for "freedom of the womb" and that women must control whether they bear children or not. The campaign against her comes at a time when criticism of foreign institutions, especially aid agencies and voluntary groups, has been mounting in Bangladesh. This campaign, too, has been led by Muslim

groups, who say the foreign institutions are undermining the basis of Bangladesh society. (Hazarika 1994, A6)

Within this political struggle, which is framed in the *New York Times* between militant Islam and the secular subjects of Bangladesh, gender and NGOs become intertwined with the success of neoliberal policies, which are all threatened by this "militant" Islam.

Burns, for example, in an article states,

> Militant leaders have used the turmoil to promote a wide agenda of fundamentalist demands, including calls for Bangladesh to be made an Islamic republic, and for the Muslim penal code, to be imposed as criminal law. They have demanded the expulsion of privately run foreign aid organizations that administer much of the $2 billion the country receives each year in development assistance, describing the agencies' efforts to foster more jobs and education for women, among other projects, as "decadent" and "un-Islamic." The demands have come just as international aid agencies have been saying that Bangladesh has begun to turn the corner, with striking gains in primary education for girls, in employment opportunities for women, and in lowering birth rates. But as the social advances have gathered speed, they have met increasing resistance from the male-dominated hierarchies in the villages where 80 percent of Bangladeshis live, particularly from the Muslim clerics at the top of the rural power pyramid. (1994b, 1)

Another Burns article continued this rhetoric and reported:

> Muslim fundamentalist groups have used the campaign to renew demands for the expulsion from Bangladesh of foreign aid organizations that disburse much of the $2 billion in annual development assistance. They say that these groups, by pressing for female education, birth control and wider women's rights, are undermining Muslim mores. (1994a, A3)

Rather than examining the multifaceted nature of NGOs and their diverse engagements with the Islamic tradition and neoliberal polices, in the *New York Times*, NGOs signal development and advancing the rights of women, which then emerge as oppositional to Islam.

The backlash against Nasrin, within what the *New York Times* conceptualized as a "majority" secular society, was pinned onto the failure of Zia to confront the "militant" Islam and eliminating it from the political sphere:

> One of the boycotting parties is a Muslim fundamentalist group, Jamaat-e-Islami. Critics of the Government's move against Miss Nasrin say that it was aimed at placating the Jamaat leaders and drawing them back into Parliament. (Burns 1994a, A3)

By drawing the "militant" Islam into the political sphere, when Islam within the culture talk of the *New York Times* needed to be relegated to the private sphere, Zia's government was accused of failing the naturally secular constitution of the Bengali people. One article reported,

> Under a stronger Government, many Bangladeshis opposed to the militants say, the militants could scarcely have hoped to turn the utterances of a writer, even one as controversial as Miss Nasrin, into a platform for creating major political unrest. Educated, urban Bangladeshis insist that the traditions of Bengali Muslims incline toward tolerance, not zealotry, in religious matters. "The Bengali mind is basically secular," said Serajul Islam Chowdhury, an English literature professor at the University of Dhaka. "The mullahs are good men, but we have never wanted them in politics." Instead of confronting the militants, the Zia Government has seemed eager to placate them. (Burns 1994b, 1)

This secular Bengali mind threatened by the radical Islam led one editorial within the *New York Times* to frame Bangladesh, at the micro-level, as constituted by two opposing civilizations:

> The Bangladesh that has been capturing attention there is a country where crowds of angry Muslims have been demanding the death of a writer accused of blaspheming the Koran. The images have been all the more stark for the fact that the writer, Taslima Nasrin, is a woman, who reacted to the death threats by fleeing to an undisclosed hideout and issuing anguished appeals to Western governments to save her life. (Burns 1994a, A3)

The Bangladesh that was making the headlines was the "angry Muslim" Bangladesh, whereas the journalist claims there also existed a world cosmopolitan Bangladesh. Burns continues,

> A point made by many here is the one suggested by the uninhibited rejoicing over Brazil's victory in the World Cup—that Bengali Muslims are in fact an easygoing and in many ways worldly people. Despite political upheavals that have included the tumultuous independence struggle with Pakistan in

1971, Bangladeshis say, their country is not a natural breeding ground for extremism. Religious zealots, they say, have always been a marginal force, all the more so since the Party of God, the fundamentalists' main political vehicle, took the side of the Pakistani army in 1971, and encouraged its followers to engage in savage bloodletting. (1994c, C3)

Bangladesh is not conceptualized as a "breeding ground" for militant Islam and the Islamic civilizational force within Bangladesh. Once again, Bengali Muslims emerge as worldly and secular. Though they are uninhibited within private realms of culture (watching soccer), they are easygoing unlike the inhibition that marks the "fundamentalist" Muslims in the political sphere (savage bloodletting).

This vision of a micro-conflict within Bangladesh with two civilizational forces failed to acknowledge the many contradictory negotiations that Zia's politics undertook within the heterogeneous political society of Bangladesh. Moreover with its portrayal of the Nasrin affair, the *New York Times* took an exceptional case as the norm and then labeled the entire Islamic tradition as "oppressive" and "fundamentalist." Though the reaction to Nasrin's book is placed into a liberal/fundamentalist dichotomy, the debate on the ground within Bangladesh as well as Nasrin's writings do not fit neatly into the categories imposed by the West and within the *New York Times*. Nasrin's book is not simply a defense of liberal democratic politics contra Islam, but rather, as S. M. Shamsul Alam (2002) argues, it is "a gendered subaltern narrative" that cannot be reduced to a binary clash between tradition and modernity that was constructed not only within the *New York Times* but also within Western discourse (236).[9]

Post-9/11

Bangladesh Post-9/11

After 9/11, the *New York Times* shifted away from micro-level clashes within the subcontinent to a narrative that highlighted the macro-level Clash of Civilizations between the United States and those who upheld Western values against "bad Muslims" signified through terror around the world. This shift into a macro-level Clash of Civilizations meant that "rather than wait for 'good' Muslims to triumph over 'bad' Muslims," Mahmood Mamdani (2004) writes, "the Bush administration [was] determined to hasten such a civil war" and was "prepared to invade and bring about a regime change intended to liberate 'good' Muslims from the political yoke of 'bad' ones" (24). The threat of "Bad" Islam was no longer framed as a problematic within a singular nation-state (micro-level) but to liberal democratic values and liberal democratic subjects globally at the macro-level—clearly visible within the discourse on terror.

Within this global clash, gender remained the key site to frame who constituted a "good Muslim" contra a "bad Muslim." Zia's victory in the October 2001 elections became tied to her alliances with Jamaat-e-Islami, even though this alliance had existed earlier. One article reported,

> It is Mrs. Zia's alliance with the Jamaat-e-Islami, which wants to turn Bangladesh into a republic ruled by Islamic law, that secular Bangladeshis find most worrisome. "Jamaat has been a nuisance, but never an electoral power," said Gowher Rizvi, a Bangladeshi who leads the Ford Foundation's South Asia office in New Delhi. "We will see more intolerance, more emphasis on Islamization. And groups like the Grameen Bank that are involved in women's empowerment will suffer." (Dugger 2001, A8)

The impossibility of political Islam within liberal democracy became clear, for it became marked by the rhetoric of intolerance, which is the antithesis of liberal politics, yet constitutive of it (Brown 2008; Schmitt (1932) 2007). The intertwining of intolerance and Islam as culture within the discourse of the *New York Times* leads to the conclusion that women's liberation would then be undercut because women could not make rational free choices burdened by Islam.

Moreover, post-9/11, the relationship between gender and Zia's politics became intertwined with the global War on Terror. It no longer remained a historical specificity to Bangladesh, but the election became part of a grander staging of the War on Terror. For example, the article continues,

> While Mrs. Zia has been supportive of the American campaign to capture Osama bin Laden, the Jamaat leader, Matiur Rahman Nizami, said in an interview that the United States did not have enough evidence against Mr. bin Laden to justify military attacks and warned that the bombing "would

definitely cause widespread anger and revulsion in the entire Muslim world." (Dugger 2001, A8)

Bangladeshi politics were now bound within the global War on Terror where criticism of US foreign policy further marked the danger of Jamaat-e-Islami as a political presence within Bangladesh. However, after raising the threat of Jamaat, the article relays that "The question is how much power the Jamaat will exercise in the new government, in which it holds two of the 59 ministerial posts" (Dugger 2001, A8). This political presence of Jamaat-e-Islami was certainly not demonstrative of any Islamization, yet now, in contrast to Zia's representations in the late 1980s, Islam became representative of Bangladeshi politics because of the global stakes in the War on Terror, which required recalibrating previous alliances and representations in which Islam emerges as a global threat in a macro-class of civilization.

Pakistan Post-9/11

After 9/11, Pakistan's representation shifted as well, as its place within US policy changed because of the need to have Pakistan as an ally in the War on Terror. The strength of Pakistan as an ally was measured within the frame of the Clash of Civilizations that centered on gender. One article argued right after 9/11 that

> The country is polarized. On one side stand sympathizers with the West who have felt increasingly marginalized in recent years and believe that the current turmoil may be a rare stroke of fortune that halts the "Talibanization" of Pakistan, a drift toward the fundamentalist Islam of neighboring Afghanistan. On the other stand the holy warriors, the hope of the country's myriad dispossessed. (Bearak 2001, A1)

This representation, however, of a dual Pakistan polarized between Talibanization/Islamization and Westernization, was thought to have global implications within the War on Terror and, therefore, was no longer framed as strictly a micro-level clash within Pakistan. The article continued and fretted that

> By drafting this fragile and fractious nation into a central role in the "war on terrorism," America runs the danger of setting off a cataclysm in a place

where civil violence is a likely bet and nuclear weapons exist. Pakistan has long been the speculated locale for one of the world's worst nightmare scenario, in which Islamic terrorists, in league with rogue elements of the military, seize control of the government and wield the vengeful sword of jihad with a nuclear tip. Islam is a growing force here. Hundreds of religious schools, known as madrassahs, have eagerly sent their students to fight at the Taliban's side. Pakistani border guards wish them well as they head to the front lines. Last Friday, in a drama repeated in hundreds of towns and cities across the country, mullahs at the Red Mosque in Islamabad followed the gentle chanting of afternoon prayers with frenzied threats of violence: Death to America! Let Americans come here to be buried. (Bearak 2001, A1)

This Islamic radicalism was framed as encroaching upon the secular urban areas of Pakistan—a fear heightened because of Pakistan's geopolitical location. In Pakistan, moving spatially, even within an urban space, could constitute a passage through centuries. Yet, now the key was how this clash was tied to the United States itself as the chants become critical to understand how the microlevel clash is also a macro-level one.

Moreover, the evidence for this move through time spatially occurred within representations of women. The article stated,

But radicalism has deep social roots here. In the cities, the turn of a street corner can seem to be time travel between centuries. Wide boulevards clogged with expensive cars become narrow lanes where shrouded women carry jugs of water on their heads. (Bearak 2001, A1)

This "bad" and backward Islam is represented by the veiled women doing domestic labor in contrast to the boulevards of expensive cars that mark progress. Here, both civilizations existed within a fractured Pakistan, and this unwholesome product was framed as a threat to American security interests and foreign policy, which required a world rendered whole in its own image.

The challenges posed by traditional Islam threatened women within Pakistan as the clash between the secular subjects and Islamic fundamentalists, within the logic of the War on Terror, swayed toward Islam. One article reported,

Meanwhile, the government is gradually handing over the rights of women as citizens and indeed as human beings to tribal elders in a society that has, to a degree, long considered women as lesser beings, family property and repositories of the family honor. Rape as a form of revenge is a common phenomenon, particularly in the southern Punjab and upper Sindh region, and the use of such violence is increasing. (Sarwar 2002, A15)

This challenge, however, was framed globally. The article continues discussing a rape case within Pakistan and reports,

> The problems involved in cases like this are not unique to Pakistan and the debate should not be, either. General Zia's notions of Islamic law, for example, were partly foreign in inspiration. This is not to shift blame but to acknowledge that forms of traditionalism and fundamentalism can in a sense be modern, even late-modern, across large parts of the world—and that they can and should be contested in modern, usually secular terms without any loss of cultural or religious identity. In Pakistan and many other places, this is the fight now. It is hardly abstract. It is fought over the bodies of girls and women, and sometimes over the bodies of boys. (Sarwar 2002, A15)

Though continuing the discourse where Islamization in Pakistan is linked to Iran, the issue now became a modern problem that is fought over the bodies of women and girls. The key to stopping this Clash was to make Islam into a private cultural/religious identity while shifting the public political/economic identity into a liberal one, thereby producing the ideal global governable subject.

Bangladesh and Pakistan Comparatively

Thomas Friedman, in his opinion article "Today's News Quiz," brings these narratives on Bangladesh and Pakistan together through the trope of a secular and liberal India. Framed as a quiz, Friedman asks questions to which he provides a response. He begins by examining the Muslim population of India and writes,

> Which brings up another question that I've been asking here in New Delhi: Why is it you don't hear about Indian Muslims—who are a minority in this vast Hindu-dominated land—blaming America for all their problems or wanting to fly suicide planes into the Indian Parliament? Answer: Multi-ethnic, pluralistic, free-market democracy. To be sure, Indian Muslims have their frustrations, and have squared off over the years in violent clashes with Hindus, as has every other minority in India. But they live in a noisy, messy democracy, where opportunities and a political voice are open to them, and that makes a huge difference. (2001, A19)

Friedman reproduces the Clash of Civilizations narrative that drove American foreign policy. There existed "good" Muslims and "bad" Muslims and the good Muslims existed where Islam became one identity within a multicultural free market society.

For Friedman, the real issue was not with Islam but an Islam outside of liberal secular values. He continues,

> In other words, for all the talk about Islam and Islamic rage, the real issue is: Islam in what context? Where Islam is imbedded in authoritarian societies it tends to become the vehicle of angry protest, because religion and the mosque are the only places people can organize against autocratic leaders. And when those leaders are seen as being propped up by America, America also becomes the target of Muslim rage. (2001, A19)

The context of Islam, the political climate within which it is embedded—a climate determined relationally with the United States, became key to understanding whether its constituted as "good" or "bad." This framework allowed Friedman to compare Bangladesh with Pakistan. He argues,

> Followed Bangladesh lately? It has almost as many Muslims as Pakistan. Over the last 10 years, though, without the world noticing, Bangladesh has had three democratic transfers of power, in two of which—are you ready?— Muslim women were elected prime ministers. Result: All the economic and social indicators in Bangladesh have been pointing upward lately, and Bangladeshis are not preoccupied hating America. Meanwhile in Pakistan, trapped in the circle of bin Ladenism—military dictatorship, poverty and anti-modernist Islamic schools, all reinforcing each other—the social indicators are all pointing down and hostility to America is rife. Hello? Hello? There's a message here: It's democracy, stupid! Those who argue that we needn't press for democracy in Arab-Muslim states, and can rely on repressive regimes, have it all wrong. If we cut off every other avenue for non-revolutionary social change, pressure for change will burst out anyway—as Muslim rage and anti-Americanism. ... So true. For Muslim societies to achieve their full potential today, democracy may not be sufficient, but it sure is necessary. And we, and they, fool ourselves to think otherwise. (2001, A19)

In order for Muslim societies to fulfill their potential, a path that Bangladesh, he believes, is on, the culture has to be rooted within a liberal democratic milieu.

To prove his theory, Friedman relies on gender—the fact that Bangladesh elected two women as prime ministers. This leads him to the conclusion that whereas Bangladesh is moving forward temporally toward a liberal democratic society, Pakistan was caught within a temporal loop of barbarism and "bin Ladenism." Ignoring the fact that Pakistanis also elected a woman prime minister, Friedman maps why Bangladesh became home to "good Muslims" while also explaining why Pakistan remained "bad Muslims" by flattening the multiple positionings and negotiations that constitutes postcolonial governmentality within a neoliberal paradigm. Friedman takes the success of two women within electoral politics and that became constitutive of the entire tradition within Bangladesh from which Pakistan is contrasted. The South Asian ideal, though still behind, within this framing, remained India as its subjects most resemble liberal secular subjects within Friedman's analysis in which Islam is flattened.

Conclusion

This essay has considered the patterns in *New York Times* that flatten the dynamism of the Islamic tradition in South Asia. In examining this frame, this essay has historicized key points that shifted the patterns of representation, which remained dependent on a particular geopolitical moment examined in the introduction of this volume. These patterns broadly render South Asian Islam coherent by contesting the very parameters of the Islamic tradition by producing a bifurcated understanding of Islam: Good Muslim/Bad Muslim. These bifurcated notions are grafted onto the very geography of South Asia in which Bangladesh comes to represent a Good Islam contra Pakistan's Bad Islam. Women are central to these debates in determining good from bad, for these patterns reiterate a colonial order of things in which women were simply the ground of the debate rather than subject or object.

Notes

1 See Lena Meari's discussion of "material ideology" within her chapter in this volume.

2   For the making of "liberal citizens" in the *New York Times* in other contexts, see Caroline McKusick's article in this volume. Literature on understandings of temporality is vast, see Fabian (1983); Koselleck (1985); Young (1990); Appadurai (1996); Mitchell (2000); Bannerjee (2006); Scott (2014). The key is, as Lila Abu-Lughod writes, "We all live in real time, our worlds marked by change, argument, and social contestation. What occurs in places that (are made to) appear timeless or backward is always a product of a long history" (224).

3   My argument about discursive shifts is not to locate clean breaks within the framing of the *New York Times*. Rather, time, as Derrida (2006) continually reminds us, is "out of joint." Therefore, temporalities continually converge and intersect, creating an assemblage of multiple temporalities that exist as contradictions, disturbances, and disjunctures. See Derrida (2006); Mbembe (2001).

4   For a critique of this understanding of agency, see Mahmood (2005).

5   For arguments about the shift of culture into the domain of politics, see Brown (2008) and Žižek (2008). Žižek (2008) in particular is helpful. He argues,

> Contemporary liberalism forms a complex network of ideologies, institutional and non-institutional practices; however, underlying this multiplicity is a basic opposition on which the entire liberal vision relies, the opposition between those who are ruled by culture, totally determined by the life-world into which they were born, and those who merely "enjoy" their culture, who are elevated above it, free to choose their culture. (661)

6   For Bannerjee (2006) "modernity appears as temporal competence, an advantage that the posterior possesses over the prior exclusively because of the former's advanced position in time" (4).

7   The literature on the relationship between women's bodies and the nation-state is large and quite diverse. For example, see Kaplan, Alarcon, and Moallem (1999).

8   For the relationship between the veil and foreign policy, see Lena Meari's chapter within this volume.

9   For this innovative reading of Nasrin's work see Alam (2002). Alam's work takes into account that though the *New York Times* and Western discourse present us with rigid division between tradition and modernity, Nasrin's work cannot be easily divided into these two categories. Also see Lamia Karim's article on Nasrin that seeks to understand the paradoxes of the various receptions of Nasrin's work across the subcontinent (Karim 2012).

References

"A Pakistani Plan for Islamic Code: Premier Keeps Election Vow by Proposing Supremacy for Religious Laws." 1991. *New York Times*, 11 April: A5.

Abu Lughod, Lila. 2013. *Do Muslim Women Need Saving?* Cambridge, MA: Harvard University Press.

Ahmad, Dohra. 2009. "Not Yet beyond the Veil: Muslim Women in American Popular Literature." *Social Text* 27 (99): 105–31.

Alam, Shamsul S. M. 2002. "Women in the Era of Modernity and Islamic Fundamentalism: The Case of Taslima Nasrin of Bangladesh." In *Gender, Politics, and Islam*, edited by Therese Saliba, Carolyn Allen, and Judith A. Howard, pp. 235–67. Chicago: University of Chicago Press.

Alloula, Malek. 1987. *The Colonial Harem*. Translated by Myrna Godzich and Wlad Godzich. Minneapolis: University of Minnesota Press.

Appadurai, Arjun. 1996. *Modernity at Large: Cultural Dimensions of Globalization*. Minneapolis: University of Minnesota Press.

Asad, Talal. 1993. *Genealogies of Religion: Discipline and Reasons of Power in Christianity and Islam*. Baltimore, MD: Johns Hopkins University Press.

Asad, Talal. 2003. *Formations of the Secular: Christianity, Islam, Modernity*. Stanford, CA: Stanford University Press.

Asad, Talal, Wendy Brown, Judith Butler, and Saba Mahmood. 2009. *Is Critique Secular? Blasphemy, Injury, and Free Speech*. Berkeley: University of California Press.

"Backward March in Pakistan." 1979. *New York Times*, 19 October 1979: A34.

Banerjee, Prathama. 2006. *Politics of Time: "Primitives" and History-writing in a Colonial Society*. Oxford: Oxford University Press.

Bearak, Barry. 2001. "In Pakistan, A Shaky Ally." *New York Times*, 2 October 2001: A1.

Bernal, Victoria, and Inderpal Grewal. 2014. "Introduction: The NGO Form: Feminist Struggles, States, and Neoliberalism." In *Theorizing NGOs: States, Feminisms, and Neoliberalism*, edited by Victoria Bernal and Inderpal Grewal, pp. 1–18. Durham, NC: Duke University Press.

Brown, Wendy. 2008. *Regulating Aversion: Tolerance in the Age of Identity and Empire*. Princeton, NJ: Princeton University Press.

Burns, John F. 1994a. "A Feminist Writer's Defiance Fuels Militants in Bangladesh." *New York Times*, 13 July: A3.

Burns, John F. 1994b. "Furor over Feminist Writer Leaves Bangladesh on Edge." *New York Times*, 16 July: 1.

Burns, John F. 1994c. "The World: A Writer Hides. Her Country Winces." *New York Times*, 31 July: C3.
"Censorship by Death." 1994. *New York Times*, 6 July: A18.
Chatterjee, Partha. 1994. *Nation and Its Fragments Colonial and Postcolonial Histories*. Oxford: Oxford University Press.
Crossette, Barbara. 1990. "Official Islam Proving Gentler in Bangladesh." *New York Times*, 15 February: A17.
Crossette, Barbara. 1991a. "Bangladeshis Keep the Hard Edge Off Islam." *New York Times*, 6 March: A11.
Crossette, Barbara. 1991b. "Pakistan's Gamble with Quick Reform: Prime Minister Sharif Risks His New Democracy with Modernization Plan." *New York Times*, 30 June: 9.
Crossette, Barbara. 1992. "Bangladesh Chief Visits Washington: Seeks to Keep Global Powers From Overlooking Nation in Forging New World." *New York Times*, 9 March 1992: A8.
Crossette, Barbara. 1993. "Conversations: Khaleda Zia; A Woman Leader for a Land That Defies Islamic Stereotypes." *New York Times*, 17 October: E9.
Crossette, Barbara. 1994. "A Cry for Tolerance Brings New Hatred Down on a Writer." *New York Times*, 3 July: E7.
Derrida, Jacques. (1993) 2006. *Specters of Marx: The State of Debt, the Work of Mourning and the New International*. London: Routledge.
Dugger, Celia W. 2001. "New Premier in Bangladesh Vows to Stamp Out Corruption." *New York Times*, 11 October: A8.
El Shakry, Omnia. 1998. "Schooled Mothers and Structured Play: Child Rearing in Turn-of-the-Century Egypt." In *Remaking Women: Feminism and Modernity in the Middle East*, edited by Lila Abu-Lughod, 126–70. Princeton, NJ: Princeton University Press.
Fabian, Johannes. 1983. *Time and the Other: How Anthropology Makes Its Object*. New York: Columbia University Press.
Friedman, Thomas L. 2001. "Today's News Quiz." *New York Times*, 20 November: A19.
Gargan, Edward A. 1991. "Divided Pakistan Torn by Lawlessness and Scandal: The Economy Is Being Remade, and Corruption Is Charged." *New York Times*, 19 November: A17.
Gargan, Edward A. 1993. "Benazir Bhutto Returns as Leader of a Poor and Troubled Pakistan." *New York Times*, 20 October: A12.
Hazarika, Sanjoy. 1994. "Bangladesh Seeks Writer, Charging She Insults Islam." *New York Times*, 8 June: A6.

Huntington, Samuel P. 1993. "The Clash of Civilizations?" *Foreign Affairs* 72, no. 3: 22–49.

Jarmakani, Amira. 2008 *Imagining Arab Womanhood: The Cultural Mythology of Veils, Harems, and Belly Dancers in the U.S.* Basingstoke: Palgrave Macmillan.

Kaplan, Caren, Norma Alarcón, and Minoo Moallem, eds. 1999. *Between Woman and Nation: Nationalisms, Transnational Feminisms, and the State.* Durham, NC: Duke University Press.

Karim, Lamia. 2011. *Microfinance and Its Discontents: Women in Debt in Bangladesh.* Minneapolis: University of Minnesota Press.

Karim, Lamia. 2012. "Transnational Politics of Reading and the (Un)making of Taslima Nasreen." *South Asian Feminisms: Contemporary Interventions*, edited by Ania Loomba and Ritty A. Lukose, 205–23. Durham, NC: Duke University Press.

Koselleck, Reinhart. (1985) 2004. *Futures Past: On the Semantics of Historical Time.* Translated by Keith Tribe. New York: Columbia University Press.

MacIntyre, Alasdair C. 1981. *After Virtue: A Study in Moral Theory.* Notre Dame: University of Notre Dame Press.

Mahmood, Saba. 2005. *Politics of Piety: The Islamic Revival and the Feminist Subject.* Princeton, NJ: Princeton University Press.

Mamdani, Mahmood. 2004. *Good Muslim, bad Muslim: America, the Cold War, and the Roots of Terror.* New York: Three Leaves Press.

Mani, Lata. 1998. *Contentious Traditions the Debate on Sati in Colonial India.* Berkeley: University of California Press.

Mbembe, Achille. 2001. *On the Postcolony.* Berkeley: University of California Press.

McClintock, Anne. 1995. *Imperial Leather: Race, Gender, and Sexuality in the Colonial Conquest.* New York: Routledge.

McLarney, Ellen. 2011. "American Freedom and Islamic Fascism: Ideology in the Hall of Mirrors." *Theory & Event* 14 (3).

McLarney, Ellen. 2015. *Soft Force: Women in Egypt's Islamic Awakening.* Princeton, NJ: Princeton University Press.

Mitchell, Timothy. 1988. *Colonising Egypt.* Berkeley: University of California Press.

Mitchell, Timothy, ed. 2000. *Questions of Modernity.* Minneapolis: University of Minnesota Press.

Mydans, Seth. 1987. "A Bank Battles Poverty." *New York Times*, 12 July: E3.

Mydans, Seth. 1988. "In Bangladesh, Women Can't Go Home Again." *New York Times*, 17 April: A8.

"Pakistan After Zia." 1988. *New York Times.* 18 August: A26.

Prial, Frank. 1980. "As Pakistan 'Islamizes,' Feminists Rise Up in Anger: Rumors of a Backward Step Waiting Lists for Girls Backlog of Cases in Courts." *New York Times*, 8 November: 2.
Purdum, Todd. 1995. "A Clinton and a Bhutto Share a Joke in Pakistan." *New York Times*, 27 March: A1.
Said, Edward. 1979. *Orientalism*. New York: Vintage.
Sarwar, Beena. 2002. "Brutality Cloaked as Tradition." *New York Times*, 6 August: A5.
Schmitt, Carl. (1932) 2007. *The Concept of the Political*. Translated by George Schwab. Chicago: University of Chicago Press.
Scott, David. 2004. *Conscripts of Modernity The Tragedy of Colonial Enlightenment*. Durham, NC: Duke University Press.
Scott, David. 2014. *Omens of Adversity: Tragedy, Time, Memory, Justice*. Durham, NC: Duke University Press.
Scott, Joan. 2007. *The Politics of the Veil*. Princeton, NJ: Princeton University Press.
Weisman, Steven. 1986a. "The 'Islamization' of Pakistan: Still Moving Slowly and Still Stirring Debate." *New York Times*, 10 August: 10.
Weisman, Steven. 1986b. "For Bhutto, A Big Issue Is Her Sex." *New York Times*, 25 August: A2.
Weisman, Steven. 1986c. "The Return of Benazir Bhutto: Struggle In Pakistan." *New York Times*, 21 September: A40.
Young, Robert. 1990. *White Mythologies: Writing History and the West*. New York: Routledge.
Zaman, Habiba. 1999. "The Taslima Nasrin Controversy and Feminism in Bangladesh: A Geo-Political and Transnational Perspective." *Atlantis* 23 (2): 42–54.
Žižek, Slavoj. 2008. "Tolerance as an Ideological Category." *Critical Inquiry* 34 (4): 660–82.

Contributors

Tanzeen Rashed Doha is the Global Racial Justice Postdoctoral Fellow at the Mario Einaudi Center for International Studies at Cornell University. Doha is an anthropologist of Islam and secularism. His ethnographic work examines problems of betrayal, hypocrisy, false worship, disbelief, and other political and moral actions and psycho-existential conditions, through an engagement with twentieth-century Islamist thought. His work has appeared in *American Journal of Islam and Society* and *Political Theology*. Doha is the founder and general editor of the journal-magazine *Milestones: Commentary on the Islamic World*.

Suad Joseph is Distinguished Research Professor at the University of California, Davis. She founded the Middle East Research Group in Anthropology (aka Middle East Section of the American Anthropological Association), the Association for Middle East Women's Studies, the Arab Families Working Group, and the University of California Davis Arab Region Consortium. She was president of the Middle East Studies Association of North America. She cofounded the Arab American Studies Association, the Association for Middle East Anthropology, and the *Journal of Middle East Women's Studies*. She is general editor of the *Encyclopedia of Women and Islamic Cultures*. She has published over 100 articles and edited or coedited 12 books, most recently *Arab Family Studies: Critical Reviews* (2018), *Arab American Women: Representation and Refusal* (2021); *Handbook of Middle East Women* (2022); and *The Politics of Engaged Gender Research in the Arab Region: Feminist Fieldwork and the Production of Knowledge* (2022). She founded the Middle East/South Asia Studies Program at UC Davis; cofounded the Feminist Research Institute, and was awarded the UC Davis Prize for teaching and research; the UC Davis Edward A. Dickson Emeriti Professorship; the Middle East Studies Association Jere L. Bacharach Life Time Service Award; and the life time service awards from the Association for Middle East Women's Studies and the Arab American Studies Association.

Rajbir Singh Judge is Assistant Professor of History at California State University, Long Beach. He specializes in intellectual and cultural history of South Asia, with a particular emphasis on Punjab and the Sikh tradition, and global intellectual history more broadly. He has published a number of articles, including in *Comparative Studies of South Asia, Africa, and the Middle East* (2022); in *Modern Asian Studies* (2022); in *Theory & Event* (2022); in *Cultural Critique* (2021); in *positions: asia critique* (2021); in *Milestones: Commentary on the Islamic World* (2021); in *Qui Parle: Critical Humanities and Social Sciences* (2020); in *History & Theory* (2018); and in *Journal of the History of Sexuality* (2018).

Caroline McKusick holds a PhD in anthropology from UC Davis, with a designated emphasis in critical theory. She is Associate Editor for the Humanities at Stanford University Press. Her PhD research focused on the practice of journalism as a way of creating gendered selfhood, based on fieldwork among Kurdish women journalists in Northern Kurdistan, in Turkey. Her writing can also be found in the *Routledge Handbook on Women in the Middle East* (2022), *Generations of Dissent: Intellectuals, Cultural Production, and the State in the Middle East and North Africa* (2020), and the *Encyclopedia of Women and Islamic Cultures Online*.

Lena Meari is Assistant Professor of Anthropology in the Department of Social and Behavioral Sciences and the Institute of Women's Studies at Birzeit University, Palestine. She has special interest in the geopolitics of knowledge production; critical feminist theory; revolutionary movements; and decolonizing methodologies. Her research focuses on the formation of revolutionary subjectivity in colonial contexts and the practices of *sumud* among Palestinian political prisoners. Her publications include "*Sumud*: A Palestinian Philosophy of Confrontation in Colonial Prisons," "Re-signifying 'Sexual' Colonial Power Techniques: The Experiences of Palestinian Women Political Prisoners," and the coedited books *Rethinking Gender in Revolutions and Resistance: Lessons from the Arab World* and *The Politics of Engaged Gender Research in the Arab Region: Feminist Fieldwork and the Production of Knowledge*.

Hakeem Naim is Assistant Professor of Teaching in the Department of History at Northern Arizona University. He grew up in Afghanistan and lived in multiple countries as a refugee/immigrant. He received his PhD in Modern Middle East history from the University of California, Davis in 2019. In his research, Dr. Naim focuses on the late nineteenth-century Islamic nationalism, colonialism, postcolonial theories, and comparative intellectual history of the Ottoman Empire, Afghanistan, and Central Asia. He has a command of various languages, including Persian (Dari), Turkish (Modern and Ottoman Turkish), Arabic, Pashto, Uzbek, German, and English. Before moving to Northern Arizona University, Dr. Naim was a lecturer at UC Berkeley and Western Washington University where he taught Modern Middle East history, History of Afghanistan, Turkey, the Ottoman World, and a seminar in historical research.

Index

Note: Figures are indicated by page number followed by "f". Endnotes are indicated by the page number followed by "n" and the endnote number e.g., 20 n.1 refers to endnote 1 on page 20.

Abu Lughod, L. 68, 72, 172
Afghanistan 9, 13, 21, 22, 82, 126
   mujāhidīn in 117–18
   Taliban control in 21
   US foreign policy 144
   women's rights 132
Ahmed, L. 68
Alam, S. M. 188
Algeria 21, 84, 85, 90
Ali, K. 131
Alimahomed-Wilson, S. 6
Allah, concept of 124–5
al-Qaʻida 115, 123, 128, 129
American masculinity 108
anti-immigrant 4, 5
anti-immigration rhetoric 3, 4
anti-Islamism 22, 105–7, 118, 125–7, 134
anti-Muslim racism 22, 106
anti-West sentiment 80–1
Arab Americans 12, 26
Arab countries 15, 42
Arab-Israeli war, 1967 11, 17
Arab nationalism 15, 18
Arab Spring 13, 23, 134, 135
Arab Uprisings 13, 134, 135
Aristotelian liberalism 124
Asad, T. 40, 120, 174
Ataturk, M. K. 44–8, 47–9
Aziz, S. 6, 73

"bad" Muslims 22, 59, 95–8, 166, 193, 194
   Pakistan 24, 68
   threat of 189
Bahrain 14
Bangladesh 9, 13, 192–4
   economic policies 168
   Nasrin case in 184–8

   neoliberalization of 175–8
   post-9/11 188–90
   resentation of 25
   women role in 167
Barlas, A. 131, 133
Bearak, B. 96
Benhabib, S. 130
Bharatiya Janta Party (BJP) 13
Bhutto, B. 172–5
   failures of 182–4
Bin Laden, O. 23, 113, 123, 129, 134, 135, 189
Black Muslim women 7
Breitbart (website) 2
British Muslims 6
Burns, J. F. 186, 187
Bush, G. W. 91, 137

Canada 7, 88, 89, 150
Can the Subaltern Speak? (Spivak) 109, 110, 134
capitalism 1, 19, 26, 37, 112, *see also* Islamic capitalism
   growth of 62
   problem for 61
   reconciliation of 20
Carson, A. 2
categorical thinking 7–8
chador 76, 79, 95, 131, 155, 158, 179
Chamoun, C. 16–17
Chartrand, S. 85
Chinese 26
Chomsky, N. 69, 106
Christians 3, 15, 16–18, 119
   Lebanon in 15
   Maronite community 18
Çiller, T. 45, 46

The Claims of Culture: Equality and Diversity in the Global (Benhabib) 130
clash of civilizations 20, 21, 26, 27, 38–43, 71, 84, 87, 118, 182, 189, 190, 193
Clines, F. 78
Cohen, R. 161
Cold War 12, 24, 117, 122, 123, 166, 169
colonialism 1, 12, 19, 26, 129, 203
 Israel in 85
color, people of 1, 6
communicative ethics 130
conservative Islamophobia 8
Covering Islam: How the Media and the Experts Determine How We See the Rest of the World (Said) 9
Crenshaw, K. W. 118
Crossette, B. 126, 132, 176, 177
Cruz, T. 4
cultural discourses 69, 73, 101
cultural practices 118, 120, 121
cultural racism 1, 67
 culture 1, 23–5, 29 n.3, 40, 56, 121, 122, 126, *see also* Islamic culture
 Bangladesh in 176, 177, 180, 195 n.5
 minority 121
 modern racialization of 71
 political 129
 Saudi Arabia in 142, 143
 southeastern Anatolia in 60
 "West" vs. the "East" 141

Davis, A. 118
decolonizing 25–7
Deleuze, G. 109
discourses
 colonialist 68
 cultural 69, 73, 101
 ethical 68, 83, 128–34
 liberal 144, 154
 Orientalist 20, 68, 142, 168, 179
discrimination 6
 race 90
 sexual 88
 veil, construction of 77–80
Doha, T. 22, 23, 42, 68, 180

East 42, 43, 47, 58, 61, 147
 vs. West 141

Ebadi, S. 159, 160
Edmonton Journal (newspaper) 7
Edward, S. H. 69
Egypt 14, 21, 84, 128, 185
Ellison, K. 2
Elmir, R. 6
El Saadawi, N. 119, 120
enemy within 98–100
England 3, 7
epistemic 106, 110, 112
Erdoğan, T. 52, 56, 63
Erlanger, S. 97
Europe
 deadly attacks in 135
 Islamophobia in 2
 population of Muslims in 3
 "productive elaboration" 40
 sexual and cultural politics in 68

fanaticism 47, 52
Fanon, F. 68
Farnsworth, C. 88
FBI 4, 5, 12, 26
feminism/feminist 105, 111, *see also* academic feminism
 hegemony of 107
 Marxist 112
 modern 112
 theory 118
 Western 108
feminist theory 22, 110, 118
First Gulf War 13
Fisher, I. 97
Foucault, M. 110, 114, 142
France 5, 6
Francke, L. B. 79
Friedman, T. L. 18, 192–4

Gaza Strip 84, 97
Geertz, C. 120
gender (gendering) 26, 27, 89
 Islamophobia 6–7
 Lebanon of 15–19
 Pakistan's politics in 172
 tradition and authenticity of 110
 violence 7
"Genealogy of Terminology" project 10
Germany 3, 6

"good" Muslims 22, 59, 73, 95–8, 193, 194
   Bangladesh in 168
   Turkey in 61
gradual change, concept of 151, 152
Grameen Bank 178–9, 189

Habermas, J. 130
hadith 111, 131, 133
Hamas 13, 87
   oppressive system of 97
   perception of 85
   women in 98
Handbook of Middle East Women (Joseph and Zaatari) 25, 201
hate crimes 1, 4, 5, 7
hate speech 2
headscarves, wearing of 51–5
hegemonic feminism 107, 110
hegemony, hegemonic 69, 107, 122–8
hijab 4, 7, 155
Hindu 13, 165, 192
hip-hugging jeans 50, 51
Hizbullah 117, 118, 123, 129
honor killings 60
honor suicides 60
hooks, b. 118
Hopkins, P. 7
Huffington Post (site) 6
Huntington, S. P. 71, 72, 168, 182

Ibrahim, Y. M. 84
ideological, ideology 43, 107, 119, 141, 142, 144
   discourse 160
   material 67
   political 6
   power 159
immigrants 6, 11, 72, 99, 203
imperial
   economic–political interests 73
   foreign policy 101
   power 141
India 7, 9, 13, 71, 110, 173, 183, 192
interests
   economic 39, 67, 69–71, 83, 161
   imperialist 100
   material 101, 167
   political 24, 39, 69–71, 83, 92, 101, 144
internal orientalism 58–61

The Interpretation of Cultures (Geertz) 120
"intersectional discrimination" 2, 6
Iran 23
   Islamic rules in 81
   state power in 115
   veiled Muslim women in 154–60
Iraq
   al-Qaʻida in 129
   US imperial aggression in 108
   war in 22
Islamic culture 23, 147, 153
   modern racialization of 71
   racial formation of 67
Islamic dress, violations of 157
Islamic fundamentalism 21, 73, 84–8, 119, 151, 179
Islamic liberalization (liberalism) 119
Islamic militancy 83, 88, 127, 150
Islamic orthodoxy 111, 112, 131, 137, 174
Islamic Republic (Iran) 12, 14, 21, 23, 113, 125, 131, 144, 154, 167, 175, 185
Islamic youth activism 47
Islam/Islamic
   capitalism 61–4
   consolidation of 23
   imposition 95
   orthodox tradition of 131
   politics 39
   racial formation of 21
   reconciliation of 20
   reconfiguration 122–8
   repression 95
   terrorism 70
   tradition 165
   violence of 92, 100
   women's rights in 130
Islamism 23, 51, 108, 109, 111–13, 136 n.7
   contemporary history 113–17
Islamist periodization 102 n.2
"Islamist Winter" 23, 134
Islamophobia
   categorical strategies of 7–8
   conflation of 2
   electoral politics 2
   escalation of 1–4
   Europe in 6
   gendered violence 6–7

hate crimes 1
  intensification of 2
  material 4–6
  Middle East in 154
  print news media in 8–10
  United States in 71
Italy 3, 6

Japanese 26, 89
Jarmakani, A. 166
Jews 3, 5, 26, 119
Joseph, S. 27 n.1, 28 n.2, 136 n.4
Judge, R. 24
Justice and Development Party (AKP) 19, 37, 39–41, 51, 54

Kamm, H. 82
Kantian liberalism 124
Kavakci, M. 56–8
Kemalists 43
Khatami, M. 131
Khomeini, A. 45, 81, 84, 114, 116, 131, 158, 159, 185
Kinzer, S. 133
Kumar, D. 8
Kurdish Women 58–61

La Ferla, R. 95
Lajja (shame) 168, 184
law (Islamic law) 24, 84, 116, 121, 122, 125, 189, 192
Lebanese Civil War 12, 17
Lebanon
  Christians 15
  Civil War 12
  gendering of 15–19
  Israeli aggression in 117
  representations of 19
Leetaru, K. 3
LeMoyne, J. 90
Le Nouvel Observateur (magazine) 116
Le Pen, M. 4
Levin, B. 4
Lewis, B. 71, 168
liberal imperialism 141, 148
liberal Islamophobia 8
liberation 93–4
Libya 2

Lorch, D. 82
Lyotard, J.-F. 118

Macron, E. 4
Mama's Baby, Papa's Maybe: An American Grammar Book (Spillers) 108
Mamdani, M. 73, 93, 189
Mani, L. 166
Maronite Christian community 18
Marxist feminism 22, 112
Massoumi, N. 6
material 4–6
material ideology 67, 70, 102 n.1
McKusick, C. 19, 20
McLarney, E. 167
Meari, L. 20–2, 41, 57, 118, 121, 148
Mecca 115–17
Media Analysis project 9–12
misrepresentation 2, 9, 11, 12, 25–7, 26, 27
modernity 50, 109, 130, 181, 188
Mohamud, H. 7
Mohanty, C. 110
Mojtabai, A. G. 75
"moral panic" 8
Mujahidin (Freedom Fighters) 13, 71
multiplicity 72, 118
  representations of 83
  veil 75–7
Muslim Americans 5, 9–11, 22
"Muslim Ban" 2
Muslim population, *see* population of Muslims
Muslim women
  anonymous mass 49–51
  good/bad 95–8
  headscarf-wearing 50
  headscarves in 51–5
  marriage of 50
  oppression of 82–3, 83
  Orientalist fascination with 50
  protecting 72
  repression of 84
  saving 72
Mydans, S. 175

Naber, N. 1, 67, 73
Naim, H. 23, 24, 45, 71, 115, 116, 167
Nasrin, T. 184–8
Nasser, G. A. 16

national origin 1, 67
negativity 75–7
neocolonialism 1, 12, 19, 26, 27
neoliberal economic policies
   Bangladesh in 24
   implementation of 37
   intensification of 40
   success of 168
9/11 attacks 4, 5, 19, 22, 92, 128, 130
   issue in Western countries 98
   victims of 108
1979 113–17
1980s 43–6
   consolidating Islamism 117–22
   veiled Muslim women in 74–5
1990s 43–6
   veiled Muslim women in 83–4
niqab 87

Obama, B. 2, 129
oil resources 14, 71
Omar, I. 2
Omni, M. 8, 71
oppression 21, 22
   Afghan women of 82
   Iranian women of 23
   Palestinian of 26
   Saudi women of 24
   veil/unveil 93–4
Orientalism/Orientalist 20, 68
   ambivalent power of 144–8
   discourses 68
   internal 58–61

Pakistan 9, 13, 177, 181, 192–4
   Afghan refugees in 82
   islamization of 169–72
   liberalization of 24
   politics 173
   post-9/11 190–2
   representation of 25
   US foreign policy 25
   women role in 167
Palestine 114
Palestinian Islamic Resistance Movement 13, 17, 85, *see also* Hamas
The Pew Research Center 3, 5
physical violence 7
political ideology 6, 21, 117

Pollitt, K. 79
population of Muslims 3, 27, 41, 192
post-9/11
   Bangladesh 188–90
   Muslim immigrants 99
   Pakistan 190–2
The Postmodern Condition (Lyotard) 118
power
   colonial 110
   liberal Orientalism 144–8
   political 115
   state 114
practices
   discriminatory 79
   material 75
   oppressive 79
   repressive 75
Prial, F. 169
print news media 26, 68
   Islamophobia in 8–10
productive elaboration 40
pro-system Islamism 38–9
psych (psychological, psychoanalytic, psychosocial) 22, 105, 106, 108, 120

Qatar 14
Quran 111, 116, 131, 133

race/racialization 5, 8, 27, 71–2, 89, 118
racial formation 8, 21
   definition of 71–2
   "Islamic culture" of 67
   processes of 69
racialization 1, 8, 26
racism 2, 6, 67, 71, 72, 121, 122
   anti-Muslim 22, 106
   Bangladesh in 176
   cultural 1, 67
   "cultural interpretations" of 120
   form of 8
   Saudi Arabia in 142
Rafsanjani, H. 159
refugees 2, 82, 88, 89, 150, 203
religion 1, 5, 6, 11, 14, 21, 27, 71, 72, 121, 180, 184
   commonality of 8
   cultural interpretations of 120
   Turkey in 44
religious fundamentalism 83–4

representational strategies 71, 101, 118, 134
representations 1
  electoral politics in 4
  media 130
  Muslim women of 25–7
  news media 14
  patterns of 19–25
  Turkish Muslim women of 39
  veiled Muslim women of 81–2
  veil of 82–3

Said, E. 9, 147
San Bernardino attack 3–4
Sanchez, J. 72
sati 165, 166
Saudi Arabia 13, 21
  American women in 94
  media representation 115–16
  oil resources of 70, 77
  representation of 23
  US foreign policy 24
  US involvement in 144
  veiled Muslim women 148–54
Sayyid, S. 111, 129, 137 n.9
Sciolino, E. 81, 94, 95, 131
Scott, J. W. 68
Second Gulf War 13
secularism, secular, secularization 18, 24, 43–6, 60, 62, 73, 106
  feminism 134
  media 134
Sex and Social Justice (Nussbaum) 124
sexism 2, 119
sexual politics 68
shari'a (Islamic law) 24, 106, 111, 114, 121, 125, 131, 133, 146
Shia Hizbullah 129
sign 82–3
Soltani, A. 6
Somalia 2
Soviet Union 13, 16, 117, 122, 171
Spillers, H. 108, 109, 134
Spivak, G. 109, 110, 134
Spurr, D. 142
structure
  anti-Islamism 118
  ethical 114
  liberal feminism 125
  political 154

shari'a 114
subjective essentialism 109
Sudan 21, 84, 123, 128
Sunni Hamas 129
Sunni Muslim 38, 42
Switzerland 15, 17, 18
symbol
  discrimination 77
  oppression 77
  violence of Islam 100
Syria 2, 12, 16–18, 70, 135

Taliban 21, 93
  emergence of 123
  Islamic legitimacy of 132
  misogyny 108
Tavernise, S. 132
terror 17, 73, 101, 188, 189
terrorism 6, 70, 73, 83, 92, 97
Thobani, S. 108, 134
Tlaib, R. 2
Toscano, A. 47
Trofimov, Y. 115
trousers 51, 63, 155
Trump, D. 2–6
Tuğal, C. 39
Turkey 45, 56
  clash of civilizations 39–43
  politics 44
  pro-system Islamism emerges 38–9
  timeline 46–7
  Westernization 47
Turkish Muslim women 20, 39, 41–3, 61, 63, 64
Turkish political groups 47
2000s 46–7
  veiled Muslim women in 92–3
2001 128–34

UK 5, 7
United Arab Emirates 14
United States 56
  9/11 attack 19
  construction of 90–2
  ethical burden of 92
  hegemony 122–8
  Islamophobia in 2
  military domination of 141
  Muslim population in 3

political-economic interests 38, 69–71, 83–5, 92, 100
  race in 71
unveiled women 73, 82, 93–4, 105
US foreign policy 9, 14, 21, 25, 142
  consolidation of 11
  materiality and actuality of 67
  neoliberal economic policies 37
  power of liberal orientalism 144–8

veil 6, 21, 68
  anti-West sentiment 80–1
  colonialist binary, marker of 80
  construction of 77–80
  cultural discourses 69
  liberation/oppression 93–4
  multiplicity 75–7
  representation of 82–3
  representations of 72
veiled Muslim women 6, 22, 67
  1980s in 74
  1990s in 83
  2000s in 92–3
  Iran in 154–60
  Orientalist approach 77
  representation of 81–2
  Saudi Arabia in 148–54
  United States in 99
verbal assaults 7
vsictim
  religious fundamentalism 84
  veiled Muslim women 81–2
victimhood 101
violence 6, 10, 108
  against Black Muslim women 7
  forms of 60
  gender based 7
  ideological justification for 43
  physical 7
  religious 137 n.8
  self-destructive 135

Wadud, A. 131
Waldman, A. 93

Wall Street Journal, The (newspaper) 9
"War Against Terror" 14
War on Afghanistan 13
War on Iraq 13
War on Terror 19, 22, 40, 63, 93, 106, 128–34
  Bangladesh post-9/11 189
  Pakistan post-9/11 190
Washington Post, The (newspaper) 3, 6
Weisman, S. R. 122, 171
West 17
  vs. East 141
  ethical responsibility 22
  harmonious wedding 63
  liberating power 90
  role of 83
  veil 80
West Bank 84
Western discourse 105
  mainstream 107
  radical 107
Westernization 40, 47, 50, 152, 190
white man's burden 87–90
White Wars: Western Feminisms and the 'War on Terror' (Thobani) 108
Winant, H. 8, 71
women's rights 48, 72, 107, 124, 130, 133
  Islamic fundamentalism 179
  Islamic law 122
  Pakistani politics 183
  pressure of 127
  violations in 118
Wright, O. 6

Yemen 2

Zaman, H. 184
Zia, K. 168, 178–82
Zia-ul-Haq, M. (General Zia's) 169
Žižek, S. 135

www.ingramcontent.com/pod-product-compliance
Lightning Source LLC
Chambersburg PA
CBHW062226300426
44115CB00012BA/2239